Ministry in the Countryside

Ministry in the Countryside

A Model for the Future
Revised and Expanded

ANDREW BOWDEN

continuum
LONDON • NEW YORK

Continuum
The Tower Building
11 York Road
London SE1 7NX

370 Lexington Avenue
New York
NY 10017-6503

www.continuumbooks.com

First published 1994
Revised edition published 2003

British Library Cataloguing-in-Publication Data
A catalogue record for this book is available from the British Library.

ISBN 0-8264-6765-2

Typeset by BookEns Ltd, Royston, Herts.
Printed and bound by Biddles Ltd, Guildford and King's Lynn

Contents

Acknowledgements   xii

The Story Since 1994   xiii
  Changes in rural society   xiii
    Political changes   xiii
    The future of farming   xvi
    Other rural businesses   xix
    The centralization of 'service provision'   xx
    The demography of the village in 2002   xxi
  Changes in the rural Church   xxiv
    The rural Church at national level   xxiv
      Work stemming from the Arthur Rank Centre   xxiv
      Other national organizations and rural forums   xxvi
      Ecumenical committees and initiatives   xxvi
    The Church and rural soceity   xxviii
      Village community life   xxviii
      Involvement with secular agencies   xxix
      Local ecumenical co-operation   xxx
      Church buildings   xxx
      Ministry to visitors   xxxi
      Village schools   xxxii
    The ministry of the Church in rural areas   xxxiii
      The factors of change   xxxiii
      The experience of local ministry in rural areas   xxxvi

Ordained local ministers   xl
The role of the stipendiary   xlv
The role of the diocese   xlvi
End piece   xlviii

PART I   THE RURAL COMMISSION   1

1   **The Initial Response**   3

2   **The Contest – Our Inheritance**   7
The social inheritance   7
The Church inheritance   10
The parson   13

3   **The Context – The Countryside Today**   16
The social context   16
The development of the rural lobby   20
The rural Church   23
The revival of morale   28

4   **The Commission**   32
The genesis of the Commission   32
The work of the Commission   34
The follow-up to the Commission   37
Conclusion   42

PART II   THE VISION   45

5   **The Vision**   47
The local focus   48
The benefice team   49
The stipendiary   50
The diocese   50
Conclusion   51

PART III   TESTING THE VISION   53

6   **Introduction**   55
The evidence   56
The ecumenical evidence   59
Evaluating 'success' in the rural ministry   60
   Attendance statistics   60
   Assessing morale   63
What is 'rural'?   66

7   **The Rural Church in Crisis**   69
Numbers   69
   Future numbers of stipendiaries   70

Criteria for deployment of: stipendiaries   70
The Sheffield Formula   70
The ecumenical factor   72
Non-stipendiary assistance   73
Money   74
The escalating cost   74
Why they won't pay   77
The principle of payment for ministry received   79
Theology   81
The people of God   81

8   **Local and Catholic**   83
What lay people say they want   84
Attitude to having a woman as vicar   85
They want a vicar they know   86
Localism as the bedrock of rural religion   88
Catholic as well as Congregational   90
Congregations need each other   91
The Free Church experience   92

9   **Models of Ministry**   95
The 'supermarket model'   95
The Free Church evidence   96
The deanery parish   97
Comparison with the Methodist Circuit   99
Minster ministry   100
Bishops-in-little   100
The French evidence   101
Minister ministry Mark II   103
Groups and teams   106
The benefits of groups and teams   107
A changed context   109
The problems of working in groups and teams   110
Parishioners want their own vicar   112
The multi-settlement benefice run as one parish   113
Parochialism – good or bad?   114
Joint worship   114
The multi-parish benefice   116
The practice of the absence of the priest   117
Satellite parishes peopled by second-class citizens   118
A vicar in every village   120
The past resurrected   120
The past transformed   121
Local group and benefice team   122
A practical example   124

10 **Setting Up a Local Group**   126
    The job description   126
    Are candidates available?   129
        Lay ministry already happens   130
        Why does lay ministry not thrive everywhere?   131
    Individuals or groups   132
    Selection of group members   133
        Testing the parish   133
        The Lincoln method of nominating candidates   134
        The role of the bishop   135
        Why the process of nomination is so important   136
    What sort of person is needed?   136
        A cautionary tale from America   136
        Needed: people who will work together   137
    Will the village accept them?   138
        Opposition to lay ministry   138
        The case of St Mary's, Comberton   140
    Making sure the village is happy   142
        Pastoral care   142
        Community involvement   143
        Care for the disadvantaged   143
        Care for the natural environment and buildings   144
        Relations between the group and the congregation   145
    Training the local ministry group   146
        Training as a group   147
        A possible curriculum   147
    The geographical boundaries of local ministry   150
        A group in each settlement   150
        A group in each benefice   151
    Welding the local group on to the benefice team   152

11 **Local Non-stipendiary Ministry**   155
    A theology of local ministry   155
        Canon Royle on local ministry   156
        Bishop Baker on local ministry   157
    Implications for the local group   159
    Implications for Readers and lay pastors   160
    Implications for local non-stipendiary ministers   161
        Local non-stipendiary ministry – training and selection   162
    Implications for non-stipendiary ministers   163
        The choice – local or apostolic?   164
        Involvement in group training   164
    Implications for retired clergy   165
    Local non-stipendiary ministry – a first-class ministry   166

12	**The Role or the Stipendiary**	167
	A new job description	168
	Holy	170
	Learned	170
	Local	171
	Apostolic	172
	Profile of the rural clergy	173
	Their attitude to lay ministry	174
	Can they cope temperamentally?	175
	The relevance of the age of the rural clergy	175
	The relevance of temperament	176
	Clergy stress	177
	Problems perceived	177
	Rewards enjoyed	178
	Postscript	180
	There is still a job to be done	180
	Autobiographical	180
13	**Diocese and Deanery**	184
	The need for a rural strategy	184
	Supporting stipendiaries	186
	The training of stipendiaries	187
	Continuing Ministerial Education	188
	The diocese and members of the group	189
	The diocesan strategic reserve	189
	Bridging the gulf between diocese and village	190
	The problems of synodical government	191
	Money, appointments and buildings	192
	What then of the deanery?	193
14	**The Ecumenical Dimension**	195
	The decline of the Free Churches in rural areas	195
	What went wrong?	196
	Theology	196
	Political context	197
	Worship	197
	The need for a trusted stipendiary to make difficult decisions	198
	The rural Free Churches today	199
	The Free Church contribution to the rural ministry debate	200
	Ecumenical co-operation	201
	Councils of churches	201
	Ecumenical co-operation in small villages	201
	Examples of co-operation	203
	The village with only one church	203
	Shared oversight and the village Local Ecumenical Project	204

15 **Church Buildings**   207
    The significance of buildings   207
    Coping with maintenance   210
       Fabric funds which work   210
       Reordering village churches   211
       The conservation lobby   213
    Other church property in villages   213

16 **Regular Sunday Worship**   215
    Worship in every church every Sunday   215
       How many churches have no Sunday service?   216
       Will people worship elsewhere?   217
    Should services be at a regular and convenient time?   217
       Stipendiary availability   218
       Fewer communion services   219
       Lay-led short services   220

17 **Mission and Evangelism**   223
    Constraints on evangelism in rural areas   224
       Popular religion   226
       Implicit religion   227
       Popular beliefs   228
       Community church Mark II   229
    What strategy for evangelism is likely to work?   229
       Communal not associational   229
       Local and personal   230
       Starting where people are   230
    An agenda for rural evangelism   231
       Pastoral care   231
       Care for community life   231
       Vibrant worship   231
       Teaching   233
       Direct evangelism   234
       Indirect evangelism   235

Bibliography   237

TO

Sue

Acknowledgements

It is no light undertaking for a parish clergyman to write a first book of this length. In my case it was made possible when the diocese of Gloucester gave me sabbatical leave, and the Royal Agricultural College, Cirencester, and the parishioners of Coates, Rodmarton and Sapperton with Frampton Mansell, cheerfully dispensed with my services for three months. My absence from the parishes was covered by my colleagues Bill Woodhouse and Jeremy Francis, and the project was financed by generous grants from the Sylvanus Lysons Trust and the Guild of All Souls.

I owe a particular debt of gratitude to Professor Leslie Francis who guided me throughout, and to Trinity College, Carmarthen, who offered me a bolthole at particular moments of stress. Jeremy Martineau, the Church of England National Rural Officer, read the first draft and gave invaluable advice at that stage; Christopher Short and Michael Winter at the Royal Agricultural College guided me through the statistics of the Rural Church Project; Anthony and Kathleen Herbert read and commented on the proofs; and Bishop Anthony Russell helped to dredge me out of those pits of gloom into which all authors must occasionally fall. But my profoundest thanks are due to Carol Treasure who typed at least three drafts of the manuscript against the inevitable deadlines, and to my wife Sue who, after the agony of it all, is still ready to support, encourage and laugh with me.

The Story Since 1994

When *Ministry in the Countryside* was published in 1994 it was welcomed as filling an obvious gap in the market. Clearly, however, a lot has happened since then, and I am grateful to the publishers for allowing me to write this foreword to the new edition.

In this chapter I first consider the major changes in society since 1994 that have had implications for those who live in villages, with particular reference to the government White Paper and to the consequences of the foot-and-mouth epidemic. I then survey the church scene, with extended sections on our eight years of experience in forming Local Ministry teams in Gloucester Diocese, and on the *Stranger in the Wings* report which I helped to write.

CHANGES IN RURAL SOCIETY

Political changes

Those who live in towns now believe that they too have a stake in the countryside. For generations, local government in rural areas has been left to those who live locally. County and District Councils have allocated resources to education, welfare, environment and recreation as seemed best to local rural people. Farmers have adapted the landscape to the needs of their industry and their sporting whims. Not any longer. The countryside is the lung that urban man needs to breathe, and New Labour is determined that urban man shall have a say on the future of a countryside which 'is needed by all and belongs to us all'.

In this the government is certainly articulating the aspiration of the majority of voters. Arguably the single most important fact to emerge from the 1991 census is that the cities are declining in population, and more people are now living in small towns and villages, even in remote rural areas. For the first time since 1700 migration to the town has been reversed. Perhaps for the first time in human history the *civis* – the city – is no longer seen as the sole focus of 'civilization'. It seems likely that the results of the 2001 census (yet to be published at the time of writing) will confirm the trend. The future of the countryside has therefore become a key political issue.

Since 1997 New Labour has signalled the change in a number of ways. It has created the Countryside Agency, which already employs a workforce of 600. The Agency is committed to ensuring that the countryside should be available to urban as well as rural people. Access for rambling is high on the agenda; so is the development of national parks and forests. Their 'sustainable land management strategy' encourages farmers to move from food production to landscape conservation. Community initiatives which show entre-preneurial flair – but cost the taxpayer little – are strongly encouraged.

The government carried out a major consultation exercise prior to the publication of *Our Countryside: the Future* in November 2000, which was certainly the most well-informed and thorough White Paper on rural issues for half a century. A principle recommendation was to bring food production and food consumption into one ministry, along with environmental concerns. So DEFRA was born – the Department of Environment, Food and Rural Affairs. Naturally farmers were unhappy about being downgraded from 'special ministry' status; and the fledgling department did not encourage confidence by their handling of the final stages of the foot-and-mouth epidemic. At times DEFRA ministers even tried to make the farming community the scapegoat for what most reasonable commentators have seen as a natural disaster fuelled by current market practices and government incompetence in the early stages.

Despite this inauspicious beginning, there are signs that DEFRA wishes to listen to informed advice. A national Rural Forum, at which the churches are represented, meets with ministers regularly, and is supported by regional Rural Affairs Forums. For many years the rural lobby asked for joined-up government thinking on rural issues with a single co-ordinating ministry. This is what we now have in DEFRA. The trouble is that most of the ministers are not recognizably rural! The hope is that this may change as Labour MPs who represent rural constituencies are drawn into the Ministry.

DEFRA also has a watching brief for Regionalization; and to help with this a Directorate for Rural Economies and Communities has been set up. For New Labour the centre of the universe is, of course, Westminster. Like every government before them they want to control everything and to have their finger in every pie. But a combination of rhetoric when in opposition and the stipulations attached to payments from the European Union has contributed to an outbreak of devolution on an unprecedented scale. Not only have Scotland and Wales (almost) flown the nest, but Regional Offices, Regional Development Agencies, Regional Forums and Regional Think Tanks are sprouting as readily as the snowdrops in spring. At the moment the jury is out as to whether they will fade as swiftly as the snowdrops: but if Regionalization does take root it will certainly constitute a revolution in the local politics of rural areas.

There are, of course, problems. The boundaries of the Regions are dictated from Brussels, and often seem unrealistic to those who live on the margins. But the promised referendums on Regional Assemblies will give a clearer idea of whether what seemed good to Scotland and Wales is going to appeal to the Regions of England. Certainly Regionalization is a significant initiative, and the Church needs to be intelligently joining in the debate. There is at this stage everything to play for.

The White Paper also made suggestions about how to reinvigorate Local Government in rural areas at County, District and Parish Council level. It is an ongoing democratic scandal that the turnout at local elections is so abysmal: but it is equally irritating to local people that decisions about all manner of local matters are determined by national regulations. The argument is circular. Local councillors complain that the voters do not bother to vote since Westminster holds the purse strings and has eroded their traditional powers: and

Westminster argues that local councillors are not fit to manage serious decisions about large sums of money – and that in any case they do not have a mandate from the voters to do so.

For years now the rural lobby have urged the government to look at the 'Commune' system in France and Germany, where the smallest settlements have the right to levy taxes and to provide services at a very local level – a system which often works very well indeed. The government has responded by suggesting that those Parish Councils 'which can demonstrate their excellence' may receive serious money to spend as they think fit on certain services. Initial reaction has been predictably alarmist, but it is to be hoped that the Church will encourage local people to rise to the challenge. This is, after all, what we have long asked for, and if it can be made to work, it could reinvigorate local democracy. It has to be said that a number of villages will be too small to fulfil the criteria for 'excellence': but the time has surely come for the emergence of 'federated' Parish Councils, on the benefice or circuit model.

A final 'political' point to note is that the perception among rural people that 'urban man' is 'interfering in our factory', and that the voice of 'real rural people' is no longer being heard at Westminster, has led to the transformation of the British Field Sports Society into the Countryside Alliance. After two unexpectedly successful marches on London, and rather too much bombastic sabre-rattling for the taste of other organizations who have been battling in the field for a generation or more, the Alliance seems to have settled down under new leadership to becoming a political force to be reckoned with. It remains essentially the mouthpiece of the hunting lobby; but all those who see the countryside as a place of work, and all those whose jobs require them to rear, care for and slaughter animals are right behind them. The strength of the Alliance was forcefully demonstrated on 22 September 2002 when over 400,000 of their supporters marched through London. This, the biggest peaceful demonstration in British history, underlined the disaffection of 'real rural people', and raised the prospect of serious unrest in the none too distant future.

The future of farming

The morale of farmers is very low. Whatever they do seems to be wrong. They are told to embrace the market economy, and when they adopt more efficient practices in order to compete, they are accused of 'raping the environment'. In the wake of some ill-researched media scare they are forced to adopt animal welfare and health and hygiene codes that cost money to implement; at the same time, the supermarkets are allowed to continue to stock their shelves with food sourced from countries where animal welfare codes are a joke. They are accused of being feather-bedding consumers of three billion pounds a year in subsidies, when in 2001 the average farm income was £3,500. The statistics from Brussels give the European perspective. They show that since 1995 the real annual income of British farmers has dropped by 70 per cent, and in 2001 their average income was 30 per cent lower than farmers in *any other* European country.

It is hardly surprising then that the suicide rate among farmers is a national scandal: and it is to the great credit of the Churches that they, through their agricultural chaplains, have played a key role in setting up the Farm Crisis Network. This is a sort of farmer-friendly version of the Samaritans, with the bolt-on of free confidential and independent advice about making a coherent farm plan. For many stock farmers, BSE directly followed by the foot-and-mouth epidemic was the final straw. Once again the Churches – via the Arthur Rank Centre and the Agricultural Chaplains Association – provided practical help and encouragement through the Addington Fund. Applications for financial help were processed within a week, and were normally associated with pastoral care and professional advice.

But what of the future? The publication of the Curry Report *Farming and Food: a Sustainable Future* in January 2002 sketches a possible scenario. Inevitably, farmers hoped to find statements of clear government support for farming and domestic food production. They looked for a pathway out of the present situation where long-term trends seem to be downwards, with, for instance, wheat being sold at the same price as it fetched in 1975. For them the central issue remains that commodity prices are too low. The failure of the report to address this will confirm the suspicion that the government is not committed to the future of British agriculture, and that it is happy to acquiesce to the present situation, where food is purchased from the 'least-cost supplier'. The volume of imported food will inevitably increase. Countries with more favourable climates, cheaper labour, and governments that subsidize their farmers will always be able to undercut home production, especially at a time when there is so little concern about the nature of imported food, and no tax on aviation fuel. The Curry Report is subtitled 'a sustainable future': but what the farmer on Grunty Fen knows is that you can only farm if you make a profit on what you sell – and that depends on commodity prices.

In contrast, the report accepts as inevitable the eventual phasing out of commodity subsidies, but offers in exchange the hope of 'modulation'. This is a way of supporting financially those farmers who farm in an 'eco-friendly' way. Within the CAP, governments are permitted to practice 'modulation', though at the moment only three do so. For there is a catch: national governments have to match fund modulation grants, in contrast to commodity subsidies that are funded in full. It is proposed that the UK rate of modulation should increase from its present three per cent, to 10 per cent in 2004, and 20 per cent in 2007. Some will see this as much-needed support for the wider rural economy and the environment; but it all depends on the Exchequer finding matching money.

The Curry Report also encourages us as a nation to recognize the dangers of consuming too much, and eating too much junk food. If British people spent more on 'good' food (not just organic food), it would provide an opportunity for farmers with the skill and entrepreneurial flair to respond to 'windows of opportunity'. Farmers' Markets are a drop in the ocean, but they do point to the possibility of inspiring the British housewife to take as much trouble over cooking and nutrition as their French counterparts – a cultural consummation devoutly to be desired!

The mushrooming of 'hobby farms' in certain areas offers opportunities to farm contractors to do the *real* work – provided they can grit their teeth and put up with the whims of hobbyists! But perhaps the major hope is that farmers will in future be paid more for 'farming the landscape', and on the back of this will be able to develop tourism-centred enterprises.

Nevertheless, what the foot-and-mouth epidemic highlighted was that many farming enterprises are no longer financially viable. Those who have administered the Addington Fund have been appalled by the stories they have heard. One way out for those who live near towns is for the farm to become a part-time enterprise supplemented by another income. But many others will want to 'retire with dignity'. To this end a major challenge for farming charities is to orchestrate systems that allow farmers – particularly tenant farmers – to buy or rent a retirement home. To their credit, the Church Commissioners are already pioneering such schemes on their tenanted farms; and the Addington Fund is now helping to alleviate the problem.

Other rural businesses

The foot-and-mouth epidemic shone a spotlight on the whole rural economy. It showed how many farm enterprises are already involved in some aspect of tourism; and how much non-farm based tourism depends on the farmed landscape. It also brought to our attention the fact that the rural tourist industry today provides more employment and earns four times as much as farming itself.

There is no doubt that rural tourism has a huge potential for growth. Three quarters of those who holiday in our rural areas are British, many of them having retired on good occupational pensions. But it is the potential for attracting foreign nationals to visit the countryside that really needs to be developed. Anyone who has toured in France or Germany will recognize how much we need to change if we are to attract those who are unfamiliar with the English language and with our way of doing things. What rural providers most need is good basic advice on how to attract the foreign customer.

Rural churches could play a part in developing such tourism. A recent initiative by the British Tourist Association (BTA) seeks to market 'Hidden Britain'. The strategy concentrates on the appeal of local people as well as local buildings. Visiting a village and mingling with a rural community as well as admiring the landscape could, it is believed, appeal to many foreign nationals. The BTA has encouraged the Arthur Rank Centre to develop a pilot project in Cumbria to see how villages can best work with tour operators to deliver such holiday packages. Certainly the popularity of rural radio and television soap operas would suggest that those who visit the countryside are as likely to be as interested in rural life – the pub, the farm, the church, the gossip – as in the rural landscape.

Light industry has developed vigorously in many rural areas, thanks to the improvement in access to the motorway system and to the development of old farm buildings as industrial units. A current government Green Paper on planning would give more flexibility to rural businesses that succeed and want to develop locally, rather than having to re-locate to the nearest town.

Rural businesses have particularly benefited from being able to offer part-time employment to local people. This costs the employer less and seems to suit the lifestyle of many local people – particularly women with young children. Obviously there is a danger that some will be exploited, but a growing number of rural people welcome the opportunity to be able to put together a 'portfolio' of part-time jobs that together pay the bills. The variety of employment offers a flexibility of lifestyle and gives a job satisfaction that the regular nine-to-five grind often cannot match.

The development of the home computer is beginning to have the effect that Toffler predicted of allowing many more people (including executives) to work from home for at least part of the week. The limitation to this development will be that Broadband Telecommunication is not, and is very unlikely to be, available in remote rural areas outside the market towns.

Among other major employers in the countryside are schools, residential homes, health care services and government agencies. In future these are likely to be located in larger villages and market towns, but they do at least provide local employment, often on a flexible part-time basis. An interesting recent development is the expansion of tertiary education for those with disabilities and learning difficulties who are now legally entitled to further education.

The centralization of 'service provision'

In *Faith in the Countryside* the Churches, in parallel with other worthy reports, argued that society had an obligation to support those village residents who are least able to support themselves. Village people had as much right to 'services' as their urban cousins. There are still favoured areas, such as the north west of Scotland, where such aspirations seem possible: but this is exclusively on the back of the European taxpayer. Where urban English taxpayers have to foot the bill, any moral imperative is generally quietly ignored. Shops and post offices in small villages continue to diminish in number. Public transport between villages usually depends on local subsidy and is therefore very variable: and this causes particular problems for those who have to use public transport to access medical facilities. Except in a handful of villages, the 'right to buy' is gradually eroding the stock of low-cost rental housing. The only two public amenities which have survived and developed, even in small villages, are village halls, saved by lottery fund grants, and village schools, saved because parents now have the right to choose where to send their children to school. (They do not of course have the right to free transport to the school of their choice – and this can create traffic jams in the most unlikely places!)

But village halls and schools apart, the government seems determined to locate all other 'services' in market towns or key villages. This is a major recommendation of the White Paper, which includes a 'health check list' of the services that should be available in such rural centres. (Interestingly, neither cultural facilities nor places of worship get a mention on this list.) It is clear that in the future those who live in smaller villages are going to be left to fend for themselves. It will therefore be all the more important for congregations in such villages to work with other volunteers to fill the vacuum. In 1994 I cited two examples of Community Care Networks masterminded by their local Churches. The need for such initiatives will not diminish – and this is, after all, what the Church has always been good at, and what has always kept Church and community in a working relationship with one another.

The demography of the village in 2002

The startling results of the 1991 census referred to earlier highlighted the extent of urban–rural migration. What this means in practical terms is that, since so many of those who can afford to do so now prefer to live in a rural area, the cost of rural housing has soared, and 'social stratification' is becoming a major problem in many areas. The census also revealed that this 'flight to the countryside' is associated with two particular age groups: couples who are bringing up young children, and those who have just retired. The onset of teenage frustration for the former, and the loss of the car for the latter, are often catalysts for a move back to town. The desire to live in a village is therefore pragmatic and variable, and this results in a highly mobile society. The demographic stability that was once a hallmark of rural life disappears, and the village becomes a variation on the suburb.

What then is the 'human context' in which the Rural Church is called to minister in 2002? The first thing to be said is that the village is no longer an industrial site, a place where people have to live because they are geographically anchored to their work. Today, most people who live in the village have opted to do so. They choose this for a variety of reasons: because they like a small settlement; because they think it is the right environment in which to nurture their children; because they find fulfilment in 'living closer to nature'; because it is a congenial place in which to work at the computer; or because they have retired and their friends live locally. For the present it suits them fine, but if circumstances change they will then choose to move elsewhere. A few stay and become enmeshed in the local place, but the majority are at heart 'colour-supplement gypsies'.

These people – particularly the early retired group – often contribute significantly to community life, and today are frequently the backbone of village organizations, including the Church. But they do have their blind spots. They are probably highly articulate, and have particular interests that they pursue with passion and defend with skill. They will for instance all know what 'local identity' means – without perhaps recognizing that their understanding of the term is highly individual and almost certainly contentious. Many of them will – thank goodness – choose to contribute to community life, but only to those specific areas of activity that interest them.

One of the most significant developments of the last 20 years has been the enthusiasm of the over-40s to retrain and to study for exams. Ten years ago the academic pretensions of the retired were typically to attend a weekly Workers Education Association (WEA) class for the study of music, pottery or local history. Today such initiatives as the offer of 'personal skill accounts' are persuading many to enrol on computer courses, to take A Levels alongside teenage students at Adult Education Colleges, and to join the select band of those privileged to appear, bedecked in mortar board, gown and the distinctive yellow and sky-blue hood, in that oval photograph frame in the living room. More and more mature people want to do some serious study – and to get a bit of paper at the end to prove it. This has major implications for local Churches.

There are still a few for whom the local place is the shop floor of industry – the farmers and countryside workers; those who continue to scratch a living, or a retirement, in the land of their ancestors. But as age increases and public transport decreases most of them migrate to the town. Some are seriously deprived, and they too are forced to move. A significant number of those who hang on are mildly deprived; and were it not for kind neighbours and loyal families, their quality of life would be well below that of their urban cousins. In just a few villages in just a few areas a very few seriously wealthy traditional landowners survive: but there is little attraction in these egalitarian legalistic days in being the squire of Puddlecombe-on-the-Marsh.

Not surprisingly, in the modern village there is a new attitude to authority. Increasingly, people are valued for who they are, not for the office they hold. They are respected for their performance on the day, not for the uniform they wear. Inevitably this puts a strain on those who bear the burden of office in rural areas: on landowners and farmers, police and professional people, councillors and civil servants – and on the clergy.

Thinking laterally, this development is linked to the 'blame culture' which holds that anyone who, for whatever reason, can be held to be blameworthy is relentlessly pursued, irrespective of who they are, or their station in life. This has a massive implication for the cost of delivering services, since whatever is delivered has to be checked, double-checked, and covered in triplicate by an army of civil servants. It is also a major disincentive to amateur volunteers who fear that they will be 'liable' if their good deeds go wrong. The transport problems of small villages would probably be solved overnight by volunteer drivers and local taxis, were it not for a blame culture which 'makes no allowances and takes no prisoners'.

What hope is there that such a multifaceted 'context' may become 'a living soul'? There are perhaps two practical possibilities. First, while for the foreseeable future major decisions are likely to be taken at Westminster or at regional level, there is some hope that local people may, through political channels, in some small way help to shape their own future. Reinvigorating local democracy is a priority for the revival of rural life. But perhaps the most hopeful window of opportunity for the Church is that the great majority of those who live in villages still have somewhere tucked inside them an inherited vision of a vibrant community where local people do things together and care for each other. If the Church can give substance to this vision and help them to fulfil their inner longings, it will have earned a valued place in the village of the future.

CHANGES IN THE RURAL CHURCH

In this section I chronicle the encouraging developments that have taken place at the national level, and go on to illustrate how the rural Church has remained true to its calling to serve society – to be the Church of the people. But my chief aim is to discuss the future of rural ministry in the light of my experiences as a Local Ministry Officer, and as a member of the working party which produced the report *Stranger in the Wings*.

The rural Church at national level

The reception given to *Faith in the Countryside* by the wider Church was muted. Nevertheless, the determination and enthusiasm of those living and worshipping in villages has been such that rural issues are now as high on the agenda of the mainstream Churches as they are on the agenda of the government.

Work stemming from the Arthur Rank Centre

The Arthur Rank Centre (ARC) at Stoneleigh played a key role in setting up the Archbishops' Commission; and since 1990 the recognized authority of the staff to speak ecumenically for the rural Churches has been consolidated. The funding of the Centre is still problematic, but the mainstream Churches have demonstrated their confidence in the ARC by the appointment and funding of staff. The URC and Methodist Churches now fund one member of staff; the Baptist Union another (on a part-time basis); the Church of England has a full-time Rural Officer who is based at the ARC; and the Director is funded by the Rank Foundation and the Royal Agricultural Society of England (RASE). Secular agencies have continued to look to the ARC to speak authoritatively for the Churches in a number of important forums. For instance, the contribution of the Churches to the Government White Paper was put together at the ARC; and the Anglican Rural Officer is currently a member of the Rural Task Force of DEFRA.

A new Director, Gordon Gatward, was appointed in 2000. A farmer's son with a PhD to his credit on the 'Theology of Animal Husbandry', he had natural links with the RASE and with the farming world. His leadership was particularly effective during the foot-and-mouth epidemic. Within days of the first outbreak, the ARC Addington Fund – first set up in East Anglia to address the consequences of swine fever – was opened. During the first year it distributed over 10 million pounds to 23,000 applicants, along with much-needed pastoral care and professional advice. The Fund has been staffed by many volunteers from the RASE and other bodies, but the farming world has not forgotten that the ARC was at the heart of the enterprise, and that it is frequently the Churches' Agricultural Chaplains who have operated the fund at a local level. Foot-and-mouth has put the ARC on the map as never before; and Ben Gill, President of the National Farmers Union (NFU) has said that 'the only organization that has come out of the crisis well has been the Church'.

The ARC acts as the operational centre for a number of important networks. The Rural Officers meet there twice a year, as does the Agricultural Chaplains Association. ARC staff have played a key role in launching and servicing the Farmers Friend Network referred to earlier; and they have also helped to consolidate the National Churches Tourism Group.

The journal *Country Way* continues to flourish. It is a truly inspiring, quality publication that every rural congregation in the country ought to subscribe to. A series of practical handbooks (by L. Francis and J. Martineau) on rural ministry from Acora Publishing, which combine serious statistical evidence with suggestions for action are now available to help rural parishes plan for the future. The latest are entitled *Rural Youth, Rural Visitors* and *Rural Mission*. A number of videos have also been produced. *Hidden Treasure* on evangelism in rural areas, is particularly effective for use in smaller parishes.

The ARC has continued to offer training in rural ministry, particularly to those who are about to take up a rural post for the first time. Courses are held twice a year, and concentrate both on the rural social context, and on issues surrounding the multi-parish benefice or multi-point circuit. Occasionally dioceses run rural courses of their own, but in general they have found that it is better to rely on the professional experience available at the ARC rather than to try and re-invent the wheel for themselves. It is also healthy for ministers to meet colleagues from other parts of the country who are in the same situation as themselves.

As a direct result of the way their work is valued the Centre was relocated in 2002 to a highly prestigious site on the edge of the Grand Show Ring at Stoneleigh. There are not too many things that the Churches can crow about these days, but the ARC is surely a glowing example of what the Churches, working together, can still achieve to influence society for good.

Other national organizations and rural forums

Other organizations continue to provide regular opportunities for rural people to meet and to plan together. The Rural Theology Association (RTA) runs an annual conference, as does the Rural Evangelism Network (REN). Hard-working enthusiasts ensure that local RTA Groups and Rural Study Networks continue to flourish. In Cheshire, for instance, the meetings are attended by as many as 70 people; and the East Anglia Association musters 30 or more for their biannual gatherings. In other areas it is more likely to be the faithful few who keep the show going; but they always manage to raise the temperature of debate on rural issues in their churches.

Further education in rural issues with tutorial back up is offered by Christian Rural Concern (CRUC); and this is now taken further by MTh, M.Min and D.Min courses in Rural Ministry offered by the Centre for Studies in Rural Ministry, University of Wales, Bangor. The residential elements of these are located at St Deinol's Library, Hawarden, and are run in association with the ARC. The course is directed by Leslie Francis, for many years a major contributor to the literature of rural ministry, and co-ordinated by Peter Francis, Warden of St. Deinol's. It is significant that in 2002 more than 250 lay members of local ministry teams and church congregations were enrolled with the University of Wales, Bangor, on certificate and diploma courses run through the Centre for Ministry Studies.

Ecumenical committees and initiatives

The Churches Rural Group (CRG), a co-ordinating group of Churches Together in England (CTE), first met in 1993. All the mainstream denominations are represented, and representatives from the Churches in Wales (CTYN) and the Church of Scotland attend. As a forum for ecumenical discussion and exchange of information, the CRG has proved very effective. In 2002 it took responsibility for the running of 'Rural Resurrection', a three-day conference brought together at the same venue residential meetings of the Rural Officers, the Rural Evangelism Network, and the CRG itself. All the key players in the rural church were there, and it was a sufficiently significant gathering to attract Sir Donald Curry as a guest speaker.

Potentially the CRG has a major role to play. The ARC would probably welcome an official link to CTE via the CRG; and both secular government and other rural organizations would be only too ready to deal with one rural church body as opposed to a plethora of denominations. Already a number of representations to government prepared by the staff of the ARC has gone forward under the CRG logo: but a committee which meets only three times a year is simply not prepared or able to take on the role of spokesperson at this stage.

Rural practitioners within the denominations have significantly raised the profile of rural issues at their national Assemblies. At both the Baptist and URC Assemblies motions relating to the farming crisis have been fully debated; and the Methodist Conference has adopted a similar motion expressing sympathy with and encouragement for farmers. The Rural Affairs Committee of the General Synod of the Church of England, which started as a support group for the Rural Officer, has developed into a full-blooded lobby group. It has organized two full-scale debates on rural issues over the last three years, and a well-attended fringe meeting has become a regular feature of the York Synod. The Committee has also just authorized an excellent study-guide (*The Grass is Always Greener* by Anne Richards), which will help urban and rural people to understand each other better.

One of the most significant jobs of the Rural Officer of the Church of England has been to run induction courses for new archdeacons and bishops appointed to rural dioceses. He has also initiated an annual meeting of 'rural bishops', which has proved extremely popular and is increasingly influential. A development of this has been to bring together the rural bishops with the senior free-church staff responsible for rural areas, to discuss specific issues (such as the government White Paper or the Curry Report).

At this stage it is too early to predict whether the latest round of Anglican–Methodist talks will lead to practical changes at grass-roots level: but most rural congregations of both denominations are only too aware of the folly of Christian disunity. There are no longer the resources or the stomach for more than one Christian presence in each settlement.

In all of these ways the rural lobby within the mainstream denominations has grown in confidence and effectiveness since 1990. The Churches are now well equipped to play a full part in the national debate about the future of our countryside.

The Church and rural society

Village community life

It would be all too easy for rural congregations, bereft of a resident clergy person, presented with ever-spiralling quota requests, and compassed about with architects and quinquennials, to concentrate simply on survival. It is a credit to their humour and native Christianity that in so many cases they do much more than that. Leafing through the pages of any copy of *Country Way* the reader uncovers a dozen examples of heart-warming community service. Frank and Griselda James run the village shop that specializes in locally-produced food, a cyber café with a library service on CD, and the area newsletter. They are also heavily involved in their LEP and in running Alpha courses. Eddie Upton, the Director of Folk South West – a folk arts development agency – is also Churchwarden of St Mary Magdalen, Stocklinch in Somerset. Jenny and Glyn Lewis run a Sunday half hour in the local residential home which is the highlight of the patients' weekend. Roger Greene, the Methodist Rural Chaplain for Cornwall, has sponsored no less than 500 applications to the Addington fund, and his phone has become so busy that Farm Crisis has paid for him to have a dedicated line installed.

A recent survey of volunteers discovered that regular church worshippers are 70 per cent *more* likely to be involved in voluntary community work than those who are not regular worshippers. This is a remarkable fact that we would trumpet from the rooftops if we were not so shy of 'good works': and it is a statistic that rings true as you look around most village congregations. It is even more likely to be true where a congregation has regained confidence and taken responsibility for its own future by the formation of an eldership or local ministry team. Burfield team started a regular coffee morning in the village hall, and has experimented with a Sunday lunch for the lonely. Weston team has produced village drama of real quality that involves even the most intractable teenagers. Ampton has revitalized the local village hall. Forton has developed two annual Riding for the Disabled pageants for people with learning difficulties, that are attended by people from all over the region. At Coxton a regular pastoral care scheme is now in place, and in Southchurch a Good Neighbour scheme offers help with everything from looking after the guinea pigs to allow a family to go on a much-needed break, to threading ten needles a week for a brilliant but now partially sighted seamstress.

It is stories like these that encourage one to believe that, despite the prophets of doom, the rural church in England can have a bright future. Within this broad spectrum of involvement certain themes emerge.

Involvement with secular agencies

At county level, 24 dioceses now have strong links with their Rural Community Council (RCC). In each case church members serve on the Executive Committee of the RCC, and in five cases the RCC Director serves on the Rural Committee of the diocese. Throughout the country the Churches are involved in the government's Regional Agenda, and in numerous cases are represented on such groups as Environmental Forums, Wildlife Trusts, Rural Anti-racism Forums, Carers Support Centres and Rural Business Development Programmes. Details of this involvement are recorded in *Celebrating the Rural Church*, published in 2000 to record progress since *Faith in the Countryside*.

Nineteen dioceses have been involved in providing affordable village housing on glebe-land. Ironically, all of the projects have faced stiff local opposition. Even in cases such as Sapperton in Gloucestershire, where the initiative was taken not by 'outsiders at county level', but by the local PCC, the issue has been deeply divisive. Perhaps that just shows how important it is! Five dioceses have used glebe-land for environmental purposes, and Ecumenical Countryside Committees have held seminars and conferences on local environmental issues.

Local ecumenical co-operation

Inter-denominational co-operation at a national level in rural areas is now a welcome fact of life. At county level, most Rural Committees are now ecumenical in membership. In the parishes, things are much more patchy. In one sense ecumenical life is simpler, in that most small villages now only have one place of worship, and most market towns have a lively Council of Churches. But this disguises the sad fact that few services of worship are truly inter-denominational: whatever their background, individuals have to fit into the inherited tradition of the church they attend.

In some areas the opportunity to set up a Local Ecumenical Project (LEP) has offered a way forward for inter-denominational co-operation. There are over 860 LEPs registered with CTE, which means that there are now many examples of shared use of premises and shared planning which are underpinned by an official agreement. *Releasing Energy* by Flora Winfield (2000) tells heartening stories of practical co-operation from around the country.

Faith in the Countryside argued that the LEP, while sometimes appropriate, was too cumbersome and frightening an instrument for the smaller village – and anyway did not address the real situation in those settlements where there was only one place of worship. To meet this need the 'Declaration of Ecumenical Welcome and Commitment' has been developed. This certainly meets the need, but the take-up has been small. The difficulty seems to be that local members of local congregations tend to be happy with the *status quo*, but it is they who have to take the initiative and 'drive' the project. It is those who are 'outside' who feel the need for change – but since they are not 'in' they are powerless to act.

Church buildings

In 1990, the Acora Commissioners were surprised to discover how many village churches had been reordered for liturgical purposes. Since then, more and more village church buildings have been adapted for multiple community use. A recent survey showed that over half of our rural churches are already used for non-ecclesiastical activities, and the Rural Churches Community Service Programme – which offered the possibility of grants to rural congregations who wanted to adapt their church building for community use – had more than 700 applications.

Most of the adaptations made or desired are relatively simple: an inside toilet; facilities for making coffee and for washing up; provision for a soundproofed crèche area; carpeting and an adequate heating system. They do not require major structural upheaval or the mass destruction of those beloved pews. But the need to implement the requirements of Disability Access legislation by 2004 will concentrate the mind considerably.

The 'Living Churchyard' project, masterminded by the ARC, drew the attention of rural churches to the potential of churchyards for environmental conservation: and this has become reflected in the literature of 'Best Kept Churchyard Competitions'. Every rural PCC struggles to keep their churchyard 'tidy', but as a result of the seed sown, questions are now being asked about conservation as well as about neatness.

There remains an issue in our multi-cultural society about public funding of a denominational church building. Those of us who live in small villages know that the parish church welcomes Christians of all denominations to its services, and is frequently used as a place for quiet reflection by those of other faiths. The visitor's books of our churches bear witness to the fact that, *pace* Philip Larkin, it is not just 'the converted' who recognize their holiness. But explain that to the urban bureaucrat who controls the purse strings of lottery and landfill site grants. Surely there is here an important job for the Churches Main Committee.

Ministry to visitors

It is often said that the notice board in a rural church is the first thing looked at by the visitor, and the last thing looked at by the local. The same local people who display remarkable imagination and energy in devising schemes for 'getting them into church' rarely seem to recognize that 'they' do come – voluntarily and unenticed – in the form of visitors. However, much has been done to rectify this visual impairment thanks to the hard work of a number of enthusiasts. The National Church Tourism Group has already been mentioned. Another important initiative has been the 'Through the Church Door' scheme that has flourished in a number of areas. *Church Watch* by

Leslie Francis vividly highlights the opportunities and the pitfalls. Nine dioceses now have officers responsible for tourism, and a further four are considering an appointment. Seven dioceses have close links with the Tourism Departments of County Councils – an unheard-of luxury in 1990 – and in many areas there are leaflets available for tourists, ranging from 'Church trails' to glossy brochures on 'our local Christian heritage'. More ambitious schemes are being piloted at national level; and the recent Acora Publishing book *Rural Visitors* will encourage parishes to respond to this vitally important evangelistic opportunity with the enthusiasm it deserves. Keeping the church open is obviously a major issue, but it is heartening to read that the Ecclesiastical Insurance Group (EIG) now recommend that the best way to keep a building safe from theft and vandalism is to keep it open and frequently visited.

Village schools

Apart from the church building, many villages still have a church school. This is a major piece of plant that is properly heated and potentially a comfortable venue for a meeting (though a small investment in adult-size chairs is needed). And yet its potential for use outside school hours as a local facility is still largely ignored by church and community alike. There is major work to be done in putting the church school on the agenda of the PCC, and in working out local ways of opening the place up for community use, during both term time, and school holidays and weekends.

When it comes to recognizing the local school as a way of exercising pastoral care for children and their parents and commending the Christian faith to them, there are signs that congregations are recovering confidence in what they have to offer. In an important article in the *International Journal of Education and Religion*, vol. 1, no. 1, pp.100–21, Leslie Francis outlines what is happening in his usual meticulous way. He draws attention to the fact that for a generation clergy have been slightly embarrassed about using the Church's inherited stake in education to 'thrust religion down their throats'. But now, thanks to the patient work of Christian educationalists who have developed RE courses which are quite obviously sensible, valuable and multi-culturally acceptable, and thanks also to parent power, which is opting for a 'Christian ethos education' in quite remarkable numbers, both clergy and congregations are beginning to see the village school in a new light. PCCs are coming to recognize that ministry to children *in the school* offers at least as much potential for positive input as ministry (via Family Services) *within the church*. It helps that, in a relatively new departure, not only do the children occasionally come to church on Sunday, and not only does the school frequently use the church building both as a teaching resource and as a venue for school 'performances', but now lay members of the congregation are being invited to take assemblies alongside the hard-pressed vicar.

The ministry of the Church in rural areas

The factors of change – manpower, money and theology

The core of this book is just what it says – a discussion about the appropriate ministry for rural areas in the 21st century. It started life as an attempt to expand the chapter on ministry in *Faith in the Countryside*, and to give it some strategic clarity. In 1994 I argued that the old model was breaking down, and that if God was to be worshipped in our villages into the next century we must act now to change the system. I suggested that, in the light of the statistical and other evidence available, the model most likely to succeed was that 'each settlement should grow its own local Christian focus', and that in due course one or more members of the group should be ordained to preside at the weekly eucharist, which should be held in every church every Sunday at a time which best suited local people. After nine years working as a Local Ministry Officer in a diocese, which now has over 40 teams up and running, I am convinced more than ever that this model remains the best on offer for the rural areas.

The practical factors which will determine the future of rural ministry are still what they were in 1994 – money and clergy numbers. In the 1990s, clergy numbers seemed to be the key factor. Then the number of stipendiary ordinands stabilized and the number of non-stipendiary clergy increased, so that there are today roughly as many ordained people ministering in the Anglican Church as there were in 1994. (Non-stipended clergy are not of course as 'deployable' as their stipendiary colleagues, and are not for instance usually available to move into a vacant rural parsonage. While most rural benefices rely on the help of non-stipended clergy, it has not in practice been possible to substitute non-stipended for stipendiary as the global numbers might give one to expect.)

Undoubtedly the key factor in 2002 is money. We now recognize that the worst blunder of the Church Commissioners in the 1980s was not their decision to invest in property, but their assumption that pensions would be met out of current income. The 'pensions time bomb', combined with a swinging redistribution of 'historic resources' (the endowments from past generations of Christians) from the ancient sees to those less well-endowed, has persuaded most rural dioceses to adopt budgets of retrenchment. They are now more than ever determined to keep stipendiary numbers within the Sheffield allocation. In 1994 I argued (see Chapter 7) that the Sheffield formula was simplistic, and that a more sophisticated formula of deployment within a diocese would allocate sufficient stipendiary clergy to rural benefices to keep the traditional show on the road. Having battled to secure the acceptance of just such a formula (which is perfectly simple to apply in a computer-literate age) in the Diocese of Gloucester, I have finally had to accept defeat. The budgetary situation is now so tight that the diocese cannot contemplate an increase in the number of stipendiary clergy, which is now so low that the Pastoral Committee has to question the viability of any benefice with a population of less than 3,000. Long before that figure is reached a threshold has been crossed, and in our context at least the old system of one village – one vicar – one vicarage has broken down once and for all. In fact, even in our urban areas the 'single cure' is now unusual.

But there is mercifully a third factor of change to be reckoned with – and that is a renewed understanding of the theology of the church. Since the first publication of this book I have developed the somewhat skimpy notes at the end of Chapter 7 into a full chapter in *Dynamic Local Ministry* (pp. 31–53), to which I must refer the reader. There I argue that we should return to our New Testament roots to rediscover a model of 'Church' which fits our present situation. There we find a DIY Church, where a collaborative authority is exercized by a group of elders, and where a congregation without a eucharistic president is unthinkable. Since 1994 key documents have helped us to reflect on this model. Robin Greenwood's *Transforming Priesthood* helped to open our eyes to collaborative ministry within the Holy Trinity itself.

The General Synod report, *Eucharistic Presidency*, along with the Roman Catholic report *The Sign We Give*, reminded us that the eucharist is an activity of the whole congregation, not just of the priest – and invited us to ponder on the paradox of a eucharistic church which, because there are too few priests, effectively denies a weekly eucharist to half its members. Further, they recommended that presidency at the eucharist should be linked to pastoral oversight: that the president at the eucharist should have a personal (pastoral) relationship with the members of the congregation. Clearly this is unlikely to be the case when, for instance, a retired priest is parachuted into a parish for a brief hour in order to 'work the magic'! Finally, we in England have become aware of the radical writings of the late Wesley Frensdorff, a former Bishop of Nevada, USA, who, like his mentor Roland Allan, memorably challenges us to rethink our understanding of priesthood:

> As Roland Allen pointed out more than 50 years ago, we have a situation in which we claim that the eucharist must be central to the life of the church wherever it gathers, *but we have locked up its presidency in a professional highly educated order.*

What this all amounts to is that our problems over money and numbers would be an undoubted disaster – but only if we assume that the running of the church should be 'locked up ... in a professional highly educated order'. If instead we:

> Dream of a church in which the sacraments, free from captivity by a professional elite, are available in every congregation regardless of size, culture, location or budget.
> In which every church is free to call forth from its midst priests and deacons, sure in the knowledge that training and support services are available to back them up.
> In which members, not dependent on professionals, know what's what and who's who in the Bible, and all sheep share in the shepherding.
> (*op. cit.* P. 2–4)

the sky remains the limit.

The experience of local ministry in rural areas

In 1994 there was precious little evidence outside Lincoln Diocese about how such local groups would work. Since 1994, however, no less than 20 dioceses in England have begun to officially introduce some form of local ministry, while over the water in the USA, Canada, Australia, New Zealand and South Africa, Anglican rural dioceses are turning the rhetoric into reality at a speed which would no doubt terrify the General Synod of the Church of England. At the last Lambeth Conference a fringe meeting on local ministry attracted 120 bishops, and overran its time by an hour. *Dynamic Local Ministry*, which seeks to give an overview of a fast-moving situation, and to tell stories rather than to give a careful assessment, received only one review in the religious press, yet has sold out within ten months. Such is the interest in a movement that is already transforming our understanding of 'Church', and bringing new hope to rural congregations. What follows in this section is a series of practical suggestions, the fruit of nine years of hard-won experience.

When the definitive guide to local ministry is written, the first point that will be made is that it is not just about patching up rural ministry: it is about changing the culture. The Victorian-Edwardian parish system was an integral part of rural culture, and its replacement constitutes nothing less than a surgical operation. Do not therefore expect to push it through in five minutes.

Do not even bother to start unless the bishop and the senior staff of the diocese are completely with you. The involvement of the bishop to give support when local people complain, to encourage when things go wrong, and to browbeat the Board of Finance into footing the bill, is essential if anything radical is to happen. Nor is it worth proceeding to nominate a team unless two-thirds of the congregation, and all of the PCC, understand and approve the change. In New Zealand a local ministry officer may work with a parish – through Sunday preachments, parish days, study weekends – for a matter of years before it is felt to be right to move on to the 'gifting day', and ultimately the 'choosing day', which will identify the local ministry team. The same pattern of long-term work with the whole congregation is mirrored in North Michigan, USA. Similarly, our experience in England leads us to believe that the Lincoln 'Getting Started' module needs to be expanded indefinitely until the time is right – even if it does make the zealots very frustrated indeed. It is an irony of human nature that no-one wants to change unless they are uncomfortable where they are: so it is often the case that it is only when the old system finally breaks down that congregations will recognize the advantages of the new wine. But so be it! A key part of the work with a parish is to persuade the congregation to think strategically, for it is only then that they will be able to identify what they believe God is calling them to do and be; and only when they have some grasp of the vocation of their *parish* will they have some sense of who they should identify as potential members of a team.

In the early stages, a 'benefice team' or 'a team for each village' is always an issue. In Chapter 10 I concluded that the optimum solution would be a 'local team in every settlement': a perfect example of the triumph of theory over experience! When small congregations begin to take an honest look at who might say 'yes', talk of a team in every village recedes imperceptibly into the background. While in almost every case each village involved can produce a few nominees, a nominee is not the same as a signed-on-the-dotted-line volunteer. Except, therefore, in rather special circumstances, most teams end up as 'benefice teams'.

The system of choosing developed in Lincoln may seem a trifle ponderous at first glance, but it seems to fit the English context and it has stood the test of time (I refer the reader to Chapter 10). In other Provinces of the Church the process tends to be more open, but that is only after much more preparatory work with the parish than we can give. There is not usually a dearth of potential candidates: some parishes have produced upwards of 40 names. It is however much more difficult to persuade those nominated to take on what is obviously a very serious commitment. In Gloucester Diocese, only two out of 40 parishes have so far sought nominations and then failed to form a team; but a number of others have had to settle for as few as five or six members.

The training offered to a team in Gloucester Diocese now differs radically from that which we initially adopted from Lincoln. We now feel that our priorities are: first team-building; second to help the team to sort out aims and objectives (what are they there to do); third to ensure that they have regular business meetings that 'work', but which are quite different in character from a PCC meeting; and fourth to teach team members how to discern and develop gifts in others. The training no longer attempts to be a crash-course in the Christian faith. To achieve these ends, all our modules now use 'transformative education' as the method of delivery, and the team tackles them with the help of a 'companion-facilitator' rather than a 'tutor'. Training in the parish is balanced by study days and residentials, which get team members away from their home territory and give them the opportunity to rub shoulders with members of other teams from other parishes. All teams begin by objecting to these 'outings', and end up longing for more of the same!

Usually there are fears that local inhabitants will not accept the ministry of lay people, even if authorized by the bishop. Obviously, there are occasions when individuals want to see a priest and no-one but a priest. Equally, it is only sensible for a parish which is embarking on forming a lay team to take every opportunity to explain to local people what is going on via the magazine, local press, *The Archers*, etc. But the evidence so far is that, if the members of the team are sensible, and are doing things which local people want to see done and which would not otherwise be achieved, they will find easy acceptance in their villages.

What has emerged over the years is that members of the team need to take special care about their relationship with other members of the congregation. There may be some in the congregation who wanted to be on the team but were not chosen. There may be past feuds, petty resentments and personality conflicts; and the disenchanted will invariably appeal over the head of the team to the vicar. It is essential: first that the team recognize from the start that they are there to energize the whole congregation, not to do it all themselves and not just to fulfil their own spiritual needs; second that they keep the closest possible links with the PCC and other church officers; and third that they open up their training modules to other members of the congregation. (If, for instance, they do a module on worship they should ensure that the organist, server, choirmaster, family service organizer, etc. are also invited.)

Teams do not just happen, and the closer the bonding of the team the greater the danger of disruption because of personality conflicts. This is why so much emphasis needs to be placed on team-building activities, and the use of well-tried training tools such as Belben and Myers-Briggs. But perhaps the greatest test of all for the team is likely to be their relationship with clergy and readers.

If the team is to change the culture – to move the parish from a 'clerical' towards an 'all-member' model for ministry – there will be major implications for the role of the clergy and readers within it. Authorized ministers are expected to lead: indeed their leadership may have been crucial when the parish was deciding whether to adopt collaborative ministry. But if the team is to develop a true leadership role, their style of leadership will be all-important. The authority of their office will need to give way to the authority of their personal gifts – a very painful process (and in the English context this can never fully happen, because the incumbent has certain legal responsibilities that he cannot devolve to lay people). There are no easy answers, and no quick fixes, and every team and each incumbent come to realize that they have embarked on a pilgrimage road which is often stony, and where no-one is ever allowed to see round the next corner. And the difficulties are compounded tenfold when a new incumbent is catapulted into a team that he or she did not call into being.

After a period of training, teams are given the bishop's licence to minister in their place – but only for a limited period. It is not healthy for the individual or for the parish that membership of a team should be a life sentence. At regular intervals (say every 5 years), the bishop makes enquiry of the PCC and the congregation; some members may go, and others may join. Always at this stage the aims and objectives of the team need to be revisited and redefined, and this is always a difficult process. Every time a team loses or gains a member the old team dies and a new team is born. This change, like every change, inevitably ushers in a time of turmoil, and teams need special guidance from their companion-facilitator to weather the storm. A particularly thorny issue is how to deliver to new team members the quality training which the others received and now take for granted. Clearly then the responsibility of the diocese to support teams does not stop when they finish their official training; it continues so long as the ministry team endureth – and this too has financial implications.

Forming a team, changing the culture, is bound to be difficult and dangerous. It does not always come off. But the potential for the transformation of individuals and parishes is there. In January 2000 an examiner from the Ministry Division (MINDIV) attended a local ministry residential on spirituality. Their remit was to assess its contribution to the training of Ordained Local Ministers (OLMs) but quite apart from that specific, what bowled her over was to be confronted by 40 or so lay people who were spiritually mature, bubbling with confidence and highly articulate about their faith. Any system that can transform caterpillars into butterflies on that scale is, she felt, worth a bit of difficulty and danger!

In conclusion, despite the many changes in the rural church since 1994, it would still seem that the best hope for ensuring that God continues to be praised in our villages at the same convenient time each week is that ministry should be focused not on an ordained individual, but on the whole congregation. Nevertheless, there are enormous practical advantages in having an ordained person in each village – *provided they are part of a local ministry group*. It is to the issue of OLMs that I now turn.

Ordained Local Ministers

The key document on OLMs to be published since 1994 is the General Synod Report *Stranger in the Wings* (1998). The working party consisted of only five people including the secretary, all of whom were, or became, enthusiasts for local priesthood, and saw it as a way of breaking the clerical mould in which we find ourselves encased – hence the title which is taken from the poem 'Mutations' by Louis MacNeice, which stands at the head of Chapter 1:

> For every static world that you impose
> Upon the real one must crack at times and new
> Patterns from new disorders open like a rose ...
> The stranger in the wings is waiting for his cue
> The fuse is always laid to some annunciation.

Sadly, the promise of that splendid opening was diluted to suit the taste of the entrenched clericalism of the House of Bishops – but at least significant points were made.

Some would argue that the localism of the rural church is an anachronism. Chapter 2 of the report discusses this argument in detail, and concludes that 'a strategy of mission which starts with 'the local' is a strategy which starts where most people are'. It goes on to point out that 'local' priesthood has been part of the Christian tradition since New Testament times. The Orthodox churches have regularly ordained local people to minister in their home villages; and the same was often true in England, even after the Reformation. Many a squire's son was sent for ordination so that he might take up the family living in the place where he was born: and many a Parson Woodforde ministered in the same parish for 30 years or more. The report concludes: 'For most of Christian history, and for much of English history too, there has been a close link between the local settlement, the local congregation and the local priest. "Local" priesthood is not therefore a new invention, but it can perhaps be seen as a recovery of healthy rootedness.'

The report commissioned a survey of all existing OLMs, and had a 75 per cent response rate. One of the most interesting results was in answer to the question 'How did you first come to recognize that God wanted you to be a priest?' Fifty-five per cent mentioned encouragement from the local congregation, and only 30 per cent mentioned a sense of personal calling. This alone marks a clear 'vocational division' between the local and the peripatetic clergy. Other questions in the survey produced a 'characteristics of OLM' profile that is shown in diagrammatic form on page 48 of the report. OLMs should be holy, pastorally aware, enmeshed with the local community and team players, and the congregation must affirm their vocation. They are called to be priests in their local place – *not* to be vicars in a variety of places. The survey reminds us that the call to 'priesthood' and the call to 'vicarhood' are not necessarily the same.

Having established the validity of the vocation to local priesthood, the report recognizes that OLMs may be regarded by some as 'second-class priests', and seeks to answer some of the objections. The licence of the OLM is local, and when he or she moves the licence will not necessarily be renewed. In a strictly legal sense this is of course true of every priest. In practice the licence of an OLM is sometimes renewed – but only after they have as it were 'served their time' and been truly accepted by their (new) local congregation. The theological *training* of an OLM is not as extensive as that of a seminary trained stipendiary: but on the other hand the *life experience* of a 50-year-old – the stuff of theological reflection – is greater than that of a newly-ordained 25-year-old graduate. Nor do all stipendiary clergy have the same capacity for theological reflection. The vicar of Coates, Gloucestershire in 1840 was infinitely less well theologically educated than the vicar of Horsley, Hampshire (John Keble) – but no-one suggested that he was therefore a second-class priest.

Perhaps the Orthodox, with four times as many years experience as the Reformation Churches, may help us here. In their tradition: 'the celebration of the liturgy is the supreme function of the priest, and his other functions are, in comparison, insignificant. Indeed they are not so much "functions" as "charisms" (gifts of the Spirit) which individual priests may have: but only if they are perceived to have them will they be licensed to teach or preach'. (*Stranger in the Wings*, 2.46).

This chimes in with the ARCIC and LIMA reports on Ministry. In these the ordained minister is held to be responsible: for 'oversight' – holding the theological 'focus'; for ensuring that the word is preached (though this does not necessarily imply that they should preach themselves); for presidency at the eucharist; and as 'icon' or representative of the Church to those beyond the congregation. The reports also emphasise the collegiate nature of all ministry. The 'competencies' of OLMs are outlined in the diagram on page 48 of *Stranger in the Wings*, and after much heated debate they *do* include the ability to speak, read *and preach* in public.

But perhaps the most important achievement of the report was to set out the educational rationale for how OLM candidates – who sometimes leave school without qualifications – can learn 'to theologize and guard the tradition'. Fresh from dourly fought battles and hard-won victories over the examiners of the Ministry Division, Wendy Bracegirdle of Manchester Diocese, along with David Leslie of Liverpool Diocese showed how – *pace* Liberation Theology – all of us are theologians in the making and we can all learn to theologize, even if we are not fluent in Hebrew, Greek and Latin. (See *Stranger in the Wings*, Appendix 5.)

In all of these ways the report consolidated the position of local ministry within the Church of England. Sadly however it failed at the last ditch. In the first place, it failed to adjudicate between 'team Led' and 'priest Led' local ministry. In the original report on OLM,

MINDIV recommended as equally valid three different 'tracks'. In Lincoln Diocese a lay team was formed, and only later might one of the members of the team proceed to ordination. In Truro an individual was identified for ordination, and a team from the local congregation was assembled around them to assist with their training. In Manchester and Southwark, where the priorities were somewhat different, there was another track which ensured that OLMs were part of a team – though the team could consist solely of authorized ministers.

It will be seen that while the first track could be a very effective tool for breaking the clerical mould, the other two tracks are all too likely to result in lots more (non-stipended) priests. It is perhaps indicative that in Oxford Diocese – which has adopted its own version of the Truro model – there are now 196 NSMs, of whom 45 are OLMs. In 1996 – before the scheme started – there were 146 NSMs. In six years, non-stipended clergy as a percentage of the diocesan staff has risen from 26 per cent to 35 per cent.

It could be argued that, far from breaking the mould, this has put back by a generation the day when congregations will recognize the need for all-member ministry. The working party, divided as it was between those whose dioceses favoured the Lincoln model and those whose dioceses were committed to the Manchester model, could not bring itself to adjudicate between the two, and in the interests of group solidarity a chance was missed to mark out local ministry as an agent for radical change.

The second issue has to do with the way in which MINDIV remains responsible for the development of OLM. Back in the early days, the House of Bishops' *Guidelines for OLM*, (1989) agreed that all diocesan schemes for the training of OLMs should be subject to approval by MINDIV. This was to ensure that OLMs were 'up to standard' and could not be accused of being second-class priests.

It has to be remembered that the remit of MINDIV is to supervize the selection of candidates for the ministry and to run the theological colleges and courses at which candidates are trained. They have no remit with regard to the training of lay people (apart from Readers). Quite naturally their staff and advisers have an overriding concern with clergy, and are expert in academic lecture-delivered theology. They are major stakeholders in the continuation and improvement of academic theological education. It could therefore be argued that, if the Church needs to shift away from a clerically focused model of ministry to one that is more collaborative in style, MINDIV and their advisers are the very last people qualified to give unbiased or even wise advice.

Since the heady days when *Stranger in the Wings* was in the process of being written, MINDIV have done exactly what the House of Bishops has authorized and encouraged them to do. They have spared no effort to ensure that OLMs should be 'proper priests who have been properly trained'. To this end they have imposed a regime for the regular rewriting of schemes and for the inspection of schemes which is so thorough that it requires the individual attention of a full-time officer in each diocese. It would be difficult for the devil to devise a more effective way of ensuring that OLMs become 'clerics'.

One must assume that MINDIV had a major input into the interim report of the Archbishops' Council on 'The structure and funding of ordination training' (The Hind Report). OLMs are seen simply as clerics who are there to assist stipendiaries. 'They will have engaged in foundational theological and ministerial studies ... before they attend a Bishops' selection conference ... and should continue formal training at a level appropriate to their envisaged ministry in the early years of ministry.' There is no recognition that they, unlike other clergy, are an integral part of a lay team who both share in their training and who themselves need to be part of the educational process. There is no recognition of their special need for 'transformative education' and for alternative methods of assessment. Least of all is there any suggestion that the OLM might be 'the stranger in the wings' whose gift to the church is that (s)he is *not* a 'cleric', but is there to help to break the clerical mould.

It was instructive to visit New Zealand where there is no MINDIV, and where each bishop is responsible for selecting, training and ordaining their own clergy. It is a system that lends itself to experiment and the taking of risks. It will probably never happen, but if OLM is to help to break the clerical mould, rather than to reinforce clericalism, what we need in England are bishops who have the nerve to take responsibility for the experiment themselves, and to remove the training of OLMs from the control of MINDIV and Church House, Westminster.

Needless to say, none of this ever appeared in the text of *Stranger in the Wings*!

The role of the stipendiary

In 1994 it was still possible to envisage a traditional role for the stipendiary incumbent in a rural benefice. In an autobiographical note that I now find somewhat embarrassing, I described how it could be done. But in 2002 the rural stipendiary as 'local vicar' is on the way out – that is the clear message of all the evidence.

The vocation of the rural stipendiary remains what it always was: to be holy, learned, local and apostolic. The underlying role of the stipendiary – to catch 'the vision' and communicate it to others, to keep the parish theologically focused, to ensure that the parish remains 'catholic', to be ready to speak out prophetically, and to carry the can if exciting experiments go pear-shaped – is still vital for the church of the future. But this role will be exercised as companion-facilitator, not as 'traditional vicar'.

In the short term – and we probably now have less than a generation in which to manoeuvre – the priority of the stipendiary will be to change the culture and to move towards all-member ministry, probably by establishing a local team among whom one or more may eventually become OLMs or readers. In the longer term, rural parishes will need just as much loving support and prophetic criticism as ever the young churches of the Greek world needed in New Testament times, and it will be for the stipendiary to meet their needs. A particularly helpful book, *Ministry in Three Dimensions* by Steven Croft, suggests that the stipendiary of the future will increasingly be called on to exercise a 'presbyteral and episcopal' role. It will be for them to discern gifts in others and to encourage vocation. It will be for them to hold the vision and to lead the transformation of the culture. It will be for them to ask the hard questions, sort the knotty problems and exercise spiritual discipline. This is already the case in the Diocese of Nevada, and I refer the reader to *Total Ministry* by Zabriskie for a description of how such a ministry can work out in practice.

Rural ministry has certainly become a 'specialist ministry', and such a development implies that Continuing Ministerial Education (CME) for stipendiary clergy should help to fit them for this new role. Anyone involved in personnel training in industry has to be a highly skilled technician: and clergy companion-facilitators will need more expertise in the subject than they picked up from college 20 years before.

The role of the diocese

The first duty of the diocese is to affirm rural congregations. Unfortunately small rural parishes tend to irritate hard-pressed diocesan officials. They make as great a demand on the secretariat as do larger parishes. The churchwardens are often extremely difficult to deal with; 'Whatever you do for them they still regard the diocese with enormous suspicion.' The problem is compounded because most diocesan officials have never lived in a small village and therefore find 'village Christianity' incomprehensible. What they need to realize is that these same villagers have kept alive the rumour of God in a context that would have driven most bishops to despair long ago. They have shown a dogged perseverance that puts them on a par with Jacob labouring for Rachel, or St Christopher at his ford – or perhaps more to the point on a par with the traditional housewife. They too are 'the saints' – even though they would not be seen dead at Spring Harvest. If the culture is to change there must be encouragement, recognition of achievement, sympathy and laughter.

The diocese also needs to encourage clergy to consider the rural ministry option. One way of doing this is to set up rural training parishes. This was a major recommendation of *Faith in the Countryside*, and it is good to hear that 16 dioceses have now done so. In the longer term this should mean that the Church will have a steady stream of stipendiary clergy – who will one day be in positions of influence – who value rural ministry and understand the problems. On the other hand, while virtually all stipendiary clergy 'taste' urban and suburban ministry as curates, few dioceses yet provide an opportunity for them to 'taste' rural ministry. This is storing up trouble for the future – for them and their families. As is pointed out in *Celebrating the Rural Church*, to be inducted to an incumbency in a rural setting is for many to undergo an enormous culture-shock. It is a shock that could so easily be avoided *if training dioceses just took rural ministry seriously.*

Apart from affirming rural parishes and encouraging rural ministry, the supreme role of the diocese is to hammer out a clear strategy for the delivery of ministry in the villages. Today there are effectively two options. The ministry can remain essentially clerical – a parson or reader in each village; or parishes can be encouraged to go for an 'all-member' model of ministry, served by 'local' priests.

If it is to be the clerical option, it will undoubtedly have to be largely 'non-stipended' clerical: *and the parishes and the clergy need to know this*. NSMs will need to be deployable, and they should realize from the start of their training that they may well be asked in the future to run a village church. The diocese needs to husband its rural rectories and to encourage NSMs and retired clergy to consider the 'house for duty' option. (Indeed a glance at the appointments advertisements in church journals suggests that this is something of a growth industry.) If local priests are to be encouraged, the diocese will need to target existing readers and churchwardens of long standing to explore their vocation to a 'local' priestly ministry; and there will also need to be a clear decision about who their line-manager will be, and how they will be supported in their potentially very lonely job. For the convenience of the clergy – for this is after all a model that reckons the convenience of the clergy above the wishes of the laity – multi-parish benefices will become single units with one PCC.

If this clerical option is to work well there are obvious attractions in encouraging the deanery, or the 'Minster' as the delivery point for ministry. For the diocesan office there are great attractions in such a system. A properly conducted survey would also probably show that such a system does make possible a number of initiatives that would not otherwise happen. The Chapter for instance can provide a valuable support network for isolated clergy. Deanery Youth Workers, Deanery Administrators and chaplaincies to government structures at deanery level were all around in 1994, and with such a model of ministry they should be possible today. However, what needs to be realized is that though those who live in small villages will go to the large village for what they need because they have to, they would still *prefer* to have their own post office, shop, school, doctor, policeman – and church and vicar. And sociologists tell us that the Church is best understood as a 'voluntary associational activity'. Note *voluntary*.

In all of these ways the diocese could endeavour to keep the old order going into the new century. It will be clear from everything I have written that I would regard this as a thoroughly retrograde strategy. But at least it has the virtue of clarity. It is a strategy that can be commended with honesty and energy by bishops and archdeacons, and has some chance of short-term success.

If, on the other hand, the diocese is to go for 'all-member ministry' sustained by 'local' priests, there will be a different set of priorities. Parishes and clergy will need to know that the future is both non-stipendiary and collaborative; and that the future depends on the local congregation themselves. And since few welcome change unless they are uncomfortable where they are, the diocese will need to eschew palliative strategies – such as 'house for duty' and forced deployment of NSMs – which will simply prolong the agony.

It will be necessary for bishops and archdeacons to be frank and honest with parishes about the future. This will not make them popular! But at the same time as being honest about the necessity for benefice amalgamations and the reduction in the number of stipendiary clergy, they do also need to do everything in their power to communicate to rural parishes 'the vision'. Parishes need, for instance, to recognize that they *can* have their own priest, keep their own church and run their own show – *if they only play their cards right. The sky is still the limit!* The former Bishop of Ludlow masterminded an enormously successful 'travelling theological circus' that persuaded droves of rural church-wardens and PCC members to 'do' theology, to get their minds round why change was necessary, and to grasp the possibilities for the future. Interregnums are opportunities for in depth study not to be missed. Archdeacons' Visitation charges tend to enter at one ear and exit from the other: but opportunities to preach can surely be transformed into opportunities to share honestly – and so to teach.

The diocese will need to set up a professional training organization to help parishes to move from where they are to where they could be – and to fund it generously. All of this may seem a tall order in the current climate of conservative retrenchment, but with courageous episcopal leadership the corner can be turned (as *Dynamic Local Ministry* shows). And what a worthwhile challenge that would be for anyone who is called to wear a mitre!

End piece

Perhaps the most encouraging news of that dire year 2001 came from a national survey on church growth. To the researchers' amazement this showed that the churches most likely to be growing are those with no more than 20 members. So there is hope – if we have the will and are prepared to take risks. As the Kiwis would say: what we need is less red tape and more pink elastic!

The Rural Commission

1

The Initial Response

On 10 September 1990, *Faith in the Countryside*, the report of the Archbishops' Commission on Rural Areas, was launched at a press conference at Lambeth Palace.

During the previous 18 months, the 20 commissioners heard evidence from a variety of people: invited experts and national leaders; clergy and lay people; people living in the country and those living in towns; young and old; rich and poor; those in work and the unemployed or retired.

In the course of 42 diocesan and four regional visits, they took evidence from over 6,000 people and listened to the views of as many more again. As the process gathered momentum, expectations of the report grew. And by 10 September it seemed – at least to the commissioners – that all rural England was agog, eager to find out what they had said.

The secretariat of the Commission did everything possible to ensure a successful launch. On the previous Monday, the 'Acora officers' from every diocese gathered in London to receive their pre-publication copies and to be briefed on how they should field the flood of enquiries from local press and radio that would come their way the next day. That evening, the trains from London to the shires carried their full quota of clergy, each engrossed in a large green-covered book.

Alas for the best-laid plans. On the Tuesday morning news broke that the release of Terry Waite might be imminent. The press conference at Lambeth was indeed full to overflowing – but the journalists were not interested in the report. That evening, the more enquiring members of the television-viewing public may have wondered why the Archbishop should be interviewed about Terry Waite in what appeared to be a cellar flanked on the one hand by the familiar figure of Lord Prior, and on the other by the Bishop of Norwich – but of *Faith in the Countryside* there was not a mention. The national newspapers followed suit, and the report was relegated to a brief mention on the inside pages.

Crowded out of the headlines at its launch, the media found the report – when eventually digested – rather stodgy. They had inevitably expected political fireworks from the successor to *Faith in the City*, and a leak the month before had whetted their appetite for another Church–government confrontation. What they got was a balanced, carefully expressed, weighty document with few brave slogans and a minimum of disposable clerical idealism. Furthermore, the future of rural England was already a well-charted area of political debate and in the social field the report said roughly what others had already said (although everyone agreed that it said it extremely lucidly). *Faith in the Countryside* was no doubt commendable, but not particularly newsworthy. So the Acora officers, crouched expectantly over their telephones, were disappointed – the commissioners, who had worked hard and given of their best, were very disappointed.

Yet despite the disaster of 'launch day', *Faith in the Countryside* is now widely accepted as a good document, and a worthy companion to *Faith in the City*. Much of the credit must go to the secretariat for making it so accessible. The general consensus is that it is exceptionally well presented, and that it also makes interesting reading. At one meeting a member of the audience declared that having taken the report to bed as a cure for insomnia, he was amazed to find himself still reading with enthusiasm at 2 a.m.! The vice-principal of the Royal Agricultural College, Cirencester, has recommended it to his students as the best available overview of the rural situation in England. And, at its local launch, the director of the Northumberland rural community council favourably contrasted *Faith in the Countryside* with a Brussels document on the rural future. The former report, he said, was 'people-concerned from cover to cover', whereas the latter only devoted some ten pages out of 600 to people's lives.

Some of this enthusiasm has to be seen in the context of a growing interest in rural life generally, and in this sense it is a report which rides on the crest of a wave. The rural lobby – which has gained enormous momentum since the early 1970s – has always seen the Church as an ally, and for the sake of the cause its members were determined that the report should succeed. Therefore, media interest or no media interest, there were powerful forces standing in the wings before the launch, determined that this report would not sink without trace.

The publication of *Faith in the Countryside* was followed shortly afterwards by a report from the House of Lords Select Committee on the future of the countryside. In the debates on this report, the Acora evidence was referred to frequently; and when Action with Communities in Rural England (ACRE) published a lobby pamphlet in the spring of 1991, its members chose to link the two reports to demonstrate how similar their analysis of the situation was.

The enthusiasm of the secular agencies has, however, to be set against a lukewarm reception by the Church. The *Church Times* review was far from enthusiastic, and during the first month the only two published letters were from correspondents who had clearly not read the full report. A consensus view might be that while *Faith in the Countryside* had served to put the rural Church on the agenda and indeed gave a vivid account of the problems, it had failed to come up with acceptable ecclesiastical solutions.

One of the difficulties is undoubtedly the size of the document. Few PCC members are used to coping with 400 pages of serious argument, and those who have tried have tended to pick up one or two banner recommendations – 'a service in every church every Sunday' is the one most often quoted – without grasping the over-arching 'vision'. The short report is an excellent summary; but inevitably, because it is a summary and so is stripped of human illustration, it fails to capture the imagination. Where (as in Carlisle diocese) deanery study groups have invested many hours in determined study of the report, the 'vision' has been perceived and 'the converted' are already busy converting others: but this has only happened as a result of two years' unremitting and imaginative preparatory work by the Diocesan Rural Officer.

The other major problem is that, in contrast to the bulk of the report, chapters 8 and 12 (ministry and finance) show distinct signs of partially resolved battles in committee. In one sense, all the material is there, but while each tree is lovingly described, the boundaries of the wood are irritatingly vague. What is lacking is a coherent vision statement which PCCs can grasp.

So, while over 20,000 copies of the report have already been sold, the number of deaneries and parishes who have as yet changed their way of life as a result of *Faith in the Countryside* is relatively few. Obviously, the diocese has an important part to play in putting the recommendations into practice, but until rural clergy and rural congregations perceive 'the vision' and recognize it as sensible and practical, little will happen.

My hope is that this book may persuade others that there is now a model for future rural ministry which is practical, positive and of the Spirit.

It is now over three years since the report was published and during that time the issues raised have been very thoroughly debated in the rural forum, and many new practical initiatives have been taken by rural dioceses. A consensus is emerging about how to tackle ministry in rural areas during the next generation. In the belief that the moment has come to give verbal form to these ideas, I shall first try to place the Rural Commission in its historical context and then go on to state simply what I perceive to be 'the Acora vision', or rather, perhaps – since we have begun to move beyond Acora – 'a vision of rural ministry after Acora'.

I shall then test the model against a mounting body of evidence on rural church life. There are the extensive surveys carried out in parallel with the work of the Rural Commission and the *Children in the Way* reports, and there are also a number of other important dissertations and papers not generally available. Examples of properly monitored experiments are few and far between, but there is also a certain amount of evidence from dioceses which have undertaken rural initiatives. In the light of this evidence I shall try to assess the value of 'the vision' and the likelihood of 'success' if it is implemented.

2

The Context – Our Inheritance

The warm reception given to *Faith in the Countryside* by rural secular agencies is evidence of the close links which exist between Church and society in the rural sector. Depending on the viewpoint, these are either an anachronistic survival from the past, or a glorious example of what should be happening in every other area of national life. Therefore if we are to understand the context of the Rural Commission, we must begin by focusing on the nature and history of rural society in England. We shall look first at our inheritance from the past, and then in more detail at important developments since 1945.

THE SOCIAL INHERITANCE

In his novel *People of the Black Mountains*, Raymond Williams describes how for 7,000 years people have settled the land and shaped the landscape. From the early hunters to the computer programmers in their Black Mountain retreat, our relationship to the countryside has been determined by 'how we survive' and 'how we choose to live together'.

Rural nostalgia has become such an industry that it is worth making the point that our villages were originally factories rather than time-share holiday developments. Nor is rural nostalgia new. The same Dr Raymond Williams who wrote *People of the Black Mountains* was Professor of Drama at Cambridge, and his seminal book *The Country and the City* shows how the 'rural idyll' was well established in English literature as far back as the sixteenth century when Virgil and Horace became essential reading for the educated Englishman. Nevertheless, if we are to understand rural areas today we must be realistic about the past, and it is worth examining just three of the most powerful current myths.

The first myth is that villages are places where the pace of life is slow and unhurried, places which are essentially for the enjoyment of leisure rather than the pursuit of work. As Nan Fairbrother said so forcibly in her book *New Lives, New Landscapes*, there is not a square inch of English landscape which has not been in part shaped by the hand of man: and this was for the most part as true in 5000 BC as it is true today. What is true of our landscape is true of our villages. Their location, their shape and their architecture is essentially functional. It used to be said that our settlement patterns were largely determined by our ethnic origins: Germanic nucleated villages in the east, and Celtic dispersed settlements in the west. It now seems more likely that methods of agricultural production, and later socio-political patterns, have been more important than cultural background. Cereal production with limited machinery makes a nucleated village seem sensible: but cereal production with better machinery on land which is divided by dykes (as in the Fens) necessitates a dispersed settlement pattern. Pastoral agriculture, especially on poor soil, leads to dispersed settlements.

The manorial 'system' which was a vital tier of mediaeval government was well suited to the nuclear village – as was the estate system of a later generation. Other acts of government had other consequences. The love of Plantagenet kings for hunting meant that in areas such as the Forest of Dean all the ancient villages are sited on the edge of the old forest boundaries; and the enclosure movement of the fifteenth century and after (a development which was both political and agricultural) turned arable land over to sheep grazing and is estimated to have forced at least 3,000 settlements to be abandoned. Even today many agricultural villages (as in north Dorset) are severely functional and, apart from the church and two or three Thomas Hardy-type farmhouses which hardly seem able to raise themselves above the clay on which they stand, there is no building built before 1800. Most of the 'prettiest' villages are actually industrial settlements. The higgledy-piggledy villages of the Stroud valleys of Gloucestershire are collections of weavers' cottages, many of them abandoned in the eighteenth century when northern mill towns put the Stroud weavers out of business; and within living memory, the picturesque harbours of Clovelly and Hope Cove in Devon (so loved by the holiday brochures) were working ports.

So while the desire of present-day inhabitants to keep industry (and cow dung) out of the village is understandable, it is important to recognize that such a development constitutes not a return to some golden age, but a break with village history.

The second myth is that in contrast to the towns, cottage life in the old village was good, wholesome and desirable. A glance at the burial records of any village church will reveal that half of those who died before 1875 were under the age of two. The human tragedy which lies behind that simple fact hardly bears thinking about, and historians of medicine suggest at least half of those deaths were a result of contaminated water and insanitary living conditions. The fact that these conditions continued well into the twentieth century is catalogued in painstaking detail in a survey of north Oxfordshire villages entitled *Country Planning 1944*. Half of the villages surveyed had no piped water, and only 2 per cent of all houses were connected to mains water, so that inside lavatories, let alone mains drainage, were exceptional. A third of the villages were not on mains electricity.

It is hardly surprising that when those who lived in the old cottages were offered the chance of a council house, they were as quick to move to it as their ancestors had been quick to move to the new towns at the beginning of the Industrial Revolution. In a memorable phrase, disadvantage is disadvantage 'even when it is thatched'.

A Fortunate Man: The Story of a Country Doctor by John Berger begins: 'Landscapes can be deceptive. Sometimes a landscape seems to be less a setting for the life of its inhabitants than a curtain behind which their struggles, achievements and accidents take place.' The idea that rural life is uncomplicated, carefree and even very different is the townsman's myth. English rural life is actually as harsh and difficult as life in town or suburb.

The third myth is that the village is a natural community. Recently

9

mediaeval historians have come to recognize that England differed markedly from other European countries in that it never had a true peasant culture. As far back as the twelfth century we find individuals owning land, and individuals hiring themselves as labourers for cash payment. This has meant that the population of our villages has always been mobile to some degree. Nevertheless, employment, locality and blood relationship have provided the common ground in which 'community' could grow. What is not sometimes recognized is that despite such fertile soil that frail plant did not automatically flourish. Richard Jefferies is an author frequently quoted by the purveyors of rural nostalgia, and yet his essay 'Village organisation' (1875) is a cry of exasperation precisely because the villages he knew around Swindon were anything but 'communities'. It is a *cri de cœur* echoed in numerous clerical memoirs of the nineteenth century, including Kilvert. In fact the picture that we find in many Victorian novelists of village community life as for the most part narrow, suffocating and dull is probably nearer the truth than the local folk museum would suggest.

It is also being recognized that the undermining of self-contained village community life began in the mid-nineteenth century. In his survey of the village of Ringmer in Sussex, *The Quiet Revolution*, Peter Ambrose examined the parish registers in detail and showed how the number of marriages outside the village rose in direct proportion to the improvement of transport: road improvements, the railway and, perhaps most important of all for courting couples, the bicycle. He also charts the part played by the opening of a reading room where working men could for the first time study the newspaper for themselves, the growth of general literacy, and the coming of the radio, in breaking down the last vestiges of localism and bringing a common urban culture into every home. So, long before the Second World War, even before widespread car ownership, villages were no longer self-contained units set in aspic.

THE CHURCH INHERITANCE

For centuries the church has had a practical as well as a spiritual influence on the life of rural people. Indeed, a 'parish' was originally a unit of church organization.

The word 'parish' seems to have been imported from France and did not come into general use until the later Middle Ages, but the missionary strategy that aimed to build a church in each settlement served by an ordained priest goes back to Saxon times and is usually ascribed to Archbishop Theodore. Landowners were encouraged to build churches and to send one of their servants to the bishop for training and ordination. In addition to what he could earn from his glebe (meaning literally his clod of earth), the priest was to be paid fees on certain occasions, and receive an annual tithe (though this was originally a voluntary donation). In pre-Conquest times the church building seems to have been regarded as the property of the landowner, and he also owned the patronage of the benefice. It was therefore a missionary strategy which fitted perfectly with contemporary society.

The parish in this form did not of course emerge overnight, and for some time missionary work in certain areas centred on minsters with only a preaching cross in each village. However by 1291, 8,000 parishes were registered (it is likely that the actual number of parishes in existence was more like 9,500) and this gives a figure of approximately one church to 300 people. Between 1150 and 1250 large numbers of churches were built and most existing churches were reordered or added to in some way, so that by 1300 almost every hamlet had its own church – though some of these were regarded as 'daughter' churches attached to the 'mother' or 'parish' church of a larger settlement.

During the high Middle Ages the parish system came under attack on two fronts. The development of monasticism led many landowners to give their churches (and the income associated with them) to monastic houses to ensure that prayers were said for themselves and their families. The monasteries often appropriated the income of the 'rector' to themselves and appointed a 'vicar' on what was in effect half salary. Sometimes a monk was sent to act as parish priest (though this was expressly forbidden by his monastic vows), and often no one at all was appointed. From 1300 on, wandering friars began to travel round the country, preaching, hearing confessions and absorbing the charitable gifts of the faithful. A good picture of the resulting tension between parish priest and friar is given in Chaucer's *Canterbury Tales*.

Throughout this period reforming bishops, such as Stephen Langton, architect of Magna Carta, sought to ensure that there were properly paid parish priests and well-kept parish churches. Their efforts to upgrade the authority of the Church succeeded to such an extent that in an almost imperceptible way the parish priest became less the man of the local lord, and more the representative of the bishop or the abbot.

Thus by the time of the Reformation most of the English countryside was divided into parishes with at least one church building served, in theory, by a resident priest. The system was already so integral a part of the government of the realm that it was almost inconceivable that it should be replaced, and yet it was strongly challenged by the Reformers who returned from Geneva after the Marian persecution. For a generation after Elizabeth's accession they tried to superimpose upon the parish system a new mission strategy based on the belief that Christ's Church finds its true expression in the congregation of the faithful. Congregations were not necessarily coterminous with the settlement, and the Reformers believed that congregations should be governed by elected elders who chose the minister. They also believed that each congregation had the right to worship in the form they believed to be 'godly', rather than according to the formularies of a Prayer Book. Opposition to the Reformers was theological, political and cultural. Hooker's writings gave formidable intellectual support to the parish system, which perfectly expressed the concept of the Christian nation state: and at first gently – but with increasing firmness – Elizabeth's bishops took measures which led to the Puritans (as they came to be called) being edged out of the Established Church.

It is perhaps the crowning mercy of the British Reformation that, except in Ireland, the extremists never became locked on to the treadmill of mutual violence that tore apart the rest of Europe. Nevertheless, the Civil War was at least in part a religious conflict between the idea of the Church as part of the framework of society and the idea of the Church as personal and independent of government control. Though the Establishment 'won', Non-conformity also remained intact, so that the events of the seventeenth century ensured both the survival of the parish system as 'normal' – and the certainty that the vision of one parish, one church, one priest, one congregation, which inspired it would never be a reality. Rather, the 'normal' village would in future be a battleground between church and chapel.

For a century Non-conformity was in retreat, but with the coming of Methodism the chapel went on the offensive. The battle was given a political edge because the church was all too often the preserve of the landowner, while the chapel represented those who wanted the universal franchise and a new social order. In retrospect, we can see that the parish system did have as its gravest flaw that it lent itself too easily to being an instrument of political government. Intended as a framework to ensure that everyone was cared for spiritually, it all too easily became a way of ensuring that everyone was controlled.

Yet the ideal survives. It survives because it encapsulates a powerful missionary aspiration: that not one inch of the realm and not one part of creation should be beyond the love and care of God as expressed through his Church. It is surely because this argument is so vivid, and its practical expression symbolized by parish church and vicar so tangible, that the parish system as received from Saxon times still has the power to inspire people living in villages today.

THE PARSON

With the parish goes the parson. While the village parson has often been a figure of fun, he has rarely been an object of hate – unlike the figures of the hypocritical bishop or the aspiring archdeacon. Chaucer – who has little enough respect for the Church – saves some of his kindest words for the parish clergyman; and Oliver Goldsmith remembers the minister in his *Deserted Village* in some of the gentlest lines in the English language.

From Archbishop Theodore onwards, church leaders have encouraged the clergy to be learned, holy and involved in community life. They have all assumed that the clergyman should be the indisputed leader of the local church, a mini-bishop. Numerous records of visitations by mediaeval bishops show how determined they were to encourage literacy among the clergy – though the visitations also show how far the reality fell short of the vision. The fact that the priest had glebe land which he himself farmed ensured that he was personally involved in the social life and concerns of the village; and we have implicit evidence of the pastoral ministry of mediaeval clergy from the Black Death period when as many as 60 per cent of them are estimated to have died.

The Reformation bishops, such as Hooper at Gloucester, immediately put in hand measures to improve the literacy of the clergy; and though the size of the dioceses and the political duties of bishops meant that such efforts were intermittent and piecemeal, by the time of the Civil War many rural clergy were by contemporary standards 'learned men'.

Ministry in the Countryside: The Rural Commission

The fact that the 'new' services began to centre on the sermon, and that the sermon could also act as a sort of local newspaper, meant that the status of the parson as a source of knowledge and a moulder of public opinion began to grow. Perhaps more significant in the long term, there emerges from seventeenth-century rural Anglicanism an ideal of simple clerical holiness which still resonates today. No one who has read George Herbert's *A Priest to the Temple, or the Country Parson* can doubt that here genuine Christianity and authentic Englishness are combined. In his three years as a country parson Herbert created an ideal for future generations. Nor was he alone, for it seems from the detailed records of the Anglican rural clergy during the Commonwealth period that many of them were holy men apparently loved by their parishioners. A number of clerical 'memorials' of the period show how a pastoral ministry to everyone in the village was recognized as part of the job, though this social concern probably began to run in slightly different channels in the eighteenth century as the clergy became more wealthy (because of Queen Anne's Bounty and the glebe allocation) and gradually edged their way into the ranks of the landed gentry. Parson Witts of the Slaughters in Gloucestershire, for instance, spent much of his time travelling to Gloucester to act as magistrate: and even Parson Woodforde, who visited assiduously, clearly lavished most of his attention on the upper echelons of local society.

Herbert's ideal was reshaped by the religious revivals of the nineteenth century. One of the manifestations of this many-sided movement was that clergy aspired to a new 'professionalism' and that professional standards began to be set by the recently established theological colleges. The holiness of life inculcated by such High Church colleges as Chichester and Cuddesdon was perhaps more monastic than practical, but it had the effect in the public mind of creating that 'pedestal of perfection' for the parson and his family which is an essential element of the rustic scene before 1914. The reordering of so many village churches between 1850 and 1914 is evidence of the part services and prayers had come to play in the parson's life. Many rural clergy were sons of the landed gentry and as such regarded themselves as part of the village hierarchy, but at least they now became less concerned about enforcing the law and more concerned about changing society for the better. The parson was certainly the moral spokesman of the village, whose job was to stamp out wickedness, but a diary such as Kilvert's shows that he also saw it as his job to inspire 'charity' among the rich. The provision of education in the village was a cause that virtually every parson took up with enthusiasm, and to their credit they often built the village schools in the teeth of opposition from squires and farmers.

P. G. Wodehouse has a particular place for the clergy in his rustic idyll, which in a way carries forward Goldsmith's parson into the twentieth century. In 'The Great Sermon Handicap' a group of aristocratic layabouts are marooned in rural Gloucestershire. To amuse themselves after a bad day at Goodwood races, they hit on the idea of betting on which parson will preach the longest sermon on a certain Sunday. There are ten parishes within five miles, each with its resident parson – most of whom show up for dinner at Twing Hall on occasion, and one of whom gives coaching to the sons of the rich during the summer holidays. It is regarded as normal and natural for the local gentry to go to church on Sunday, where the main feature of the service is the sermon. There is no sign that going to church has any influence on belief or way of life, except perhaps to reinforce the 'Code of the Woosters' about what 'decent living' involves. None of the clergy in Wodehouse is unpleasant, and it is assumed that they perform a valuable social function in the rural community, particularly in the running of fêtes, the governing of schools, and the extracting of money from the wealthy for charitable causes. There is even one younger clergyman who has a Blue for rugby and has served his clerical apprenticeship in an East End boys' club, who is the hero of two of the stories. One of these revolves around the assumption that a parson who pinches a policeman's helmet, even for the sake of the girl he loves, should immediately resign his living. Burlesque this may be, but it has its roots in real popular perception. For when the Rural Church Project (1990) asked rural lay people what they thought the job of the parson to be, their responses bore an uncanny resemblance to the job descriptions of the parsons of rural Woostershire.

3

The Context –
The Countryside Today

THE SOCIAL CONTEXT

Change has always been a characteristic of village life, but what so stimulates our appetite for rural nostalgia is the pace of change since 1945. Farming had for generations been a bad master, but at least it provided employment; after 1945 though, as a result of mechanization, fewer jobs on the farms were available for people living in villages. The immediate effect was a decline in village population and particularly the abandonment in the 1950s of the old insanitary farmworkers' cottages.

What saved English villages from the depopulation experienced by many European areas was the second commuter revolution. The coming of cheap train services to the big conurbations meant that between the wars many of the rural areas within range of the main lines had become in effect dormitory suburbs – a transformation charted by Pahl in *Urbs in Rure*. (The very word 'commuter' originates because those buying a season ticket were able to 'commute' the full cost of the fare.) In the 1960s, with more widespread car ownership, it became possible for those working in provincial towns to put a greater distance between their workplace and their home, so that they could work in the town and live in the village. They were originally encouraged to do this because they could buy village cottages for conversion very cheaply, though the supply of these did not last long. Nor were commuters the only emigrants from the towns. With growing affluence, more people opted to retire to the country villages that they had visited when on holiday. The extent of retirement migration is now well documented, and the value and importance of young retired people to the revival of village 'community life' can hardly be over-stated.

The desire of the population at large to live in villages continues, and the development of the motorway system and of new techniques of communication and patterns of work seem to have encouraged the exodus from the towns. The census for 1981 showed for the first time a trend which has been confirmed by the 1991 census: that the population is indeed deserting the conurbations for the rural areas. This is a trend which has implications which we are only just beginning to understand.

The second commuter revolution may have saved the village from depopulation, but it has changed its nature. Villages which were industrial settlements are becoming dormitory suburbs, and there are financial implications. It is possible to argue plausibly that society should ensure that those who have to do essential work in isolated areas should enjoy 'a standard of living consistent with human dignity'. It is less easy to make a case for the urban taxpayer subsidizing those who have deliberately chosen to live in a village to enhance their personal quality of life. The argument centres around 'the provision of services to villages'.

Local authorities and public utilities, determined to reverse the appalling living conditions revealed in wartime surveys, set about improving rural services. By 1960 most villages were on mains water and electricity, and improvement grants meant that outside lavatories were fast becoming a thing of the bad old past. In the early 1970s it seemed possible that village-dwellers might soon enjoy the same level of service provision as their urban cousins. However, this altered suddenly in the mid-1970s when the OPEC countries trebled the price of oil. This jolt to the system, along with other factors, signalled the end of the open-ended welfare state and the start of increased preoccupation with costs. Financial analysis showed that it cost three or four times as much to 'service' a house in a village as to 'service' a house in the suburbs. Similar exercises persuaded commercial firms, doctors, bus companies, and even the church, that villages made little economic sense. From the mid-1970s on, despite valiant efforts by rural groups and individuals – and particularly by the Rural Community Councils –there has been a steady withdrawal of 'services' from smaller villages. Even in areas which have adopted a vigorous 'key village' policy, decline in such sectors as educational and hospital provision is still evident. The situation first gained national attention because of a lengthy correspondence in *The Times* in 1978: and indeed what we have now come to regard as 'the rural bandwagon' can be seen to originate in this influential exposure of the problem.

Increasingly, the 'solution' adopted by government and local authorities is to target resources on that group in the population which is perceived as local to the region – in many cases, one-time farmworkers and their families. Current housing policy provides a good example of the trend. On the one hand, strong planning regulations protect most villages from major development, while the pressure from the private sector for rural housing is channelled into 'key' villages (thus in effect transforming them from villages into towns). In the interests of containing the pressure at a reasonable expense to the taxpayer, there is even serious discussion of the policy of building new villages on green-field sites – such as newly abandoned military camps. On the other hand, it is recognized by most authorities that 'local' people and their families should be able to continue to live in 'their' village. Since central government policy has brought council house development to a standstill, and indeed many units have already been sold under the 'right to buy' legislation, this can only be done by providing rented accommodation, shared equity and low-cost housing through Housing Associations. Since this is possible only if cheap land is available, the planning regulations are 'bent' to allow 'social development' outside the designated building area (or village envelope). So we have one planning law for the rich and another for the poor – but for once, operated in the interests of the latter.

Perhaps the most dramatic effect of these developments has been a change in the understanding of 'community'. Ronald Blythe's *Akenfield* caught the mood of the pre-1938 village with its shared employment, shared entertainment and blood relationships, but it is a fleeting image. The reality now is that few village families go back more than a generation, and that the two-car family can form its own networks and choose its own entertainment. Pre-war community life was enforced by circumstances: today, 'community' is a 'voluntary associational activity'.

The different groups who now live in villages have different ideas about what 'community life' involves. Local people tend to 'identify' with the village just by being there, while newcomers see membership of the village as a club activity which involves 'participation'. Some assume that 'the community' should be a hierarchical structure as in pre-war days: while others assume that 'the community' should be a happy family of equals. Anthony Russell has aptly described the modern village as 'a battle ground for competing interest groups'.

Perhaps the one issue above all others which divides the modern village is work. As we have seen, historically the village was a place of work – as it still is for farmers, and is assumed to be by local people whose ancestors worked on the land. The newcomers, by contrast, have come to the village precisely because for them it is the place where they do not work, and they see it as the locus of leisure activity and recreation. The group that has suffered most in this particular conflict has been the farmers, who have traditionally regarded the countryside as 'the shopfloor of Britain's largest industry'. They lost their control of district councils to the newcomers in the 1970s, and now they even find themselves in a minority on 'their own' parish councils. Not only are the long-ignored footpath laws being enforced in the neighbourhood of the village, but carefully mown suburban-style verges make it well-nigh impossible for farmers to drive stock or heavy farm machinery through 'their own' streets.

The 1980s brought further discomfiture for the farming community. It was in these years that public attention first focused on agricultural practices such as straw burning, the removal of hedgerows and the draining of marshes; and indeed the last two were eligible for agricultural grants until 1987, even though farmers were already producing far more corn than was 'needed'. There was a growing recognition that the Common Agricultural Policy needed to be reformed, and a first step towards this reform was taken via the introduction of milk quotas. For the first time since 1945, the all-powerful farming lobby found themselves out in the cold.

What added passion to the criticism of modern farming was the parallel emergence of a near-obsession with healthy eating. Because of 'salmonella in eggs' and 'mad cow disease', farmers who had been used to playing the part of 'The Picture of Health' found themselves recast overnight as 'The Spectre of Disease'. Yet, to add insult to injury, the Pop Larkins of farming are still the favourites of the television ratings, and 'Rural England' is still used by advertisers to sell everything from cars to carpets.

Nor did public interest stop short at healthy eating. The concern for environmental issues that is an increasing theme in domestic politics has not surprisingly found its focus in rural England. It is arguable that green enthusiasts would do much more for the environment if they concentrated on making urban living attractive once again, and yet it is the rural scene – country sports, nitrate pollution of water, forestry, access to land, landscape planning, wildlife habitats and so on – which consistently makes the headlines.

THE DEVELOPMENT OF THE RURAL LOBBY

The developments outlined above amount to a rural revolution, and the future of our countryside is now high on the national agenda. Apart from action on the Common Agricultural Policy, the government recognized public concern by creating the Countryside Commission with responsibility for the rural environment, and by raising the profile of the Rural Development Commission (RDC), which now has special responsibilities in a number of designated Rural Development Areas (RDAs).

The new situation demands that people understand the issues and argue a clear political case, and rural lobby groups have become better organized, more professional, and more articulate than a generation ago. In 1980 Rural Voice was formed, an alliance of ten voluntary organizations. The aims of the alliance are set out in an explanatory leaflet:

> We seek to represent the need of those who live and work in rural areas. We provide a forum for discussion of rural problems, analyse the impact of policies on rural areas, and seek to make government and media more aware of rural needs. We look to raise self confidence in rural communities and increase the ability to provide local services for ourselves.

The members of Rural Voice are: Action with Communities in Rural

Areas (ACRE), representing the county Rural Community Councils; the Arthur Rank Centre, representing the churches; Council for the Protection of Rural England (CPRE); Country Landowners' Association (CLA); National Association of Local Councils (NALC); National Council for Voluntary Organizations (NCVO); National Farmers' Union (NFU); National Federation of Women's Institutes (WI); National Federation of Young Farmers' Clubs (YFC); and Rural, Agricultural and Allied Workers' Section of the TGWU.

There are of course other very important voluntary groups working in the countryside, such as the Ramblers Association and the Nature Conservation Trusts; but the emergence of Rural Voice, combining as it does such a diverse range of interests, is in itself something of a miracle, and marks a new determination among thinking rural people to return to consensus politics after a generation of near civil war in our villages.

The fact that the Church is represented on Rural Voice is largely a result of work based on the Arthur Rank Centre at Stoneleigh. Set up with his usual prophetic flair by the late J. Arthur Rank, its brief was to be a fully ecumenical chaplaincy to the National Agricultural Centre. It has always sought to train the spotlight on rural people and their needs and has had a series of distinguished directors – Peter Buckler, Anthony Russell and John Clarke. In the 1970s the Arthur Rank Centre took major initiatives on such issues as the agricultural tied cottage, rural housing associations, explaining modem agriculture to the general public (farm interpretation), and the problems of farming families. It acted as host to the Agricultural Chaplains Group and to the Methodist Church in Rural Life Committee, and has run numerous clergy and lay conferences on rural issues. Above all, the Arthur Rank Centre ensured a supply of country people who were also theologically articulate christians who could contribute Christian insight to the national debate about the future of rural areas.

The great strength of the Arthur Rank Centre was its involvement with rural sociology. It is arguable that village life seemed so impossible in 1970 largely because no one could understand what was happening. Rural sociology was the tool that gave people the chance to see the wood for the trees. Anthony Russell is an outstanding communicator and those who heard his early lectures bear witness to the way in which they saw clearly for the first time as a result of listening to him. His little book, *The Village in Myth and Reality,* so slim yet so profound, had an electrifying effect on tens of thousands of rural people. Here at last was someone who understood them, and affirmed them. Later, Howard Newby and others carried on the good work, but for church people at least it was Anthony Russell who began the creative process.

A few more detailed examples will give some indication of what has been achieved by a small number of individuals, all of whom drew strength from the Arthur Rank Centre.

(1) In the field of rural housing, Moira Constable of the Rural Housing Trust, originally based at the Arthur Rank Centre, is acknowledged as a national authority. So much so that when the government decided to expand its number of Rural Housing Trusts, she was asked to manage the initiative. The Centre also represents the churches on the London-based Rural Housing Forum.

(2) The Arthur Rank Centre first started to encourage debate about 'Stress in the farming community' in 1985. Now that public attention has focused on the escalating suicide rate among farmers, it is the often ecumenical Agricultural Chaplaincy teams who have been ready to take a leading role in setting up 'Farmers' Friend' telephone networks.

(3) Jesse Sage, the ecumenical Agricultural Chaplain in Kent, has from the early 1970s pioneered links between the English and European churches. In 1978 and 1980 he organized group visits by the Agricultural Chaplains Group to Brussels and to Bavaria. One aspect of this work was the setting up in 1991 of the Ecumenical European Rural Churches Network.

(4) The debate about the environment is, of course, a global rather than a purely rural issue. To the discussions about modern farming methods and farm animal welfare, the Agricultural Chaplains have been able to demonstrate their command of the hard facts. They submitted a detailed paper to the Rural Commission which has since been published in *Modern Churchman*.

(5) Eve Dennis of the Council for Nature Conservation has been

seconded to the Arthur Rank Centre and has run a remarkable campaign to alert diocesan glebe committees, diocesan advisory committees and the property divisions of the Free Churches to issues of conservation. She has followed this up with an initiative on conservation in churchyards which is likely to change our whole conception of churchyard management (and 'Best Kept Churchyard' competitions) over the next decade.

It is not surprising therefore that when in 1980 the rural lobby groups joined to set up Rural Voice they should ask the Arthur Rank Centre as an inter-denominational organization to provide the Church representative. The move to include the Church was suggested by Jeremy Martineau, then Agricultural Chaplain to the diocese of Bristol and also chairman of the newly formed ACRE. As ACRE representative, he urged that while it was not practicable to have a representative of all the denominations on Rural Voice, the Arthur Rank Centre would be readily recognized as representing their joint rural interests. He went on to be chairman of Rural Voice during the important formative period of the organization.

THE RURAL CHURCH

It is not easy to generalize about the situation of the Church of England, and the rural Church in particular, in the post-war period, because many of the indicators point in contradictory directions. At one level, the Church continued to attract considerable, if declining, support, and church attendance remained the most significant participatory activity in English society. Though the long-term trend was downward, there were significant increases in ordinands in the years after the war and as a consequence of the two Billy Graham missions.

However, the Church was conscious that the climate in which it operated was now markedly less friendly, and the emergence in the 1960s and 1970s of a more strident and aggressive secular culture made the Church seem an outdated and increasingly irrelevant institution. At the intellectual level, the theory of secularization first propounded by the sociologists of religion in the 1960s, which predicated the inevitable decline of religion as a factor in human affairs, was widely accepted. At the social level, the erosion of such conventions as 'the English Sunday'

– and a disposition to regard all traditional institutions with suspicion – severely reduced the influence and support which the Church had previously enjoyed.

Inevitably in the villages the effects of these changes were often unappreciated or ignored, but slowly it was recognized that while in previous generations the parish church occupied a position of precedency over all other village activities, it now found itself increasingly marginalized in the day-to-day life of the rural community. Certainly it remained important for the major family occasions (baptisms, marriages and burials) and for significant events such as Christmas and Easter, Harvest and Remembrance Sunday; but progressively the rural Church found itself trapped in modes of expression and styles of life which no longer resonated with the new culture and lifestyles that were a product of the 1960s and 1970s.

In the mid-1960s many country parishes were served by elderly clergy, largely dependent upon glebe and endowments for their income, in churches where the worship comprised 'the early service', choral Mattins and Evensong, and in parishes where almost all activity and the finances were under the direct control of the clergyman and his wife. Many were trained in a relatively high view of priesthood, and finished their theological study long before the 'Honest to God' debate began in earnest in the theological colleges. Many recognized that rural society was changing, but – being prejudiced against sociology – they had no tools with which to understand what was going on around them. They often felt despised by their urban colleagues and abandoned by the hierarchy, most of whom were completely ignorant of rural ministry at first hand. In the 1960s rural ministry was still regarded at theological colleges such as Cuddesdon as a sanctuary for those who were lazy or tired, or who had some other 'important' job to do as well. As against the many new books which became available on urban and suburban ministry, nothing on rural ministry was published between 1960 (*The Country Parish Today and Tomorrow* by West) and 1975 (*Groups and Teams in the Countryside* by Russell).

Perhaps worst of all was the depression and isolation of many rural incumbents. In a correspondence that followed the suicide of one rural priest in 1960, one letter to *The Times* painted this sad picture:

The trouble with village congregations is not that they are unfriendly but that they are exiguous and shamefully unadventurous, and the unhappy clergyman is daily depressed by the surrounding atmosphere of lapsed Christianity, apathy and fecklessness. He is personally unaccepted by the 'county' because he is poor and by the village because he is educated.

The rural chapels fared no better. In the Horncastle Circuit six village chapels closed between 1945 and 1970; and though the Methodist Church at least had a Church in Rural Life Committee, until 1968 it had a 'revolving' membership and met only once a year. Connexional records suggest that ministers tended to leave rural Circuits as soon as possible, and an increasing number of rural Circuits were amalgamated. As with Anglicans, a major reason for low morale among ministers was the way in which urban concerns dominated the Connexion. John Clarke, now director of the Arthur Rank Centre, recalls that in the 1960s the 'divisions' accepted without question that 'a small church was a failed church' – and judged ministers accordingly.

There was one crumb of comfort. It is from the 1960s that we can date the emergence of the practical rural ecumenism which is so influential today. Church and chapel still represented different sections of society and offered different styles of worship, but at least – faced with a steady fall in support – they usually had the wit to bury the hatchet and start working together.

In retrospect it is amazing that in the face of such obvious perplexity and disillusion the Church Assembly took no specific action. The Council for the Church and Countryside, set up with his usual prophetic foresight by William Temple, was allowed to disappear in 1948; and beyond publishing *The Land, the People and the Churches* in 1945, the British Council of Churches 'Rural Questions Committee' did little more than encourage the revival of Rogation services.

However, various reports and decisions of the Church Assembly directed to the Anglican Church at large did begin to change the life of the rural Church root and branch. The Paul Report of 1964 drew attention to the fact that rural clergy were responsible for far fewer people than those working in the urban areas. Leslie Paul's thesis was based on the assumption that it is the duty of the Established Church to offer pastoral care to everyone living in this country; and he therefore suggested that clergy should be located where people lived, not tied to a parsonage house or a church building. It is worth noting that this argument which links clergy deployment with total population is one which appeals to the classical Anglican understanding of the vocation of the national Church. It ignores, as Anglicans have always tried to do, the existence of Roman Catholicism and the Free Churches.

Nevertheless, *Faith in the Countryside* does recognize that the main thrust of the Paul Report was sensible and fair. What finally led to the adoption of Paul's recommendations in the Sheffield Report (GS 205) was the catastrophic decline in the number of Anglican clergy. In 1964 there were 15,488 full-time clergy; in 1974 there were 10,922. Something had to be done to ensure that enough clergy went where they were 'needed', and the Church Assembly agreed a formula to determine how many were deemed to be 'needed' in each diocese. The formula was given financial teeth because the Church Commissioners 'subsidized' clergy up to the set figure, but any clergy above that number had to be paid for in full by the diocese. Of course each diocese was at liberty to deploy its 'Sheffield clergy', much as it had done in the past: and in large urban dioceses such as Chester, which had to gain clergy rather than shed them, the number of rural benefices was left much the same as before. The rural dioceses, however, had to adopt new measures. Hereford in particular, under the leadership of Bishop John Eastaugh, not only determined to reduce clergy numbers to the Sheffield figure as soon as possible, but also adopted Leslie Paul's criteria for the allocation of those left. As a result, while between 1956 and 1986 the total number of clergy in the diocese fell by 43 per cent, the decline in the number of rural clergy was 57 per cent. During the same period the number of those serving in Hereford and the market towns actually increased by 36 per cent.

The 'strategy' adopted was of course the 'multi-parish benefice', which in any other generation has been called 'pluralism' and roundly condemned. No one pretends that it is a perfect solution, because no priest can be truly 'local' in a village in which he does not reside. Nevertheless, it has meant that, despite disillusion, frustration and near bankruptcy, most villages still have a parish church which is open and a priest who is in some sense 'their man'. The ship may be wallowing in high seas – but it has not yet sunk.

Another report to the Anglican Church which affected the rural areas was *Partners in Ministry* (The Morley Report), produced in 1967 as a

follow-up to the Paul Report. This dealt with the deployment and payment of the clergy, and while a number of its recommendations about
deployment have never been implemented, the plans for a new deal on
pay were put in place in the 1970s. As a result, all parish clergy in the
Church of England are now paid more or less the same stipend, irrespective of whether they are Vicar of St Martin-in-the-Fields or Rector of
Upper and Lower Slaughter. In the process, villages have 'lost' their
glebe and their endowments have been pooled; and while in a minority
of cases this has meant a net loss of income, for the great majority of
villages it has been a notable blessing. It means that clergy can now take
a rural job without the fear of a catastrophic drop in income, or the worry
of having to administer glebe.

The Endowment and Glebe Measure ironed out the inequalities
between the parishes within each diocese. The process is to be carried a
step further by the Historic Resources of the Church of England Measure
(GS 733) which aims to deal with the inequalities between the 43
Anglican dioceses. Over a period of years the endowment and glebe of
the ancient (usually rural) dioceses is being notionally transferred to the
younger (often urban) dioceses, and this has inevitably contributed to
enormous increases in the quota of those dioceses affected.

The situation of the Anglican clergy has changed in two further ways.
First, they have accepted the principle of enforced retirement (at 70 or
72) in return for a pension, and (very generous) help with the purchase
of a retirement house. Second, many large old parsonages have been sold
and replaced with (relatively) modest detached houses set in a quarter-
acre or so of garden. This transfer of the priest from the old rectory to
the new one graphically symbolizes his change in status, and as such has
significance for the role of the Anglican Church within the village.

In these ways the Church Assembly and its successor, the General
Synod, have influenced the rural Church. Yet none of these measures is
exclusively, or even mainly, concerned with the rural areas. Indeed in
each of them the rural Church appears as conservative, inefficient and
overweight, and altogether a thoroughly bad example to the rest. It has
been left to a few individuals who love and work in the countryside to do
something positive to help.

THE REVIVAL OF MORALE

An account of the revival of morale in the rural Church must begin with the initiative taken by Bishop Maurice Harland in the diocese of Lincoln in 1947 when he set up the South Ormsby Group Ministry. A report on the experiment was published in 1960 (A. C. Smith, *The South Ormsby Experiment: An Adventure in Friendship*) and this inspired Bishop Launcelot Fleming to repeat the strategy in the diocese of Norwich. In ten short years in the face of – as he saw it – a desperate situation, this kindest and most beloved of bishops imposed group ministry on one of the most conservative areas of England, and got away with it. There have of course been problems, but one of the most important results of this initiative was that it attracted a number of imaginative younger clergy to serve in villages. One of these was Anthony Russell, whose book *Groups and Teams in the Countryside* (1975) became a catalyst for discussion on rural ministry throughout the country.

From Norfolk the story moves to the Arthur Rank Centre, then under the leadership of Peter Buckler, to be joined in 1973 by Anthony Russell. The official concern of the Centre was for rural *society*, and so it was natural that it should provide the secretariat for the Agricultural Chaplaincy network; but the staff also gave major encouragement to other groups who were primarily concerned for rural *ministry*. They provided a venue for meetings, gave secretarial support, and built up a library for researchers.

The concerns of rural ministry were put firmly on the map by the Hereford Consultation of 1976 organized by Laurence Reading. There was an air of freshness about this conference and a sense of conviction that important new ideas were beginning to take shape. A happy coincidence was that one of the speakers was James Prior, then Minister for Agriculture, later to be chairman of the Archbishops' Commission on Rural Areas. The momentum was carried forward at Lincoln in 1978 and Durham in 1980 at conferences organized by Ian Beckwith and Ian Calvert respectively.

In the wake of these consultations, a number of initiatives were taken. At Bishop Grosseteste College, Ian Beckwith launched a training programme in rural ministry. In Suffolk, David Woodwards used his rectory as a centre for rural training. At Dovedale, Anthony Hodgson set up a diploma course in rural studies validated by a local polytechnic.

Though not all of these initiatives succeeded, they generated a great deal of enthusiasm and contributed to a growing body of 'wisdom'.

A number of the individuals already mentioned founded the Rural Theology Association (RTA) in 1981 with Mervyn Wilson as the first secretary. The association aimed to bring together in small informal groups those living and working in rural areas to study the theological as well as the sociological implications of the changing 'context'. A series of RTA 'occasional papers' developed into the quarterly journal *A Better Country* which, under the editorship of Anthony Herbert, has over the last ten years provided a forum for the exchange of ideas and information. The work of the RTA culminated in the splendid Scargill Conference of 1990 which both signalled a new confidence about the future of rural ministry, and also began to explore the dimension of 'green theology' – which since then has come to assume such significance throughout the Church. The report of the Conference, *The Rural Church – Towards 2000*, sold out within months of publication.

Another organization, the Federation for Rural Evangelism, brought together rural mission groups and churches of widely differing theological background who found that they shared a common purpose and common approach. This was reflected in the publication of the first and second *Workbooks on Rural Evangelism* (edited by Ian Calvert in conjunction with Jimmy Hamilton-Brown of Partners in Ministry), to be followed by E. Bailey's *Workbook in Popular Religion* and P. Croft's *Workbook for Deaneries*. These were the first practical handbooks on rural ministry to be published for many years, and with their mixture of sociology, theology and practical examples they gave rural church people something solid to bite on. The Federation, with its regular conferences, meant that the Decade for Evangelism did not catch the rural Church on the hop. Evangelism in villages is possible, provided that the context is understood and respected, and there are now organizations – such as Barry Osborne's Rural Sunrise – ready to give small congregations sound practical advice as to how to go about it.

In 1983 the new spirit abroad in the villages was given direction by the Tiller Report which, being written by one person, has a zeal and clarity which inspires. In two vivid insights Tiller affirmed what had been best in the traditional parish system and laid the foundation for a coherent strategy for ministry. First, he identified the local congregation as the basic building block of ministry and recognized its members as the frontline troops whose job was not to hold up the edifice but to spearhead the advance. Second, he called on all baptized Christians to recognize that their baptism 'ordained' them for collaborative ministry. As some would see it, it was ill advised of him to suggest that the stipendiary clergy should be diocesan or deanery staff, but that is a detail which should not detract from the thrust of the argument. (Also, although the Report is offered to the Anglican Church it recognizes the necessity for ecumenical co-operation wherever possible.) What Canon Tiller gave to the Anglican Church was a clear strategy for the future which, from the village perspective, looked as if it might 'fit'.

The multi-parish benefice, for all its faults, did concentrate the mind, and lay people began to realize that the future of the Church, for good or ill, lay in their hands. The keen ones found there were courses available to help and affirm them in their work. Besides those already mentioned, such centres as Lee Abbey, Scargill and Harnhill put on courses for rural laity; and Holy Trinity, Brompton sent out a wave of missionaries into the shires. Some dioceses had 'Scargill Conferences' which brought together an equal number of clergy and laity. Others developed highly professional courses in the Christian faith for laity; or, as in Salisbury's case, courses to train laity as 'lay pastoral assistants'. Shared or collaborative ministry seemed to many to make natural practical sense in the multi-parish benefice in a way that it did not under the old order of one parson, one parish.

Like the Anglicans, the Methodists were hit hard by the culture changes of the 1950s and 1960s. Their response was to set up the Border Experiment in the area of the Welsh Marches from Shrewsbury to Chepstow. The idea was to close small village chapels and bus members into local market towns such as Clun and Leominster. *Country Pattern* (1970), the first report of the Methodists' Church in Rural Life Committee, sets out the theory behind the practice:

> We have made plain our belief that a small society cannot be the whole church to its members and to the community. . . . Its members should be brought into a wider circle.

And later:

The most effective unit for evangelistic effort is the reorganisation of our work into larger societies.

The experiment was not perhaps a 'success', but it did have the effect of alerting Methodists to the problems of rural churches. In 1968 Alan Davies reconstituted the Church in Rural Life Committee, with John Clarke as secretary, so that it became an effective instrument for change and research within the Connexion; and in 1970 Bill Gowland held the first of a regular series of conferences on rural ministry with the subtitle 'You cannot redeem what you do not understand'.

The Baptist and Congregational Churches had more difficulty in coming to terms with the problem since according to their ecclesiology every congregation is in itself the full 'catholic' Church, and there is therefore little theological reason for those regional or national structures which, in the case of the other denominations, were at least capable of taking bold initiatives. This process was reversed for the Congregational Church when they joined with the Presbyterians to form the United Reformed Church (URC) in 1972. Presbyterianism has a strong central structure, and among other changes this led in 1976 to an important new arrangement whereby stipendiaries were paid nationally. The URC included a commitment to ecumenical co-operation in the Scheme of Union, and its churches have played a disproportionately large part in the membership of rural Local Ecumenical Projects (LEPs). Revival of morale within Baptist churches, by contrast, has often been associated with a fundamentalist biblical theology which has made close co-operation with the other denominations more difficult.

So, despite much uncertainty and not a little disillusion, there were in the 1970s signs of revival in all the denominations with a major stake in small villages. In retrospect, it can be seen that a growing confidence within the rural Church was beginning to parallel the growing concern about 'secular' rural issues; and in many areas a new generation of sociologically aware villagers on their rural bandwagons discovered rural churches which were not dead but resurrecting.

4

The Commission

THE GENESIS OF THE COMMISSION

In 1985 the Archbishop's Commission on Urban Priority Areas published their report *Faith in the City*. It won immediate attention and is arguably one of the most effective reports that the Church has produced this century. One of the reasons why it was so timely was because, as we have seen, this was precisely the moment when public attention was switching from town to countryside. Quite rightly, the Church drew attention to the desperate needs of those whom our society was in the process of abandoning.

Nevertheless, the pressures on rural areas did not slacken, and the need for the Church to reorganize 'deep rural' as well as 'inner city' ministry was highlighted by three events. On 25 May 1984 the Agricultural Chaplains Group wrote to the *Church Times*, commenting on the report *The Historic Resources of the Church of England* which was then being debated in diocesan synods. It included the paragraph:

The rural areas bore the brunt of the Sheffield cutbacks: and it needs to be recognised that, with the 'redistribution of resources' it will be the rural church which suffers again. Is it unreasonable to ask that, in the process of 'redistribution' some money be allocated to help redevelop an effective ministry in rural areas.

The letter had no effect on the issue in question, but it was a long and closely argued piece and was the catalyst for an important development. Peter Nott, then Bishop of Taunton, had come to recognize the gravity of the situation, and was encouraged by the letter to bring together a small group of bishops and senior churchmen to consider the future of the rural Church.

The second event came a year later in 1985 when Leslie Francis published *Rural Anglicanism*. As the Archbishop said in his preface: 'Dr Francis has written a timely and devastating book. . . . His research clearly demonstrates that the countryside is now as much a pastoral challenge to today's Church as the inner city.'

Whatever the suggested inadequacies of the research methods used, Francis's book at least had the effect of attracting wide publicity. It concentrated public attention on the needs of village churches and there were hundreds of rural lay people who were ready to support his analysis, and to thunder in diocesan synods that 'something needed to be done'.

1986 saw the publication of *The People, the Land and the Church* the report of a year-long consultation process in the diocese of Hereford which, masterminded by Richard Lewis, one of the Agricultural Chaplains and now Bishop of Taunton, confirmed the gravity of the situation; but it also showed evidence of a recovery of morale – even a growing expectancy of revival among the laity. In the same year, Anthony Russell's *The Country Parish* brought together in readable, lucid, accessible form the lectures on the rural Church which he had been giving for a decade, and it was immediately welcomed as a magisterial statement of the case. His analysis of the rural Church was certainly not as despondent as that of Francis, but he too agreed that urgent problems needed to be tackled.

The omens were propitious, and in May 1986 Peter Nott (by then Bishop of Norwich) and Anthony Russell produced a report to the Standing Committee of the General Synod which made the case for the appointment of an Archbishops' Commission on Rural Areas. This was published as a Green Paper (General Synod – Miscellaneous 247), and comments were invited. That autumn the pressure for a commission grew, and the last stumbling block was removed when the Duke of Westminster agreed to contribute handsomely to the costs. In July 1987 the Archbishop of Canterbury was able to tell the congregation at the Royal Show Service that

> I have just accepted the request to set up an Archbishops' Commission on Rural Areas. . . . It is a recognition that over the last ten years our nation has come to place enormous value on the countryside. . . . The churches (who have such long experience of rural ministry) have a duty to contribute their considered wisdom to the growing national debate about the future of the countryside.

He continued:

> You who live and worship in villages will know only too well that over the last twenty years we have done a hatchet job of Beeching proportions on the village church. . . . Your cry has been heard. We do realise that there is a crisis of confidence; that there is a need to bind up wounds, to reflect and ponder and listen to what you have to say about your future.

The Archbishop articulated precisely the anxieties of rural Christians, and at the same time linked them with the national concern about secular rural issues. In this way he effectively identified the dual agenda of the Commission.

THE WORK OF THE COMMISSION

Invitations to join the Commission were issued personally by the Archbishops, and inevitably some obvious names were passed over in the interests of achieving a wide spectrum of representation. There was a majority of lay people, most of them experts in some aspect of rural life; and all the mainstream churches in England were represented. Since the Commission was to hear and assess evidence, rather than simply to write a report, neither practical rural experience nor committed church membership was considered to be a necessary criterion for membership. In the event, a number of 'consultants' had to be called in to fill certain gaps in expertise, particularly in relation to the 'church' section of the agenda.

The method of hearing evidence was threefold. A number of experts were commissioned to produce papers on specific issues, most of which were subsequently printed as appendices to the report, while other experts were invited to make presentations to meetings of the Commission. Organizations and individuals who wished to do so gave evidence and this was received either in writing or verbally. This London-based evidence was balanced by a 24-hour visit by four Commissioners to each of 42 dioceses in England; and a 48-hour visit by eight Commissioners to four outlying regions – the North-East, the North-West, the Welsh Marches and the South-West. In this way, the Commission received evidence from at least 6,000 organizations and individuals, and part of its stature as a report is that it really can claim to represent the views of rural people. Nevertheless, it was a very ambitious programme, and particularly in the second working year it is arguable that the pressure to fulfil the programme diverted energy and attention from preliminary drafting of chapters for the report.

The work of the Commission hinged on the secretariat, housed in Church House, Westminster. They were an excellent team who never counted the hours worked, and much of the credit for *Faith in the Countryside* must go to Ewan Harper and Jeremy Martineau for the way they inspired such loyalty to the cause. Most of the evidence was presented to sub-committees, each of which had a particular remit. With the help of the secretariat, drafts were made and circulated to the full Commission with a request for comments. Full meetings tended to deal with major policy issues rather than textual details, while alterations and additions to the text were usually secured by individual members in personal negotiation with one of the secretaries. In general therefore, while the members of the secretariat had an important influence on the report, they did not control it. The chairman and vice-chairman were outstanding, and it is to their credit not only that it was a unanimous report, but also that the Commissioners got on so well together and were prepared to invest so much personal effort in the enterprise.

From its first meeting, the Commission decided to accept the twin agendas suggested by the Archbishop in his Stoneleigh sermon and to devote half their time to analysing the 'rural context' and the other half to suggesting how the Church should minister within that context.

Though there was obviously an overlap, the context came first, and the Church's ministry second – a prioritizing which naturally had implications. Since the Commission began work not, as had been intended, in October 1987, but in January 1988, effectively four months had already been lost. During 1987 'the context' was studied, drafts of chapters were made and revised (sometimes, as for the environment chapter, three or four times), and this phase was officially completed at a residential meeting at Rugby in February 1989. Despite obvious gaps, it is generally agreed that the first half of the report is a well-presented and polished piece of work. Unfortunately, over a year had been spent on the process, and the four lost months were never made up. There were no introductory papers on church issues as there had been on secular ones and, despite valiant efforts by the secretariat, the sub-committees were slow to produce drafts. In fact, there were no overall drafts of the three most 'difficult' chapters available until spring 1990, with the result that the issues on which there was general agreement are covered in the report with model lucidity and brevity, while the more contentious issues are all too often identified but not resolved. Nor was there time to digest the different emphases of chapters 7–12 and work them into a single coherent vision.

The last residential meeting was at Almondsbury, Bristol, in May 1990, and was largely devoted to two chapters. Lord Prior, as a 'typical lay person', insisted that he should be able to understand the chapter on theology, and this meant two days' agonizing redrafting for the 'theologians' group – but with excellent results. The chapter on organization and finance proved a major battleground between those lay people with business experience who believed that the Church, and particularly the Church's finances, were badly managed and that this needed to be said, and others who felt that to concentrate on this issue would divert attention from the main thrust of the report. A compromise was reached whereby the chapter concentrates on the breakdown of communication between the village church and the centre, and commends the principle of 'subsidiarity' (that all decisions should be taken as close to the grass roots as possible). It was attacked by some members of the General Synod as being visionary and impractical, but it needs to be recognized that it very faithfully represents the views of village clergy and lay people as conveyed to the Commissioners on their diocesan visits.

At the end of such an emotional marathon the Commissioners gathered at Almondsbury did not have the energy to tackle the chapter on ministry in any detail, though this crucial chapter needed a residential to itself. First, it needed to be meshed in with those on worship, ecumenism and finance. Second, the Commission had put in hand a major piece of sociological research on the rural clergy known as the Rural Church Project, the main conclusions of which have now been published as *Church and Religion in Rural England*. The preliminary presentation of the results of this research was not made until April 1989, and the significance of the findings – which are critical to any discussion of rural ministry – had not really penetrated into the draft of chapter 8 of *Faith in the Countryside*. In the event it proved impossible to arrange another residential meeting, and the chapter had to be stitched together by a hard-pressed secretariat ever-conscious of the printer's deadline.

THE FOLLOW-UP TO THE COMMISSION

Faith in the Countryside was welcomed by secular rural groups (see Chapter 1), and the quality of the report makes it all the more likely that at a national level the views of the churches on countryside issues will be listened to with respect. At county level, Christian influence has been more patchy in the past, and in the future it is likely to depend not so much on one or two well-informed individuals as on 'the rural group'. One consequence of the report is that such groups have been set up in most rural areas, often on an ecumenical basis.

They have two major functions: first, to advise the Church on rural matters, and second, to speak for the Church on rural issues. To do this, the members of the group must live and work in the countryside and be familiar with the specialist language of the rural debate. The rural group is therefore much more akin to an advisory committee than to a pastoral committee.

A few areas (such as Northumberland) already had a rural group, and it is perhaps worth describing the Gloucestershire group, formed in 1984, in some detail. Membership is by invitation and is half clerical, half lay. The director of the Gloucestershire rural community council is a member of the rural group, and the Rural Adviser sits on the executive committee of the RCC. Another member is a former district planning officer, and through him close links are maintained with the county council. Two of the founder members of the Gloucestershire Rural Housing Trust are members and one of these is also on the diocesan glebe committee. (This latter link is proving fruitful in relation to rural housing.) The former chairman of the rural group is now county chairman of the National Farmers Union, and a clerical member of the group represents the Church on the county farm safety committee. Two of the group were founder members of the local Farmers' Friend Network (a Samaritans-type telephone helpline). Another clerical member represents the churches on the Council for the Gloucestershire Countryside. The group runs the Church Tent at the local county agricultural show and this is an annual chance to keep relationships with other rural organizations well oiled. Obviously the group will in the future also have an important role in relation to developing rural ministry; but in Gloucestershire's case, there is no doubt that the group is appropriately (loosely) linked to the Board for Social Responsibility rather than to the Board for Ministry.

At parish level, one aim of *Faith in the Countryside* was to re-establish that tradition of church participation in village life which was the hallmark of the Church of England. In an interesting piece of sociological research on yoked parishes (multi-parish benefices) in Minnesota, USA (1980), Crile showed that a congregation's involvement in community life was directly related to where the minister lived. The further away the parsonage, the less the involvement. While no English survey covers exactly this ground, the 1991 Rural Church Project does show that full-time ministers in multi-parish benefices allot less than 3 per cent of their time to village community activity. If this trend away from community involvement is to be reversed, practical steps need to be taken.

A number of parishes have already implemented one of the Acora recommendations by allocating one PCC meeting each year to discussions about community life in the village. They invite to this meeting members of the parish council, WI, village hall committee, and other local organizations. Where the village has already done a 'village appraisal', this has provided a useful framework for the discussion. First reports suggest that the other organizations are pleased to be invited and that this is a simple and practical way of keeping community issues on the church agenda.

If the village church is to be involved in building bridges, it needs to do something to heal the rift between farmers and newcomers. On top of all their other troubles, many farmers have found themselves under attack in their own backyard from a group of people who, however articulate, are ignorant of modern farming practice. As its contribution to Food and Farming Year 1988, the Gloucestershire rural group encouraged every church to set up a farm visit in their village (June is the best month), as an effective variation on the Rogation procession. Over thirty villages responded and in many cases the exercise has been repeated in subsequent years.

One of the most remarkable examples of Church–State collaboration anywhere in the country must be the Community Care Network set up by the dioceses of Winchester and Portsmouth in collaboration with Hampshire County Council. Two full-time workers service 'community groups' in more than 200 Hampshire villages. Each group is run on the same lines as a local volunteer bureau in that the group organizer connects those who want help with those who have volunteered. In practice, there is a danger that the group becomes no more than a voluntary car scheme but, in principle, people may ask for help with anything from feeding the cat while they are away for the weekend, to helping to cope when an old person is suddenly discharged from or taken into hospital. A similar group run by church members in Dymock, Gloucestershire, won second prize in the county Village Ventures Competition in 1991. A particularly touching request was from a keen seamstress whose sight was failing and who wanted a volunteer to thread ten needles for her each fortnight. In 1992 the Joseph Rowntree Foundation published a guide aimed at setting up a local community care group (D. M. Clark, *Good Neighbours*); and there is currently great interest in such schemes from Social Service Departments charged with implementing 'Care in the Community' in rural areas. Clearly, initiatives such as these could put the church back at the heart of village life and provide a credible springboard for evangelism.

Thus there has been good progress in following up the social section of *Faith in the Countryside*. Obviously not all the recommendations have been implemented, but the rural Church has now established a practical framework in which to pursue aims and objectives. At national level, Christians now occupy influential positions where they are contributing specifically Christian insights to the rural debate. In 1993 John Clarke, the director of the Arthur Rank Centre, became chairperson of Rural Voice, and it is to be hoped that the Centre will increasingly be recognized as the inter-denominational focus for this work. At county level the development of rural groups will, under sensitive management, link the churches to local secular authorities. At parish level there is on offer a simple practical agenda which makes straightforward village sense. Obviously, the 'cause' will advance at a different pace in different places depending on personalities and commitment, but the guidelines are there.

There remains one caveat. Nothing can happen unless local congregations flourish: everything that has been said presupposes a supply of country people who are committed Christians. That supply will dry up unless church life in our villages is vibrant enough to produce them.

As we saw in Chapter 1, church support for *Faith in the Countryside* was lukewarm. Nevertheless, the bishops neatly sidestepped any attempt by the General Synod standing committee to starve the report at birth. Between them they found the money to pay a Rural Adviser to the Archbishops: and even before the launch, Jeremy Martineau was appointed and had set up his office at the Arthur Rank Centre, Stoneleigh.

Following the pattern very helpfully set by the Archbishop's Commission on Urban Priority Areas, it seemed natural for dioceses to appoint an Acora officer with a similar brief to the Acupa officer. Similarly, the existence of an Acupa committee naturally suggested the formation of an Acora committee. All this had begun to happen before the launch itself and the initiatives have been consolidated over the last 18 months. The first Acora officers' national meetings held at Stoneleigh have been positive and lively – and, more important, very well attended.

Needless to say, since this is the Church of England, each diocese has its own way of doing things. Some of the nominated Acora officers have so many other responsibilities that they cannot possibly give the job the time it needs. Not all of them have yet formed a rural group to support their work, and not all of them have yet found a strategic place in the diocesan structure. The great majority of dioceses, however, have taken the report seriously, made sensible appointments, and are beginning to take into their synodical system the existence of a rural group whose job is to further the aims of the report. Most dioceses have already discussed the report at the Synod and sent it on for further consideration to deaneries and parishes.

The effect of this positive activity at diocesan and county levels has undoubtedly been encouraging for members of the rural Church. This is 'their' report, and at last the national Church seems to be taking them seriously. Many Acora officers can bear witness to the fact that whenever they have spoken to rural audiences, they have been heard with enthusiasm. The difficulty, as with every report, is to translate this enthusiasm into practical changes.

The diocese of Canterbury invited every parish to appoint a lay Acora representative to work with the diocesan rural group, and over 120 have responded. The diocese of Carlisle was able to draw on the Opportunity for Volunteers scheme funds to appoint deanery representatives. Over 1,000 of the parish study packs provided by the Archbishops' Officer have been sold; so the process is beginning.

In his *Report of Two Years as Archbishops' Rural Officer* (October 1992), Jeremy Martineau notes a number of ongoing initiatives. Ten dioceses have run their own CME courses on rural ministry in which he, as Archbishops' Rural Officer, has taken part, but he believes that rural clergy now need training in how to encourage local ministry as well as in the understanding of the rural 'context'. CPAS and the Churches TV Centre are producing a video for those who lead worship with small congregations. A major survey of rural parishes has been launched to try to discover the factors in the life of the church which 'make the difference'.

The initiative with the greatest potential for the future has been the launch of the ecumenical magazine *Country Way* for those living and ministering in rural areas. It is a thoroughly professional publication, and the first issues have been full of interesting articles, useful reviews, and reports of positive ventures that are going on around the country. By Easter 1993 nearly 3,000 people had taken out subscriptions.

In July 1993 the General Synod appointed Martineau as the first Church of England National Rural Officer, a three-year post. It also created a Rural Affairs sub-committee, to be located with the Board for Mission. This is the first time that the General Synod has accepted financial responsibility for the support of rural ministry.

Also in the summer of 1993, the Churches Rural Group had its first meeting. This is a council set up under the auspices of Churches Together in England which makes formal the close ecumenical co-operation which has been such a feature of the rural scene since the 1970s.

Another encouraging development is the recent appointment of a working party on non-accredited lay ministry, and a projected working party on accredited lay ministry. At the moment, as *Faith in the Countryside* pointed out, no General Synod Board is responsible for lay ministry; but if local ministry is to be 'collaborative' the Synod needs to authorize a body which can oversee and encourage the training of the lay members of local teams, as well as the priests.

CONCLUSION

In some ways the most exciting feature about the Acora process was the decision to visit every diocese in the country. The evidence was of course anecdotal and is of a different nature from a statistical social survey. Nonetheless, as a way of testing the spirit and potential of the rural Church it had value, and in a number of important ways the experiences gained give *Faith in the Countryside* its freshness and individuality.

Two things stand out which transcend the many different stories. The first is the need for confidence. As has been said, 'ten is either twice five or half of twenty'. The Commissioners' notes on diocesan visits record that in Ely diocese there is a pair of hamlets, both within the same benefice and hardly a mile apart. Both are agricultural hamlets with a few commuters; both have attractive mediaeval churches, with the fabric in reasonable order. One hamlet 'feels' dead. The church is locked and the key kept in the next village but one. There are two services a month, attended almost exclusively by outsiders, people who used to live in the hamlet – and only by a handful of them. The other hamlet bristles with footpath signs 'welcoming caring walkers'. The churchyard is adorned with flowerbeds, and the church door is open. There are no pews (providential woodworm), and the comfortable chairs are arranged in a semi-circle around the nave altar. There are new hymn books and a array of bright tapestry kneelers. The noticeboard and 'tract stall' are exemplary. What one hamlet has and the other lacks is Christian confidence.

Secondly, the overwhelming impression is not of gloom but of optimism. The sheer number of enthusiastic laity that the Commissioners met convinced them that, far from being a non-starter as has always been argued, lay ministry in villages is a real possibility. What they need are clear, simple guidelines for establishing local collaborative ministry.

The next chapter seeks to set out the basic principles for future rural ministry as recommended by *Faith in the Countryside*. The hope is that a simple presentation of 'the vision' may help to commend this rural report to the rural parishes, and give them the confidence to believe that a positive future is both possible and within their grasp.

The Vision

5

The Vision

There is a parson-shaped hole at the centre of every parish. In village after village visited by the Commissioners the cry was 'what we really want is a vicar of our own'; and two-thirds of the clergy interviewed in the Rural Church Project believed that – ideally – each parish should have its own priest. In the same survey, parishioners were asked what they considered to be the job of the vicar. With remarkably few 'don't knows', they identified the following six key features:

(1) *Pastoral* – the pastoral work of the clergy in visiting parishioners and especially those in trouble.

(2) *Community involvement* – involvement in parish and community life, and in engendering community spirit and solidarity.

(3) *Anglican representative* – being representative of the Church in the community.

(4) *Taking church services* – the clergy's role in leading weekly worship and officiating at baptisms, weddings and funerals.

(5) *Teacher* – spiritual and moral teacher and proclaimer of the word.

(6) *Father and shepherd* – a particular way of describing the care of the priest for his people, and introducing the dimension of 'holiness'.

It is a remarkable tribute to the work of parish clergy over the last century that parishioners put such value on the work of the vicar and understand the nature of that work so well. Our difficulty is that we are no longer in a position to operate the old system. There are three major reasons for this:

(1) That there are a third fewer Anglican clergy active today than there were in 1965 and, whatever allowances are made, the numbers of stipendiaries working in villages is likely to fall even further.

(2) That in the present financial climate fewer and fewer villages are likely to be prepared or able to pay for their own vicar even if one were available.

(3) That our renewed understanding of the theology of ministry calls in question a system which gave such power to the priest and laid such burdens on him.

How then are we to square the circle? *Faith in the Countryside* believes that God is challenging us to provide ministry in our villages – locally, collaboratively, and on a non-stipendiary basis.

THE LOCAL FOCUS

There will be as many variations on the theme as there are villages in the country, but the Commissioners identify the settlement, with its church and congregation, as the basic building block. They encourage each settlement to grow its own 'local Christian focus'. There is already a Christian focus in the village in the shape of the church building, and this should be cherished, not complained about. The human focus will be, not an individual as in the past, but a group of people who represent the Church in that place. This group could be anything from two or three individuals to the whole congregation. Members of the group will be nominated by the PCC and trained by the diocese. There may be included in the group: deacons, retired clergy, non-stipendiary clergy, Readers, lay pastoral assistants, churchwardens and other members of the PCC. *Faith in the Countryside* believes that there is no longer room for denominationalism in villages, and therefore, if at all possible, local ministry groups should be ecumenical. The group may therefore include elders and local preachers of other denominations.

The members of the group, along with the incumbent, will exercise a collaborative ministry in the settlement, and their ministry will be authorized in some clear way by the bishop (and representatives of other churches as appropriate). One or more of them may test their vocation to the local non-stipendiary (ordained) ministry, but this is itself a ministry which will be exercised in collaboration with the others in the group, not in isolation from them.

The job of the members of the local group will be to minister in their settlement so that the place and those who live there may be 'transfigured from glory to glory'. To do this they will need to meet regularly to plan how to exercise pastoral care, how to encourage community life, and how to ensure that teaching and spiritual nourishment is available. They will also need to pray for their village, not just privately at home, but together in church on weekdays as well as on Sundays. There will normally be worship in their church every Sunday at a time which is found to be convenient *for those living there*. This will inevitably mean that not every service is taken by the incumbent. It will be the responsibility of members of the group to help to plan services so that local people participate fully in the acts of worship, and so that they include local concerns as well as the concerns of the world-wide Church.

THE BENEFICE TEAM

This local ministry group will be part of a benefice ministry team which will normally be the responsibility of an incumbent. This too will vary in composition depending on who is available and on what the local set-up happens to be. At one end of the spectrum there may be a three-parish benefice in which only one settlement has a local group, whose members are authorized to operate solely within their own village. In this case, the benefice ministry team may consist of the incumbent, the other 'staff' (if there are any) and the members of the group, and may on occasion include churchwardens and treasurers from all three parishes. At the other extreme there may be a 'team ministry' which covers 15 settlements, each of which has its own local group, and in which each member of every group is authorized to minister throughout the team ministry's area. In this case, the benefice ministry team may consist of all the members of all the groups, plus all the team 'staff' – and churchwardens and treasurers on occasion. In addition to a village hall in which to meet, there would clearly need to be operational sub-committees; but whatever the local details may be, the underlying principle is that ministry should be local, collaborative *and catholic* (in the original sense of 'worldwide').

There is obviously a danger that the local ministry group could become so preoccupied with local concerns that it loses sight of the wider love of God for his Church and the world. One of the principles of an episcopal Church is that the local parts need to work together for the good of the whole body. That is why the local groups must be welded into a benefice team, and why the role of the stipendiary, who in a resonant phrase is 'the one from outside', is so vital.

THE STIPENDIARY

In his report, Canon Tiller recommended that the stipendiary clergy should be 'diocesan' priests rather than 'parish' priests. His suggestion was rejected, and yet in one sense that is exactly what the rural stipendiary of the future will have to be. On the one hand, stipendiaries will still be the parish priests of (local) benefices, but, on the other hand, within those benefices they will be the bishop's representative whose first job is to exercise the *episcopē* (oversight) of the Church universal. It is an enormously demanding and challenging job, and the incumbent will need firm support from other clergy in the deanery (the chapter), from diocesan officers, from a spiritual director, and perhaps from some other support group or support mechanism outside the benefice.

THE DIOCESE

The diocese has a number of support roles to perform. It needs to have a clear overall strategy which is communicated to incumbents and local congregations. This strategy is *not* a blueprint, but a framework of aims and principles in which local objectives can be identified; it is also the responsibility of the diocese to encourage local congregations to set objectives, and then to monitor progress.

Secondly, dioceses must take on the training and authorization role. Most incumbents have neither the time nor the expertise to do it all themselves. Furthermore, if local ministry is to be credible, it needs diocesan – and preferably national – authorization.

Thirdly, the diocese needs to build up a strategic reserve to cover retreat and to reinforce advance. There will be some parishes who give up; these need to be declared 'mission areas' for a set period of time during which they receive extra help. If at the end of that period they still cannot develop their own local ministry, that settlement will have (at least temporarily) to be abandoned. At the other extreme there will be benefices which grow so fast that they need extra help. There may be an opening for a youth worker, or for setting up a chaplaincy to a school or to a group of commercial enterprises. Parishes should be able to make applications for project funding (on the same lines as the Church Urban Fund) and the diocese needs to be able to respond.

CONCLUSION

The future of the rural Church is in the hands of local people. The evidence of *Faith in the Countryside* is that many will welcome and respond to this challenge. It is not just that this will keep the system running at minimum expense, but that it will also lead to effective rural evangelism. Evangelism is a question of 'being' and 'doing' more than of 'saying'. It has always been true that the most effective evangelism has been the attraction of the Christian life as embodied in people and communities. It has been calculated that 85 per cent of us become Christians as a result of someone else's personal example, and that only a small number do so primarily through the power of the spoken or written word – although these things obviously have a vital place in our *development* as Christians.

Closely related to this is the fact that the most effective evangelism normally occurs at the local level. The neighbourhood is the context for evangelism through personal example – often the words of neighbours are the most powerful ones. Knowledge of and commitment to a locality, whether one thinks in terms of a village or a county, is a vital element in evangelism.

Certainly this vision is 'dangerous'. It demands great sacrifices of the rural laity, and great flexibility and humility from the rural clergy; but given the problems ahead, it also offers real hope of a thriving future for the rural parishes.

Testing the Vision

6

Introduction

> I was to learn later in life that we tend to meet any new situation by reorganizing; and a wonderful method it can be for creating the illusion of progress while producing confusion, inefficiency and demoralization.

So, it is alleged, wrote Caius Petronius in AD 65. The Church is beginning a process of drastic reorganization in rural areas, and it is very important that this process leads to solid progress rather than further demoralization. There are a number of models of ministry being canvassed as 'the answer to our problems' at the moment, and it is inherently unlikely that they can all be right. It is therefore essential that their likelihood of success be tested against the hard evidence we have. I believe that 'the vision' outlined in Chapter 5 will appeal to many rural people, but with regard to the deployment of stipendiaries and the future survival of congregations it is not enough just to have bright ideas. In this chapter I shall first outline the evidence available and comment on its relative value. Then, since the concept of 'success' is central to any idea of evaluation, I shall examine what this might mean in the rural context; and finally in this chapter, I shall offer a definition of 'rural'.

THE EVIDENCE

The chief source of the statistical evidence about the rural Church used in this book is provided by the Rural Church Project, summarized in *Church and Religion in Rural England* by Davies, Watkins and Winter. 572 clergy from the five dioceses of Durham, Gloucester, Lincoln, Southall and Truro responded to a lengthy questionnaire, and this was supplemented by 101 face-to-face interviews with rural clergy and 489 interviews with their parishioners, selected at random from the church electoral roll and the secular electoral roll. Questions covered belief, attitude to the incumbent and the local church, worship, mission strategy, and how the clergy spend their time. It is an academic work of sociological research written by authors of real authority in the field of rural affairs, and is the most comprehensive picture of the rural Church ever published. As such, it provides a secure basis for decisions made about the future of rural ministry. It is, however, important to recognize that the research uses two different survey methods, and it is necessary to distinguish between evidence from the questionnaire and evidence from face-to-face interviews.

To provide background evidence for the General Synod Board of Education's *Children in the Way* report, a survey was carried out in 1988. Twenty-two dioceses co-operated and 72 per cent of the questionnaires were returned. The detailed results have been published by the National Society as *Continuing in the Way* (Francis and Lankshear, 1988). The questionnaire was devised to assess the contact between churches and young people in their area, but it also included background questions about the parishes and asked for a list of services held on two Sundays in November 1987. *Children in the Way* made use of the statistics considered to be relevant to the report, but many more questions could have been asked of the data collected. The data are still available and there are already examples of the use that might be made of them if the money could be found to access information. They are particularly relevant to rural ministry. The following publications by Francis and Lankshear are all statistically meticulous and very relevant: 'Ageing clergy and the rural church' in *Ageing and Society*; 'The rural rectory: the impact of a resident priest on local church life' in *Journal of Rural Studies*; 'The impact of children's work on church life in hamlets and small villages' in

Journal of Christian Education; and 'Do small churches hold a future for children and young people?' in *Modern Churchman*.

General statistical evidence on the rural Church in Suffolk is available in *Rural Anglicanism* by Leslie Francis. The survey covered the whole diocese including urban areas, and no attempt was made to distinguish between urban and rural. This evidence is supplemented by the 'impressions' of a number of ordinands visiting particular rural parishes.

The results of the Church of England census, published as *Christian England* by Peter Brierley, are not as helpful as might appear on the surface. They do show denominational strengths in rural areas and indicate which 'churchmanship' is likely to produce more people in the pews as a percentage of the total population. However, they do not indicate which 'ministerial strategy' is most successful – nor, for that matter, whether Evangelicals are operating a consciously eclectic strategy. Furthermore, the church growth statistics are themselves suspect since they cover only four years (1985–89) rather than ten years (1979–89).

People, the Land and the Church by Lewis and Talbot-Ponsonby (1987) was the report of a year-long rural consultation carried out in the diocese of Hereford. Like *Faith in the Countryside*, it is not based on statistical evidence, but does claim to reflect what rural Christians in that area think and feel about the Church.

A valuable example of face-to-face interviews with rural clergy is *Parson to Parson* by John Stewart, Rector of Langton Matravers in Dorset. During a sabbatical, Canon Stewart visited ten rural clergy, staying with each of them for a week (in his own caravan) and talking to them about their jobs. It is a fascinating, and sometimes deeply moving, account of rural ministry in 1989 and can usefully be set alongside J. Richardson's *Ten Rural Churches*.

A number of shorter papers are also valuable. The contrast between urban and rural attitudes to the Church and the clergy is illustrated by *Church and People on the Longhill Estate*. The contrast between rural and urban deaneries is drawn in a dissertation 'The role of the laity in the rural church', presented to the University of Southampton by Stephen Cope. Ripon diocese has written up its experience of establishing local ministry groups in the report entitled *Two Years On – Local Ministry in 1985*; and Lincoln diocese has carried out a similar exercise in its presentation to the Advisory Board for Ministry (ABM) on local ministry (1990). Reg Legg's book *Lay Pastorate* covers his experience of setting up local ministry, and *Delectable Mountains* by Moira Mathieson describes a local ministry project in the USA.

Evidence on the working of rural groups and teams in Norfolk is available in Anthony Russell's *Groups and Teams in the Countryside*. This is supplemented by the Hempnell Group (Lathe, 1986), and on a national scale by the General Synod reports *Team and Group Ministries* (1985), and *Team and Group Ministries: Report of the Working Party* (1991). An unpublished paper by Alan Pyke, 'Where are we going in rural ministry' (1985), records the results of a questionnaire sent to the archdeacons in three eastern dioceses and includes useful material on groups and teams.

Evidence on 'popular religion' is available in a number of papers by Edward Bailey published by the Network for the Study of Implicit Religion. Reference will also be made to an unpublished dissertation 'The theodicy of Eastington' by Noel Baker.

Formerly the best book about 'success' in the rural Church was by an American, Carl Dudley, *Making the Small Church Effective* (1978). Now that Robin Gill's long-awaited book *The Myth of the Empty Church* (1993) has been published, we have English evidence of the importance of 'over-provision of pews' in rural areas which clearly needs to be taken into account when analysing the effect on morale of half-empty churches.

Diocesan presentations to Acora sometimes provide useful evidence on particular projects, as do a number of diocesan papers that are beginning to appear as consultation documents on the general theme of 'Towards a Rural Strategy'. I have made particular use of those from the dioceses of Norwich, Salisbury, Winchester and Lincoln.

The rural ecumenical scene is researched in a report on councils of churches. *Churches in Fellowship* by L. J. Francis and K. Williams (1990) analyses the replies from secretaries of councils of churches who were asked what was happening locally and how effective they thought their council was. Another extremely helpful survey is *Methodism in the Countryside – The Horncastle Circuit 1786–1986* (J. N. Clarke and C. L. Anderson, 1986). This is a detailed historical survey of a Lincolnshire Circuit and includes a wealth of statistical material.

A number of books and papers suggest ways forward for rural ministry. There are some excellent ecumenical publications including the *Workbooks* on rural evangelism (Calvert, 1977, 1984), *Half the Denomi-*

nation (Baptist Church, 1983), *And Is There Honey Still?* by Salsbury (for the URC) and a number of Federation for Rural Evangelism papers, also articles in the RTA journal *A Better Country,* and other RTA publications such as *The Rural Church: Towards 2000.* The Bishop of Sherborne has written an important paper on the ideal of 'minster ministry', and this is most attractively fleshed out in *The New Springtime of the Church* by C. Donaldson (1992). Robin Gill's *Beyond Decline* is an important contribution to the debate, and *The Country Church* by Robert Van der Weyer will frequently be quoted, for it is full of good ideas forcefully expressed. These papers and books carry the authority of their particular authors, all of whom have experience of rural ministry, and as such are valuable contributions to the discussion. However, none of them makes any serious attempt to test their theories against the statistical data available. Valuable though they are, what the Church particularly needs at this juncture is firm statistical evidence and properly monitored experiments.

Finally, there is one publication which is essential reading for anyone interested in local ministry in rural areas. So many dioceses are now contemplating the ordination of local non-stipendiary ministers that the Advisory Council for the Church's Ministry (ACCM, now reconstituted as the Advisory Board for Ministry, ABM) set up a working party under the chairmanship of the Bishop of Stafford, which produced the report *Local NSM.* This was presented to the House of Bishops, who in January 1991 agreed a series of 'Regulations and Guidelines' for local ministry which are printed on pp. 37ff. of the report. Diocesan schemes are to be locally approved by the Diocesan Synod and nationally approved by the House of Bishops, and a detailed scheme for training has to be commended by ABM.

THE ECUMENICAL EVIDENCE

The previous section described rural ministry in Christian rather than denominational terms, and it will be urged throughout that village congregations should be 'Christian' rather than exclusively 'Anglican'. However, just as *Faith in the Countryside* was addressed specifically to the Church of England, so 'the vision' has now to be tested in the context of Anglican organization. That does not mean, however, that Free Church evidence will be ignored – as has so often been the case in the past. Clearly, there can be a problem in that the Free Churches' traditional theological understanding of Church and ministry differs from that of traditional Anglicans: but there is for instance already an uncanny similarity between the Methodist Circuit and the large multi-parish benefice, and it would therefore be foolish not to listen to what Methodists have to say on that subject. Free Church evidence will therefore be offered where it seems relevant, while a full chapter is allotted to formal ecumenical relations in rural areas.

EVALUATING 'SUCCESS' IN THE RURAL MINISTRY

'The church exists so that everyone in our village may experience God's love as real – and respond to it.' That is how one group of villages eventually came to describe their overall aim. Another village set as its goal 'that this place and those who live here may be transfigured from glory to glory'. These are not simplistic evangelical programmes, and yet they do involve counting heads. For generations, and for obvious theological reasons, rural parishes have resisted the temptation 'to number the people': after all, Christian 'success' is defined by a failed preacher nailed to a cross. Yet the very fact that the Decade of Evangelism/Evangelization is fully ecumenical does suggest a growing consensus that numbers can no longer be ignored.

Attendance statistics

Church and Religion in Rural England tells us that on an 'ordinary' Sunday between 8.1 per cent and 1.4 per cent of the total population attend an Anglican church. The smaller and more rural the benefice, the higher the percentage attendance; and conversely, the larger and more urban the benefice, the lower the percentage attendance (p. 211, Table 42). The research also tells us that 49 per cent of all parishioners questioned claimed that they had been to church three or more times during the past year – apart from attending baptisms, weddings and funerals. At Christmas alone, 51 per cent of the population of the rural villages claim to go to church (a figure which of course includes carol services as well as midnight mass). The figure rises to 75 per cent if you include those who say they have been to a baptism, wedding or funeral during the past year – a truly astonishing figure.

On the face of it, these are encouraging statistics and suggest that the most 'successful' Anglican churches are actually the rural ones. Robin Gill, however, believes that things are not as simple as they first seem. In *Beyond Decline* (1988), he points out that these figures are exclusively Anglican, and in his very important book *The Myth of the Empty Church* (1993) he shows just how difficult it is to arrive at accurate church attendance figures, or to compare the membership figures of one denomination with those of another. Gill also suggests that the highest churchgoing rates as a percentage of the population (taking into account all the denominations) may well be in pockets of the suburbs rather than in small villages. Be that as it may, what Gill is absolutely right to do is to remind us that the success or otherwise of the village church is not defined by comparison with the inner-city church, but by seeing it as a percentage of the total population. Those Christians who believe in personal salvation and personal judgement will be appalled by the fact that on an ordinary Sunday 92 per cent of the population of the village do not worship in the local church.

Leslie Francis and David Lankshear have underlined how bad the situation is by drawing our attention to other figures. In *Rural Anglicanism*, Leslie Francis showed that the number of baptisms and confirmations had fallen steeply; and the survey carried out for the *Children in the Way* report (General Synod Board of Education, 1988), published as *Continuing in the Way* (Francis and Lankshear, 1988), showed the extent to which the Church has ceased to have contact with over 90 per cent of children and young adults who, the Youth Officer of the diocese of Gloucester claims, 'are leaving the Church at the rate of three hundred a week'.

Church membership statistics based on the numbers on the church electoral roll have to be treated with caution. Traditionally there was a reluctance in villages to draw a distinction between 'the village' and 'the congregation' and this often meant that all who claimed to be C of E were included on the roll. It was only the need to draw up new lists for synodical government, and perhaps more importantly the tendency of dioceses to base their quota calculations on electoral roll numbers, which led to 'rationalization'. It is suggested therefore that while electoral roll figures before about 1980 should not be used to measure church growth, from then on they do provide an increasingly valuable statistic.

An interesting dissertation presented to Southampton University by

Stephen Cope, 'The role of the laity in the rural church', also uses electoral roll statistics, and his findings suggest that the rural parishes are in this respect performing less well than those in urban areas. When the electoral roll number are considered as a percentage of total population, they show that the very rural areas have shown a sharp fall in numbers in the early 1980s, in contrast to the urban and suburban deaneries, which have shown an upturn in the numbers over the last ten years.

The 'church growth' statistics available are suspect, either because they ignore key factors or because they are presented as simplistic 'proof' of Evangelical methods. The Rural Church Project tells us that 'Evangelical' incumbents are likely to have more people in their churches than 'Catholics', but it does not tell us how many of those Evangelicals operate a consciously 'eclectic' strategy. Not only does *Christian England* by Peter Brierley ignore this issue, but on examination the statistics of growth he uses are not as helpful as they at first seem. Had the Church census been able to compare the 1979 attendance figures in a particular church with the 1989 figures in the same church, this would have been extremely valuable, but apparently that was not possible. Instead, on this occasion (1989), each incumbent was asked whether *he or she* believed there had been growth in the parish since 1985. At the very least, it is likely that the Evangelical growth ethos put strains on the memories of the Evangelical incumbents faced with such a question; nor does it give us any handle on those individual parishes which have grown or declined since 1979, and reasons as to why they might have grown or declined. Furthermore, since the only variable used is 'churchmanship' rather than 'ministerial strategy', *Christian England* does not give the evidence about growth needed to make an informed decision about 'which strategy works best'. The *Children in the Way* statistics may still yield some helpful data, but only if the money can be found to 'band' the rural parishes surveyed by use of a 'ministerial strategy variable'.

What is perhaps most worrying is the suspicion that the (relatively) high attendance figures in village churches are the product of the (relatively) high ratio of stipendiary ministry to total population, and of a rural culture which is fast disappearing. So while the village church still has the edge on the urban church in numbers worshipping (as a percentage of the total population), these figures give little cause for smugness, and do not in themselves provide a satisfactory measure of 'success' – particularly if we are looking at potential for growth.

Assessing morale

The howls of protest which greeted the publication of *Rural Anglicanism* focused on the accounts of the visits to village churches by a number of ordinands. Nevertheless, in retrospect these reports seem much truer to life than the cold accuracy of numbers because they begin to get to grips with what the rural Church in Suffolk *felt* like. To estimate the 'success' of this or that form of ministry in rural areas there needs to be a more complex pattern of statistics which will reflect the 'feel' of a congregation. Hugh Searle from Ely diocese made this point in a paper, 'Evaluating the rural church', submitted to the Acora Commissioners. In it he argues that, as with the police force, most of what the Church does is in response to demands, and much of the most important work in both crime detection for the police and evangelism for the Church is done not by stipendiaries, but by members of the 'laity'. It is therefore very hard to measure the 'effectiveness' of Church or clergy. There is, however, an alternative concept of 'significance': this would focus on the 'significance' of the village church for the life of the village and those living in it, though this involves a basic change of emphasis in that when measuring 'significance' numbers are less important. He suggests that indicators of significance might include:

Do the church building and churchyard show signs of being looked after with care?

Are information and a visitors' book provided for visitors?

Is the church open and are people encouraged to drop in for prayer?

Is the minister in demand for baptisms, weddings and funerals?

Do the minister and active laity participate in local community events and organizations?

Is the church magazine also a community magazine?

Does the church actively support the local school, toddlers' group, over-60s, etc.?

Does the church promote fundraising for causes outside the village – such as Christian Aid?

In the same vein, John Clarke, director of the Arthur Rank Centre and himself a Commissioner, presented a paper to the Commissioners on the subject of 'measuring success' which began:

> A 'successful' rural church is usually expected to have the same characteristics as any other 'successful' church – large congregations, a suite of buildings designed for a variety of purposes, a multitude of activities on the premises every day of the week, e.g. women's meetings, men's meetings, uniformed organisations, youth clubs, badminton clubs, drama groups, mothers and toddlers clubs, playgroups, lunches for senior citizens, a 'drop-in' club for the leisured or the unemployed, etc., with, of course, 'their own minister'. There will also be considerable involvement by individuals in the life of the community in which the church is set. They will be especially prominent in the various charitable and aid organisations in the town, OXFAM, Cancer Relief and so on.
>
> What has just been described is a particular type of church set in suburbia or in a town centre. We should not expect a church in rural Africa to be anything like that, no matter how 'successful' it is. Neither should we expect all the churches in this country to be identical in style. A 'successful' rural church or inner city church will look very different from a 'successful' suburban church. Therefore, a rural church should not be classified as weak or as a problem, just because it does not conform to the standards of 'success' appropriate to the suburban church. A small church is not a failed large church: it is a different sort of animal.

He goes on to point out that small numbers are a result of a small population, not a sign of failure, and that they dictate a different strategy. Small numbers will mean that the church does not run its own organizations, but joins in with those already at work in the village. They will mean fewer church activities because with fewer people everyone will have to join in everything. Instead of Sunday schools and children's services, there will be all-age worship. He quotes Carl Dudley, who writes in *Making the Small Church Effective*:

> In a big world, the small church has remained *intimate*. In a fast world, the small church has remained *steady*. In an expensive world,

the small church has remained *plain*. In a complex world, the small church has remained *simple*. In a rational world, the small church has been the *anchor*. In an anonymous world, the small church *calls us by name*.

If these are some of the criteria by which the 'success' of the small church should be measured, what sort of questionnaire is needed to provide the required information?

In addition to the statistics of those attending church on Sunday, etc., there needs to be information on the indicators of significance suggested above. Other questions might include whether a fellowship group or a youth fellowship meets, not perhaps weekly, but for two termly sessions a year; and whether this is supplemented by an annual parish day or weekend. Is there regular all-age worship, and how do laity participate in offering worship? How far does the congregation join in group activities with the other villages? Finally, other questions would try to measure how much contact the minister and members of the PCC have with those who are not members of the congregation; and, if possible, parishioners selected at random should be questioned about their attitude to the church. These are some of the indicators which would give information on the 'life' of a church and so enable estimates to be made regarding the effectiveness of one strategy of ministry as against another.

Sadly, not even the Rural Church Project does this, though it does give a number of useful insights. Perhaps the nearest attempt at such a survey were the supplementary questions to Francis's *Rural Anglicanism* questionnaire, which tried to ascertain what contact the local church had with young people. The results, almost entirely gloomy, were confirmed as almost wholly accurate by the national survey which provided the background for *Children in the Way* (General Synod Board of Education, 1988). Nevertheless, while recognizing that there is not yet anything like all the information needed, it is obviously better to make use of what information is available than to ignore all the evidence and proceed simply on the basis of a 'hunch'. What this discussion certainly highlights is the need for the 'success' of experiments to be monitored in as full and imaginative a way as possible for only in this manner can they be of value to the Church at large. An early and enormously influential example of what can be done was *Groups and Teams in the Countryside*, edited by Anthony Russell. It is hard to point to other similar examples in the field of rural ministry.

WHAT IS RURAL?

Finally in this chapter there needs to be a definition of what is meant in this book by 'the rural Church'. It has been said that a village is a place which the inhabitants believe to be the centre of the universe. This highlights one aspect of rurality, which is of course shared with many an urban Coronation Street. It has also been said that a village is an island in a sea of green which can be reached by crossing a Tarmac causeway. Any definition of 'rural' must do justice to both the human and the geographical aspects of country life. In a useful section in Chapter 3 of *Church and Religion in Rural England*, Davies, Watkins and Winter note that:

> The simplest and probably most useful way of distinguishing between urban and rural areas is the relative proportion of open countryside found in an area. Wibberley (1972) regarded rural areas as essentially those parts of a country which show unmistakable signs of being dominated by *extensive* (as opposed to *intensive*) use of land. (p. 57)

This simple and commonsense functional definition unfortunately has inherent problems. It does not allow us to classify the small market town, the army camp estate, the mining or fishing village; but, most important, it leaves out of account the social and cultural aspects of rurality which mean so much in practice. A more satisfactory definition is offered in *Regional Studies* (1986) by Cloke and Edwards, who have devised a 'comprehensive rurality measurement' to classify district council areas on a scale of rurality. This is based on information derived from the 1981 census and follows a similar classification based on the 1971 census. There are 16 variables; ten of them directly concern population – its level, density, distribution, the distance from large centres of population and migration. The assumption is that the more sparse the population and the greater the distance from an urban centre, the more 'rural' a district. Other variables include more social factors such as jobs in the area and amenities. The four categories of rurality thus derived are 'extreme rural', 'intermediate rural', 'intermediate non-rural' and 'extreme non-rural'.

However, even this, since it is based on census statistics which go no lower than district level, does not get to the heart of 'the feel' of a place. Furthermore, as everyone knows, two villages which are geographically only a mile apart can be sociologically very different. This is why Russell's division of villages into 'urban shadow', 'accessible', 'less accessible' and 'remote or marginal' (depending on how far they are from a large conurbation), while conceptually very helpful, is ultimately inadequate (*The Country Parish*, p. 3). In *The People, the Land and the Church* by Lewis and Talbot-Ponsonby, the point is well made:

> It needs to be stressed that there is really no such thing as rural life if by that phrase we mean a stereotype or amalgam of assorted averages. Even the comment about four countrysides is open to misunderstanding. I tried fitting the parishes in this deanery into them and ended up very confused. I agree that there needs to be some sort of key of understanding to which people can refer but its approximate quality and the fact that categories are not necessarily mutually exclusive needs to be stressed very strongly.
>
> Even in this diocese of Hereford, the east is different from the west and Gloucester might be another world! (p. 24)

In the last resort, statistical data need to be checked by asking local people how they categorize their own settlement. This is what was done in the Rural Church Project, and the results are analysed on p. 59 of *Church and Religion in Rural England*. It is interesting to note that clergy working in mining and fishing villages did not describe these settlements as rural. Clearly, in their minds rurality was still inextricably linked with agriculture.

Recognizing, then, how impossible it is to do more than give a series of rough and ready categories, market towns first need to be isolated into a class of their own. The key factor here is not so much size of population (which varies enormously from area to area) as the fact that 'the market town' is a local centre to which people come from outlying smaller settlements. 'Industrial villages' are again a separate category and usually come complete with their own set of problems, but they are undoubtedly a very important part of the rural scene. Then, although numbers are often misleading, settlements of less than 1,000 population must usually be regarded as 'villages' (unless, as may occasionally be the case, the inhabitants see their settlement as a market town). Anywhere larger than this should be categorized on the basis of how local residents see their own settlement.

A village of less than 100 inhabitants with no public services except a telephone kiosk would normally be classified as a hamlet. In certain parts of the country, however, the proliferation of hamlets is historically part of a dispersed settlement pattern, and the public buildings, such as the church, the village hall, pub and shop, are usually located near a key crossroads. Tradition and the practicalities of daily life may mean that such a 'handful of hamlets' still regard themselves as together forming a village; and here too it is necessary to ask local residents how they see themselves rather than simply relying on demographic statistics.

Finally, by way of definition, it needs to be said that since the 'rural crisis' focuses around the multi-parish benefice, the main concern of this book will not be with the market town or the large industrial village but with those benefices which cover more than one settlement.

7

The Rural Church
in Crisis

The brief historical survey given in Chapter 3 argued that although the rural Church is beginning to recover after a period of major decline in the 1960s and 1970s, it is still going through a major crisis. Chapter 5 was based on the assumption that this is the case; this premise now needs to be tested. This chapter analyses the crisis and in particular argues that there is a grave shortage of stipendiary clergy and money to pay them. It is further suggested that even if there were enough of both, our theological understanding of ministry has changed, and that a clerically dominated parochial system is no longer appropriate.

NUMBERS

In this section two related issues are raised. First, whether the number of stipendiary clergy available to the Church of England is likely to decline in the next decade. Second, by what criteria the Church at national and local level should deploy stipendiaries as between urban and rural benefices.

Future numbers of stipendiaries

The first issue is swiftly dealt with. Despite all the efforts to recruit for the ministry, there are fewer stipendiary parish clergy active today than in 1892, and there will be fewer in 2002 than in 1992. The General Synod Ministry Co-ordinating Group's *The Ordained Ministry: Numbers, Cost and Deployment* gives the number of clergy active in 1988 as 10,660 and the situation since then has not changed for the better. (It is not believed that the proposed ordination of women to the priesthood, taken in conjunction with the consequent resignation of male priests, will make a significant difference to the overall figure of stipendiaries available for deployment.) It seems probable that by the turn of the century there will be approximately 9,800 stipendiaries, a drop of 800 from today's figures, or a decline of 100 a year. These are the stark facts which every diocese has to face.

Criteria for deployment of stipendiaries

How will a decline in stipendiary numbers affect the *rural* ministry? Will the cuts be made, as has largely been the case in the past, in rural areas? The answer is almost certainly 'yes', because in the eyes of most diocesan pastoral committees the needs of a parish with 10,000 inhabitants are 'obviously' greater than the needs of a group of settlements with 1,000 inhabitants.

While accepting the basic premise that 'numbers of inhabitants' are an important factor in pastoral policy, it is important to realize that there are many other factors which *ought* to be considered. This is such an important issue that we need to consider these factors in detail. Such a consideration must start from the Sheffield Formula itself.

The Sheffield Formula

The Sheffield Formula emerged from a House of Bishops Working Group in 1974 (General Synod Paper GS 205). There were four weighting factors – diocesan population (8), diocesan area (1), electoral roll (3) and number of churches (3); and on a combination of these factors the Group calculated a 'fair' distribution of the number of clergy for each of the 43 dioceses. How these clergy are deployed is a matter for each diocese to decide, but many pastoral committees have unquestioningly assumed that the Sheffield Formula, with its particular weighting factors, should also be the 'correct' basis for deployment *in the diocese*.

There are however many flaws in the formula. *The Ordained Ministry* (referred to above) itself recognized a number of the problems. The Working Party point out that to rely on membership of the electoral roll as the sole criterion for membership does not adequately reflect the situation, and so 'we have decided to change to the ratio adopted by the Church Commissioners for their purposes'. There are grave problems connected with the allocation of male and female deacons (who are not included in the Sheffield calculation) and the Working Party point out that this has caused problems for Boards of Finance trying to budget ahead. The report also suggests that the formula is now seen not as an instrument of expansion, but as a means of limitation. 'Is hiding behind the Sheffield Formula a deterrent to the Church's mission? Does it prevent dioceses from developing strategies to expand the ordained ministry where, on a less mechanistic approach it ought?' (VI. 49).

Faith in the Countryside attacks the Sheffield Formula from another angle. The Commissioners note that many of the more rural dioceses have found it necessary to give a higher weighting to space and the number of churches than was built into the original formula:

> This therefore meant that, although they had accepted the national formula for their total diocesan allocation, they found that its application at a local level proved unsatisfactory if an adequate rural ministry was to be maintained. In effect two formulae were being applied: the national one according to Sheffield and a local one according to the perceived pastoral needs and constraints of rural circumstances which did not fit into Sheffield's statistical framework. This was the evidence from several rural dioceses which claimed that their rural ministry was in danger of breaking down if clergy numbers were further reduced.
>
> This discovery bore out the argument put to us by the Rural Theology Association (RTA) in its evidence that the Church of England, in its acceptance of the Sheffield formula, had failed to appreciate the rural factors of space and scattered population and seriously underestimated the time required to serve a group of churches. (8.44–45)

The ecumenical factor

Faith in the Countryside goes on to make the point that the formula ignores the ecumenical dimension entirely, and it reveals that this was – not to put too fine a point on it – a deliberate conspiracy of the Working Party to secure the desired aim of reallocation between the dioceses:

> The Sheffield Report did in fact devote considerable time and space to ecumenical considerations and, in an appendix, effectively conceded one of the above points, namely that if ministers of the other main Christian churches were taken into account then Christian ministerial coverage in urban areas was much heavier than their report assumed. Indeed, had this approach been taken in 1973, it would have led to a flow of clergy from the province of York to that of Canterbury and from the urban to the rural dioceses. We were left firmly with the impression, from our reading of the Sheffield Report, that the ecumenical dimension was rejected because it did not assist those who wanted a more urban Anglican priesthood rather than because it presented insurmountable difficulties. These were inconvenient statistics which argued against the goal that was desired. This is made explicit in a report by the Ministry Co-ordinating Group in 1981, reviewing Sheffield:
>
> > Present strengths of Anglican and non-Anglican clergy in town and country made it inevitable that any method of ecumenical deployment is bound to result in urban dioceses losing and rural dioceses gaining a number of Anglican clergy, thus reversing the intention of the Sheffield formula. (8.47–48)

The effect of including clergy of other denominations in calculations about deployment can be seen not only as between urban and rural dioceses, but also as between small villages and their neighbouring market towns. For instance, Cirencester in Gloucestershire has a total population of 20,000 and is surrounded by a network of multi-parish benefices none of which contains more than 2,000 inhabitants all told. The contrast seems extreme. But there are resident in Circencester no less than four full-time stipendiary ministers of religion besides the four Anglican clergy; and if all of these are included there is one stipendiary minister of religion to 2,500 of the population. While recognizing that this bald ratio needs adaptation, it does show how unfair it can be to make no allowance for the ecumenical factor.

The argument usually advanced against such a weighting is that the Free Churches do not see themselves as having a responsibility for the whole population; and that since Free Churches are usually eclectic and draw their congregations from surrounding villages, it is difficult to work out an acceptable weighting factor at local level. Nevertheless, the following points need to be made.

First, that co-operation already takes place. In chaplaincy work the armed forces, prison authorities and health authorities specifically recognize the different denominations (usually financially), and the clergy involved co-operate to share the work load.

Secondly, now that the bad old days of church–chapel rivalry are in many places a distant memory, it is an absolute priority for the churches to work and plan together. The evidence to be offered in Chapter 14 suggests that the time is ripe in the rural areas to try to implement the Anglican vision of pastoral care for all, which undergirds the Sheffield Formula, *in co-operation with the other Christian churches*. It is for this reason above all that the Sheffield Formula should be adjusted to make allowance for 'the ecumenical dimension'.

If the Sheffield Formula is to be changed as suggested, rural dioceses will have to take action at a national level. What the above discussion has at least shown is that when pastoral committees deploy stipendiary clergy at local level they should not regard the original formula as sacrosanct.

Non-stipendiary assistance

Another variable which a realistic formula needs to recognize is that today most benefices could not function without a variety of 'extra' ministers. The diocese of Gloucester publishes a cycle of prayer so that each parish may be remembered regularly. Almost every parish lists not only an incumbent, but other ministers – retired clergy, non-stipendiary clergy, Readers, lay pastoral assistants – who are part of the 'official ministry team'.

In *Church and Religion in Rural England*, the authors 'look at the full range of types of staff working in the parishes' and show clearly that virtually no parish is actually run single-handed (Tables 28–30, pp. 150–2). They also show that while the 'totally rural' and the 'urban' parishes have minimal extra help, the market towns and suburbs are overflowing with resources. On average, the latter have one and a half times as many full-time assistants, twice as many part-time assistants, half as many stipendiary staff, and two and a half times as many non-stipendiary staff as rural and urban parishes. In Cirencester in Gloucestershire, in addition to the Anglican and Free Church stipendiaries already mentioned, there were living in the town in 1992 two non-stipendiaries and six Readers, besides a retired archdeacon, two retired canons, and at least five other retired Anglican clergy. Not every market town is so fortunate, but the time has surely come to recognize the part played by the ministry team in exercising pastoral care for the parish, *and to build this into the deployment formula.*

MONEY

In this section I examine first why the financial crisis has occurred; secondly, why rural parishes are beginning to refuse to pay their quotas; and thirdly, whether the situation is going to lead to dioceses adopting the principle that parishes must pay for the ministry they receive.

The escalating cost

In a prophetic paper written in 1981, Christopher Newton, then Rector of the Swan Team Ministry in Oxfordshire, predicted that by 1995 the parishes in his deanery would not be able to pay their quota. He suggested that we should therefore have to make do with fewer stipendiary clergy and that we should immediately start planning for that day. His figures seemed unnecessarily alarmist at the time, but they have proved all too accurate. In the little village of Coates in Gloucestershire the quota has risen from £550 in 1978 to £5,000 in 1992 (or by 264 per cent, allowing for inflation). The sums having to be raised via the quota by the diocese of Gloucester over the last few years have been as follows:

	Quota totals:	
	1987 –	£1,392,654
	1988 –	£1,554,933
	1989 –	£2,002,905
	1990 –	£2,132,577
	1991 –	£2,477,056

The reasons for this scale of inflation are beginning to be understood, at least by PCC standing committees. At root it is the need to fund an increasing percentage of the cost of the stipendiary clergy, who in 1992 cost about £30,000 each. The Morley Report recommended a series of measures which would put the payment and conditions of employment of the clergy on a new footing. In the past, clergy had operated as professionals, accountable to no one but the bishop, and most of them paid heavily for the privilege. The suggestion was that in the future they should in effect be employees, accountable to bishop *and congregation*, and in return for this surrender of 'independence' they would be rewarded by reasonable pay and excellent conditions of employment. The clergy were initially very uneasy about the deal, but have come to see that the relative security of employment and the very significant extras offered, particularly in retirement, are well worth the minimal sacrifices so far required. The laity, who often saw the measures as a victory for common sense (and local influence) over an antiquated clericalism, are only now beginning to realize the cost of victory; for it is they who are having to fund the agreed package.

The cost of training clergy has escalated because Local Education Authorities are much less willing to give grants for vocational training than they were in the 1960s. The cost of housing the clergy has not diminished, and the downturn in the housing market has hampered attempts to recoup costs by selling off unwanted parsonages. It must be admitted that the job of housing committees has not been eased by a sustained counter-attack from rural benefices. Plans to sell off 'old' rectories are condemned, and plans to build new housing in old rectory gardens are fought in district planning committees with all the vigour and guile that the affronted villager can deploy. Much the largest cost has been the provision of an excellent pension, the level of which is tied to the current stipend, and a loan scheme for the purchase of a retirement home. The cost of all this is borne by the Commissioners, and it is expected that by 1995 as much as 54 per cent of their entire income will have to be spent on retirement provision alone. (In 1988, *The Ordained Ministry* suggested that a high point would be reached in 2005 when 40 per cent of total income would be needed for retirement provision (p. 48). The most recent forecasts indicate the subsequent deterioration of the situation.) The Commissioners have been called on to fund these improvements, which are all over and above anything envisaged in 1960, and it is interesting that the first draft of chapter 12 of *Faith in the Countryside* included recommendations that the Church Commissioners Pensions Fund should be separately managed. The inevitable result, since their resources are limited, is that there has been less money available for the Commissioners to pay stipends, and the responsibility for this has been progressively transferred to the dioceses, and so to the quota.

Stipends have meanwhile continued to rise, even during a period of recession, and by comparison with the financial situation of many in the congregations it may seem that clergy are now well enough paid. Nevertheless, *Faith in the Countryside* made a strong case for a further improvement in clergy stipends to keep them on a par (after allowance for accommodation, etc.) with the salary of the head teacher of a village primary school (12.61). Comparison is made with the payment of chaplains to the forces, hospitals and prisons, and the figure of £14,000 p.a. (at 1990 prices) is suggested. Two factors are also highlighted: the 'necessity' for a rural clergy family to run two cars (in some Anglican provinces the parish provides the business car); and the appropriateness of paying an honorarium to those clergy wives who choose not to go out to work, and so are inevitably involved in 'secretarial' work for the parish. The tone of the report is that in return for such payment the stipendiary must be ready to be assessed, to be retrained, and 'told what to do and where to go' by the bishop; and perhaps a system of supplementary payments (12.66–67) would be necessary for a time. The key point is that if the Church (meaning in effect the laity) wants effective, well-trained, dedicated and visionary clergy in the rural ministry, it must be prepared to pay them a 'reasonable' salary.

The problems of finance have been further compounded by events. The rural dioceses have been badly affected by decisions following the publication of *The Historic Resources of the Church of England* (Church Commissioners, 1983). This report, which was as hard to oppose as the Endowment and Glebe Measure, has had the effect of cutting down in real terms the contribution of the Commissioners to those dioceses with inherited wealth. It means that in a diocese like Gloucester the full cost of any increase in clergy stipend has to be found in full from the quota. To this add the present recession and the unwise investment policy of the Commissioners themselves, and the cup runneth over. In 1988 *The Ordained Ministry* stated that:

The assumption is that the Commissioners' income for these purposes will increase by 1.8% in real terms each year, and diocesan investment income and glebe taken together by 10% each year. We estimate that to achieve the required expenditure would, on these projections, require a real increase in giving of 0.7% in each of the seven years 1988–1995.

The consensus of the chairman of Boards of Finance was that

dioceses would find the necessary resources to maintain the clergy, and additionally that a modest increase in the stipendiary clergy could be financed.

Clearly, four years is a long time in economics. In 1993 it became clear that the Commissioners would actually be able to contribute far less to stipends than had been predicted in 1988, and as a direct result a number of dioceses are now planning to cut the number of stipendiary clergy. Among them is Lincoln (see *New Times, New Ways*) which, with 549 parishes and 666 churches, plans to reduce its stipendiaries from 306 to 282 posts 'because of increasing non-stipendiary ministry and financial restraint'.

Why they won't pay

For all of these reasons, quotas in rural dioceses have escalated far beyond their level of ten years ago and far beyond what was expected in 1988. Nevertheless, the average giving per weekly attender in the rural dioceses is low by comparison with urban dioceses (*Church Statistics 1991*, pp. 932ff.). Is it then a case of 'can't pay' or 'won't pay'? It will first of all be useful to consider the sociologial and historical reasons why the problem seems so great from the village perspective.

First, small villages have genuine problems. The census material for 1991 will no doubt tell us that the socio-economic grouping figures for most rural areas are higher than for inner-city areas. However, they will also probably show that while the number of older and retired people living in rural areas has increased, the number of young people (age 15–30) has decreased. So while no one would doubt that a number of rich people live in each village, we should remember that, as Brian McLaughlin showed in his analysis of rural deprivation, it is likely that

20 per cent of the population of most villages are still living on or below the official poverty line (e.g. are in receipt of some sort of social benefit such as rent rebate). A significant number of people from these households are probably on the church electoral roll.

Secondly, small numbers have a special impact on finance. A benefice with 1,000 population and 50 on the electoral roll may have a quota allocation of £10,000 p.a. This means £10 p.a. per head of population, but £4 per week for each member on the electoral roll. Similarly, the cost of raising £20,000 for fabric repair is £20 per head of population and £400 per electoral roll member.

Thirdly, a point well made by *Faith in the Countryside* is that the travelling expenses of a multi-parish benefice incumbent are often four times as great as those of an urban stipendiary (10,000 miles and £2,000 a year is common) (12.76).

There are also historical factors which need to be recognized. The crisis seems worse because of a perceived breakdown in communication between the diocese and (rural) parishes. Many parishes do not understand where the quota money goes, and the reason for this is not just obtuseness on their part. In Gloucester in 1959 only 7.3 per cent of parochial income was on average needed to meet the quota, compared with 50.3 per cent in 1989. In 1960 the parson was paid by someone else, and there was vociferous complaint because for the first time the parish had to find money to pay some of the bills on the parsonage. Expense claims were almost unheard of. In the 1970s everything changed. 'They' at the diocesan office confiscated 'our' glebe, sold 'our' parsonage, and removed 'our' parson. In the 1980s, having stripped us of 'our' assets, 'they' increased the quota tenfold, and now expect us to pay the new parson (who lives six miles away) for the petrol he uses to visit us. In one generation not only do the goalposts seem to have been moved, the game itself has been transferred to another pitch. As it was so aptly put to the Acora Commissioners:

> Within the lifetime of some of the people in this place, the vicar has changed from being the person who distributed money to those who were the chief charge on the community, to now being the chief charge on the community himself.

Looking at the view through the villagers' windows, it is hardly surprising that there is a problem, and undoubtedly one of the great challenges for rural dioceses over the next five years will be to explain what the quota is for. The Bishop of Dorchester has written:

> The Acora report is right in seeing the financial problem not so much as money per se but as the problem of centralism. I am sure in the future that money will have to be controlled much closer to the point at which it is raised and people will not be happy to see huge sums being moved into a central fund.

Taking all these factors into consideration, we have to conclude that while it should just be possible at the moment to raise the money needed, it seems likely that unless there is a much better understanding between the dioceses and the parishes than is often the case at the moment, and if quotas continue to rise at double the rate of inflation, more and more small parishes are likely to default in their payments.

The principle of payment for ministry received

The final point that needs to be made in this section on money is that, in the circumstances described, dioceses are bound to come under pressure to tie stipendiary ministry to payment of quota. Stipendiaries could be deployed to those congregations who are prepared to pay for them. This is the underlying strategy of the URC and Baptist Churches. It can also be seen at work in the Episcopal Church of America, where it is coupled with a wide variation in stipends which many outsiders find frankly distasteful. The corollary is that those areas which cannot pay have no stipendiary clergy, or are declared to be 'mission areas' dependent on the charity of wealthy congregations. Theologically there is no doubt that much could be said on both sides, but in practice it is difficult to see how the Church of England could with a clear conscience continue to enjoy its inherited wealth while adopting a policy of abandoning the poor. In one sense, therefore, this strategy is a non-starter.

On the other hand, there is growing resentment in many dioceses about those parishes who 'won't try'. Every diocese is always on the point of changing its system for calculating the quota. This is because the Board of Finance is torn between the need to get the quota paid and the desire to allocate the quota 'fairly'. In Gloucester diocese the 'Emerson Plan' (based on the Lichfield formula) was adopted as 'eminently fair' because it took into account the sociological potential of parishes to pay rather than their current track record. The plan survived (just) the halcyon days of the mid-1980s only to collapse in 1990 because an increasing number of parishes (with potential but no hard cash) defaulted. The formula was changed to take account of actual income rather than potential, and as a result in 1991 the diocese was able to collect 95 per cent of the quota again. Nevertheless, the willing horses are growing increasingly restive. Congregations would acquiesce in subsidizing inner-city multi-racial parishes in Gloucester and Cheltenham, but they are understandably less happy to underwrite single-cure benefices who pay nothing to the quota on principle, and who have consciously rejected any thought of a stewardship campaign. As a result, a discussion paper has been put to the Board of Finance which seeks to give some recognition to the principle that a parish should pay for the ministry it receives, and suggests that those who cannot pay should be forced to come to the diocese cap in hand to beg for a subsidy. Some such arrangement may well become a normal part of the system in many dioceses within the next few years.

One practice commended in *Faith in the Countryside* is already leading in this direction. The report gives an example of what is done by Lincoln diocese to express the situation (p. 287). It commends as even more effective the policy of Rochester and Blackburn, who allow the parishes to pay part of the stipend direct (12.59). In the diocese of Rochester, stipends have been divorced from quota altogether. Each parish fixes the stipend of its incumbent within the minimum and maximum limits prescribed by the diocese, and pays what is needed after the contribution from historic resources. Grants are made available for parishes which cannot afford the minimum. The diocese feels that more money is forthcoming from parishes when what is given is seen to be so directly related to the incumbent's stipend, and this is reflected in Rochester's position at the head of the league table for clergy stipends. At the same time, the diocesan quota is so much lower because it does not have to support stipends and is therefore both psychologically and in reality less of a burden on parishes.

The evidence seems to suggest that such a system is successful in getting the quota paid, but it is paid on the assumption that a parish pays for the ministry it receives. There is an obvious danger: for when a rural diocese authorizes local ministry groups (which are non-stipendiary) in villages which have formerly had a stipendiary priest, it is probable that those parishes will no longer expect to pay for ministry which they no longer receive.

Perhaps most important of all, behind the problem is the natural reluctance of clergy, brought up in the old ways, to sing for their supper to their own congregations. It was difficult enough to get them to ask for their expenses. Yet one thing is clear: in the interests of the rural Church there needs to be as soon as possible an honest and open debate about how much ministry costs, how much ministry is worth, and who foots the bill.

THEOLOGY

The number of stipendiary clergy in office is declining and will continue to decline at least until the end of the century. For numerous good, even laudable, reasons the quota in rural dioceses is likely to rise at a rate well above that of inflation, and as a result some dioceses are already preparing to cut back on stipendiary posts. But even if there were clergy available and even if there was money to pay them, there are theological reasons why the Church should resist the temptation to return to the sort of clerically dominated ministry inherited from the past.

The People of God

The implication of thinking of the Christian community as 'the People of God' has been so well expounded in the last 20 years that it will not be necessary to argue the case in detail here. The insights of such theologians as Karl Rahner, Edward Schillebeeckx and John Macquarrie were brought together in the General Synod booklet *All Are Called: Towards a Theology of the Laity* (1985). The Working Party under the Bishop of Oxford (Patrick Rodger) published a series of essays as an aid to discussion of the issues involved. The Working Party produced a 'Common Statement' which begins:

> Because all human beings are made in the image of God, they are called to become the People of God, the Church, servants and ministers and citizens of the Kingdom, a new humanity in Jesus Christ. Though we are tainted by our sinfulness, God's wonderful grace and love offer us all this common Christian vocation.

All are called, irrespective of colour, wealth or natural ability; and though different people exercise different functions within the Church, there are no grades of Christians. The Common Statement continues:

> This call comes to us all for all our days and years, and for all of our activities. It is for our churchly ministries, for our ministries with families, friends and neighbours, for our 'Monday morning' ministries and for our 'Saturday night' ministries.

It is this insight about vocation which is the starting point for John Tiller's assertion in *A Strategy for the Church's Ministry* that Christians are in a sense ordained by baptism to exercise 'ministry'. John Macquarrie defines this ministry in *The Faith of the People of God* (p. 85):

> All Christian ministry is participation in Christ's ministry. It is clear also that Christian ministry belongs in the first instance to the whole people of God, for the whole people is incorporated by baptism into Christ and therefore shares in his saving ministry. This corporate ministry of the whole people is stressed by the use in the New Testament of the collective noun: the people constitutes a 'royal priesthood'. Expressions such as 'ministers and people', though commonly used, must be reckoned unfortunate, for they obscure the fact that the ministers themselves belong to the people of God, and that the whole people has a ministry.

Such a view of ministry as collaborative suggests a different and challenging role for the priest in a rural benefice, and Chapter 13 will examine whether such a role is likely to appeal to today's stipendiaries. At this point it is sufficient simply to register that in a perhaps heavensent way our reduced resources and our understanding of the theology of ministry come together, and both point in the same direction.

8

Local and Catholic

Chapter 5 states both that the basic building block of any rural strategy should be the local congregation worshipping in the individual settlement, and that to maintain the principle of 'catholicity' 'the local group must be welded into a benefice team'. Since these twin assumptions are the linchpin of the strategy recommended, and since they are the touchstone against which all other models on offer will be tested, they need to be justified.

Behind the assumptions lies a principle which is simple but radical: that church officers exist to serve the congregation, not vice versa. The practical reasons for accepting this principle have already been suggested – namely, that in the small villages of today it is usually the laity rather than the priesthood who have to endure the slings and arrows of front-line trench warfare. Nor, as we saw in Chapter 3, does the history of the Church of England since 1945 suggest that 'Father always knows best'. In the present situation where there are not enough stipendiaries to staff every village, and where stipends are increasingly dependent on direct lay giving, the hard reality must be that if the Church does not listen to and serve the laity, village churches will close. The theological reasons are just as cogent, and are symbolized by the sign Jesus gave to the apostles about the nature of ministry when he washed their feet before the Last Supper.

So while stopping short of commending a policy of listening only to lay opinion, and doing only what lay people want, the best hope for establishing vibrant Christianity in rural areas is for church officers to listen to the laity; and this they can now do in a systematic way by studying the findings of the Rural Church Project. Some will retort that the lay people questioned were theologically uneducated, traditional and timorous – and probably uncommitted fringers to boot. No doubt they were, but that does not mean that their views should go unheard.

WHAT LAY PEOPLE SAY THEY WANT

The evidence is presented in chapters 5 and 7 of *Church and Religion in Rural England*. Page 118 analyses the responses to the question 'What exactly is it that you feel you belong to in the Church?' and concludes:

> There would seem to be some justification for saying that being a member of the Church of England means more to many people than simply having been brought up in it or being C of E for the purpose of form filling.

It then elucidates what this means in terms of parish life. First, 87 per cent of respondents thought that it was important for a parish to have its own church building; this evidence is dealt with in more detail in the next chapter.

Secondly, 75 per cent believed that it was important or very important for a village to have its own resident vicar (*Rural Church Project*, Table 4.1.83). Perhaps not surprisingly, those aged over 65 and those from the church sample who have always lived in the village are most insistent about this, but the feeling is general across the categories (Table 4.1.87). Interestingly, when questioned about whether it was important that the vicar himself had a rural background, 61 per cent said it did not matter (Table 4.1.63), and only 39 per cent thought it was important that he should be married (though 50 per cent of the church sample thought he should) (Table 4.1.68). In other words, almost anyone is better than no one. The view of lay people was endorsed by two-thirds of the clergy, who believed that, ideally, each parish should have a priest of their own.

Attitude to having a woman as vicar

Anglican parishioners were asked a number of questions about their attitude to having a woman as a vicar (*Rural Church Project*, vol. 4, pp. 178–88). Some 27 per cent said that it would affect their view of the church positively, 11 per cent said it would affect their view negatively, and the rest said it would not affect their view of the church. Only 8 per cent said that they would not accept communion from a woman priest, and 11 per cent that they thought a woman should not conduct marriages. Not surprisingly, the older age groups are more likely to be against women priests, while younger people are more positively in favour.

These figures back up the anecdotal evidence from different parts of the country. Commissioners met women deacons who were priests-in-charge of benefices in deep rural locations in Suffolk, Nottinghamshire and the Forest of Dean, and a number of others who were curates in rural benefices. There were obvious problems about the celebration of communion, but rather to the surprise of the women themselves they had experienced very little opposition even though they were all ministering to very conservative communities.

When women are ordained as priests, it seems therefore that they are likely to be welcomed as potential stipendiaries by the majority of rural Anglicans. One concern must remain, which was well expressed in an article in the *Church Times* entitled 'Fresh problems in keeping a rural presence' (12 March 1993). Because of the geographical size of rural benefices, those parishioners who feel unable to accept the ministry of a woman priest will be considerably more inconvenienced than those of the same persuasion living in a large town – for the former may not be able to find a 'traditional' church anywhere in the vicinity.

They want a vicar they know

Lay people had a remarkably clear idea of what they wanted the vicar to do, as indicated in detail in the following table.

TOTAL SAMPLE: VIEWS ON THE JOB OF A VICAR

Job of a vicar	Parish sample N	%	Church sample N	%	Total sample N	%
Pastoral	183	54	77	52	260	53
Community figure	86	25	41	28	127	26
Services/rites	71	21	39	26	110	22
Christian teacher	73	21	40	27	113	23
Anglican representative	24	7	8	3	32	7
Father/shepherd	20	6	15	10	35	7
Other combinations	3	1	1	1	4	1
Don't know	17	5	3	2	20	4
Refused/DNA	4	1	1	1	5	1
Total	481		225		706	

Note: Totals represent the total number of references to all categories. Therefore the percentage figures total more than 100. Parish N = 341; Church N = 148. Total N = 489. The average number of categories per respondent for the parish sample was 1.35, and for the church sample 1.45.

Source: *Rural Church Project*, Table 4.1.55.

The above table shows clearly that the pastoral role is seen as of paramount importance; and the Rural Church Project investigates this further and suggests that since many parishioners expect to use a clergyman they also expect to be able to know him personally.

The laity were asked 'Would they ever approach a clergyman for assistance of any sort', and 66 per cent of the general sample and 82 per cent of the church sample said they would. They were then given a range of possible situations and answered as follows:

SITUATIONS FOR POTENTIALLY REQUESTING
CLERGY ASSISTANCE

Actual request	Number of positive responses			
	Parish sample N	%	Church sample N	%
Seriously ill	211	62	122	82
Advice/guidance	203	60	118	80
Relationship	68	20	62	42
Marriage/baptism/ confirmation	209	61	107	72
Financial	11	3	12	8
Bereavement	232	68	123	83
Total	341		148	

Source: *Rural Church Project*, Table 4.1.46.

ACTUAL REQUEST(S) FOR CLERGY ASSISTANCE

Actual request	Parish sample		Church sample	
	N	%	N	%
Yes	90	26	63	43
No	247	72	85	57
Don't know	3	1	–	–
Refused/DNA	1	1	–	–
Total	341	100	148	100

Source: *Rural Church Project*, Table 4.1.47.

While it could be argued that since very few (26 per cent) of the general sample actually ask the vicar for assistance, it is not necessary for *the vicar* to 'know' all his parishioners, it is obviously expected that *they* should be able to 'know' (or at least recognize) him.

The fact that this is ceasing to happen is illustrated in the Rural Church Project by questions to the laity about 'whether they knew the vicar'. In the five dioceses, 29 per cent of the general public said they knew their vicar reasonably or very well; and 34 per cent said they knew him, but not very well. Some 13 per cent said they did not know him at all, while 23 per cent said they had never met him. The overall figure suggests that about a third of the general public were without contact with or knowledge of their vicar. On analysis, we find that the vicar is less well known in those villages where he is non-resident (though the evidence about the smallest villages is somewhat complicated) (*Church and Religion in Rural England*, pp. 124–5).

The rural clergy are very conscious of the problem, and *Church and Religion in Rural England* (pp. 111–15) illustrates how much trouble they take to ensure that they continue to minister to the whole community (70 per cent try to do so, as against 23 per cent who see themselves as serving a gathered congregation). Something of their difficulty is shown by the fact that on average they allocate only 3 per cent of their time each week to 'community activity' (*Church and Religion in Rural England*, p. 75). Nevertheless, the fact that they still try is obviously appreciated, since, when asked whether they would prefer the services of a non-resident vicar or a part-time parochially based minister, no less than 80 per cent of the church sample and 55 per cent of the general sample voted for the full-time stipendiary (*Church and Religion in Rural England*, p. 175).

The normal strategy of the Church is to deploy stipendiaries on the principle that 'everyone should be covered by someone' and that the services of the Church should be available to all. There is less agreement on what those 'services' should be. It has been assumed that clergy should be available to baptize, marry and bury parishioners. They should also ensure that services of worship are available for people to attend (though whether this means 'a service in every settlement every Sunday at a reasonable time' is already unclear, as *Faith in the Countryside* pointed out). What the Rural Church Project shows is that the rural people interviewed expected something more. They expected to know their vicar personally.

Localism as the bedrock of rural religion

We shall look in more detail later at what personal 'religion' means to rural parishioners, but the evidence so far examined is summed up by Michael Winter and Christopher Short in a paper published in the *British Journal of Sociology* (September 1993):

> I rest my case that a sense of belonging is, in fact, strong though it need not necessarily be associated with high levels of church attendance and participation in church activities. This belonging, as demonstrated by views on clergy and church, is much more than just a sense of nominal membership of a national established church. It is a real emotional and, equally importantly, practical attachment to the church and its ministry which goes beyond rites of passage.

After carrying out the Rural Church Project survey, the authors summed up their conclusions as follows (*Church and Religion in Rural England*, p. 26):

> It is easy to debate the nature of Anglicanism in terms of a three-fold order of ministry set amidst Prayer Book, the place of Reason in interpreting scripture, and Church Tradition. A better way of characterising the Church, however, might be in its parish organisation and ethos. The Parochial System constitutes the Church of England. It is the parish not the diocese, the priest and not the bishop, which forms the centre of gravity of Anglicanism.

The Tiller Report identified the local congregation as the basic building block in any strategy for ministry and that insight (without of course all that went with it) has been carried forward into the Lincoln Local Ministry Scheme. The Lincoln submission to the Advisory Board for Ministry (1990) begins with an appreciation of the local church (p. 5):

This appreciation of the local community is part of a wider reaction within society against over-centralisation, but it is also a theological response to the God who reveals himself in the particular and the ordinary, who expresses himself through the lowly servant or the small group of believers. The local church is an expression of the one, holy, catholic and apostolic church, which with all its imperfections is a sign of God's kingdom. Or as Hans Küng has put it: The local church is the church and can fully represent the cause of Jesus Christ. It is only in the light of the local church and its concrete realisation that the universal church can be understood (*On Being a Christian*, 1978, p. 480).

In *Moving Forward* the Bishop of Norwich suggests that localism has the blessing of the Lambeth Conference. In a paragraph intended to encourage small congregations he records:

There was evidence from a number of parishes with tiny congregations, who expressed what amounted to a sense of guilt just because they were small. In our section of the Lambeth Conference we did some work centring on the question, 'What is the right size for a Christian community?' We looked at the evidence of the New Testament, the early Church, and more recent evidence such as the formation of what are known as Base Communities in Latin America. A characteristic of such a community is that it should be small enough for people to know each other personally, and large enough to provide a variety of gifts, and with sufficient members that it did not disintegrate when one or two were absent. The conclusion was, to live an authentically Christian life, a community ought to be less than 20 people. We went on to agree that when a congregation exceeded 30 or 40 it should find ways to meet not just as a large group but as smaller groups as well. Therefore the small congregation should take heart, and indeed never forget our Lord's own words, 'Where two or three

are gathered together in my name there am I in the midst of them'
(Matthew 18.20).

The argument is persuasive, but questions needed to be asked about how
rural people themselves see the situation. What the evidence suggests is
that to concentrate on the local is to start where people are, and where
the clergy who know the local area best know them to be. It means that
in contrast to every other 'solution', the church which adopts this model
starts swimming with the current and not against it. It is also the only
model which unreservedly recognizes the laity as the front-line troops
who are served by the stipendiary clergy: and the more the laity are
asked to do for themselves and the more they are asked to pay towards
the stipends of the clergy, the more important this factor will become.

CATHOLIC AS WELL AS CONGREGATIONAL

Thus the available evidence points to the local settlement as the basic
building block for a future rural strategy.

Chapter 5 suggests that every local ministry group needs to be welded
into a benefice team. First and foremost, this is to ensure that the local
church remains part of the Church catholic. In *Moving Forward* the
Bishop of Norwich has a section headed 'Local and Catholic':

> There is no such thing as an isolated Christian; always we are mem-
> bers of a community. So the concept of a purely individual parish or
> congregation living a kind of private life is a contradiction in terms.
> In Christ we belong to each other and the more a local Christian
> community lifts its eyes beyond its own horizons to the deanery, the
> diocese, the nation and the world, the more catholic and distinctively
> Christian its life will be (p.16).

After two years of consultation within the diocese, the Bishop of Norwich returns to the same theme in *Moving Forward II*:

I am all for affirming the importance of locality, of the individual character of each community, but the kind of obstinate individualism which is still present in some [villages] is frankly a death wish.

There are of course other denominations who would not put such an emphasis on catholicity, but it is clear from all the available diocesan literature on the subject that there would be no question at all of the Church of England authorizing local ministry unless there were strong safeguards to ensure that the 'local' church remained 'catholic'. This was the view of the Working Party who produced the report *Local NSM* for the Advisory Board of Ministry. On pp. 8ff. they describe the 'necessary marks of LNSM' and the first is identified as 'Catholic order in the service of the local church and community'. Many of the other guidelines and regulations seek to ensure this; and certainly one of the most practical ways of maintaining catholicity is to ensure that the local group is part of a strong benefice team.

Congregations need each other

There is another reason for insisting on the group being part of a team, and that is that every congregation at some stage needs the support of other congregations. It is arguable that when a Christian group is newly established and expanding rapidly it will bring more people into aware-ness of the reality of God's love if it can go its own way and be unhampered by rules and regulations and the demands of 'catholicity'. This is one way of understanding the success of the House Church Movement, and of other evangelical and charismatic churches spot-lighted in Brierley's *Christian England*. It can also be seen as a factor in accounting for the extraordinary success of Welsh Non-conformity during the last century, and the proliferation of chapels there. Churches, however, are not always young and adventurous; they become middle-aged. When the climate of opinion changes and there is a need for hard decisions and new initiatives, the advantages of catholicity become apparent for, as has been said, 'the walls that surround are also the walls that support'.

The Free Church experience

The Free Churches have practised collaborative ministry for 400 years, and it needs to be recognized that without local ministry groups there would be no village chapels at all. The Methodists in particular grew at a phenomenal speed – initially not because of ministers, but because of lay groups authorized by Wesley himself. The history of the Horncastle Circuit, for instance, shows how the rise in membership *preceded* the coming of resident ministers. The Free Churches were also surprisingly successful, both in sustaining membership against tough political pressure, and in expanding when religious allegiance became truly free in the nineteeth century. In this sense, the experience of the Free Church has been very similar to that of the House Churches today and supports the contention that the best way to expand churches fast is to give local ministry a completely free hand.

The problem comes in the next generation when charismatic fervour gives way to consolidated piety. Here the Free Churches offer two very different models. The classic model is that of the independent congregation where power is vested in the congregation to elect elders who call the minister. The congregation runs its own affairs and is only very loosely, if at all, linked with any national federation. This has all the advantages of localism in that full responsibility rests on the shoulders of the congregation (and it was a model well suited for weathering the opposition of the English Establishment, which was generally shown in social ostracism rather than physical attack). However, it also has all the disadvantages of localism in that there is no external authority able to enforce unattractive but necessary decisions.

The alternative model, which is offered in England by Methodism, vests authority in the central 'Conference' (with a membership half clerical and half lay). Local groups (or Causes) are welded into Circuits which are constituent parts of Districts which together form the 'Connexion', and what is decided by Conference is authoritative for every Methodist Cause. Most important of all, ministers are paid and deployed centrally. The Border Experiment (see pp. 30 above and 96 below) is a good example of how this enables Methodism to make bold experiments which involve draconian decisions, and it is unthinkable that such an experiment could have been effected by either the URC or Baptist churches. *Methodism in the Countryside – The Horncastle Circuit*

1786–1986 by Clarke and Anderson is the account of one Lincolnshire Circuit and chronicles the enormous mutual support that existed in the early days, with one village Cause 'church planting' in the next village down the road. It also records the way in which in harsher days the Circuit provided mutual support for small village Causes and enabled a number of them to close while still retaining effective oversight of members. It is probable that a sequel written today would show how a new wind of hope is beginning to blow throughout the Circuit.

It seems that in this century the latter model has been much more successful than the former in maintaining the Free Church tradition in villages. In 1950 the Baptish Union of Wales had 330 stipendiary ministers, but in 1991 there were only 119 and, of these, 22 were over 65. In 1991 there were 557 churches in the Union and 56 per cent of these recorded that their numbers were in decline, while only 12 per cent (68 churches) registered an increase in membership. Some 80 per cent of their rural churches had no full-time ministry and many did not hold regular weekly Sunday services. Since all major decisions rest with members of the local congregation, they, being human, can rarely bring themselves to make the hard decisions that are absolutely necessary for revival – such as introducing a minister with new ideas, or changing the form of service, or amalgamating with another local church. By contrast, though the Methodists have closed many village chapels they have so far managed to keep open over 4,000 others, and have kept alive Methodist *membership* in many villages where there is no longer a chapel. The lesson to be learned from the Free Church experience, therefore, is that when experiments need to be made and hard decisions taken, it is an advantage if localism is balanced by a strong central authority.

Many small Anglican rural churches also need support within the Christian family. The Bishop of Norwich again:

Some of the saddest responses come from very small parishes, like one with a fortnightly congregation of two, a parish share of £300, and an impossible task of keeping their church in repair. But why should this tiny parish see itself in isolation? They are part of a benefice of other parishes, part of a deanery, part of a diocese. . . . The tragedy is *that teamwork is not part of their experience* (*Moving Forward II*, p. 16).

At some stage in its life, every congregation will find that it needs to be part of a team for practical as well as theological reasons.

9

Models of Ministry

Chapter 8 suggested that 'to concentrate on the local is to start where people are', but that the local congregation must also relate to the wider Church. This chapter examines some of the models now being used in the light of this previous discussion.

THE 'SUPERMARKET MODEL'

In this model, small churches (corner shops) are closed and the congregation is offered transport to a larger place of worship (a supermarket).

In Anglican circles today there is a great deal less serious talk about closing village churches than there was a decade ago. A few village churches were closed, and there are still bishops, archdeacons and incumbents who bear the scars to prove it. *Church and Religion in Rural England* (p.158) quotes two of them:

'I shall always be known as the vicar who closed B——.'

'I shut two churches in my urban phase: you have to leave if you do it.'

The significance of church buildings as part of people's 'religion' is examined in detail in Chapter 15. Briefly, 83 per cent of the incumbents questioned for the Rural Church Project believed that it was important to have a church in each settlement; and its aesthetic beauty did not matter much one way or the other. Among parishioners, 83 per cent of the general sample and 95 per cent of the church sample believed that it was important for a parish to have its own church: while a very high 78 per cent of the church sample had visited a church to look around during the previous year. Obviously, for most rural people, church buildings have their own special charisma.

What this evidence suggests is that the 'religion' of many people living in villages is 'locally attached', and this explains why, when 'their' church is closed, they do not travel to worship elsewhere. Thus the paramount reason for keeping churches open is not aesthetic but evangelistic: that closing a church cuts down the number of those who worship God regularly.

The Free Church evidence

This has been the experience of the Free Churches. Small congregations fade away or grow weary and closure follows. Neighbouring congregations of the same denomination 'help' so far as they can, but it is usually up to the remnant to decide where to go on Sunday when their own church has closed; and the fact is that *many of them cease to worship anywhere*.

The one denomination which did for a time adopt the 'supermarket' model as a coherent strategy was the Methodist Church in the Welsh Border area around Clun and Leominster in Herefordshire. A number of village chapels were closed, and the congregations were offered transport into the Methodist churches in the market towns. The experiment was monitored and is evaluated in *Border Experiment*. It was not a success in so far as half of the members made 'homeless' by the closure of their chapels did not transfer membership to towns. The central churches continue to thrive, but 95 per cent of their members now come from the towns and the immediate hinterland. The 'problem' of small village communities is still a major worry to Methodists, and is invariably on the agenda of their Church in Rural Life Committee; but as a result of this one experiment properly recorded and learned from, the accepted wisdom is still that the 'corner shop' is preferable to the 'supermarket' model.

Conclusion

It seems unlikely therefore that there will be significant pressure from the centre for the rural Church to abandon the 'corner shop' model. Stipendiaries may be withdrawn over the horizon, but the branch surgery will be kept open. Local congregations may decide on closure in the face of a crumbling fabric (see Chapter 15), but such closure is likely to be experienced as a 'sad necessity' rather than as the 'leading of the Spirit'.

THE DEANERY PARISH

In this model, the deanery is constituted as a single group or team ministry. In the Anglican Church the idea that the rural deanery should be the basic unit for mission was suggested in the Tiller Report (1983).

Tiller's starting point was that

i) The local Church, as the Body of Christ in a particular place, should be responsible for undertaking the ministry of gospel in its own area.
ii) The Bishop, as chief pastor in the diocese, should be responsible for ensuring that each local Church has, from within its own recourses or from those of the diocese, the ministry which it needs.

Tiller believed the local church should function at three levels:

133. The local Church is therefore envisaged here as at one and the same time the deanery, the public congregation and the cell. There need be no confusion, because it simply means seeing the Church is organised locally in different ways for different purposes. Its components may be listed as follows:
i) the deanery synod, with a clearly briefed deanery mission committee (this would replace existing deanery pastoral committees);
ii) a diocesan ministry team of priests and deacons working with the deanery mission committee;
iii) a certain number of public congregations, each with a parochial area and church council, and a leadership team or eldership;
iv) a certain number of cells, some of which would be directly related

to the deanery mission committee, and some of which would be units of the parochial congregations.

This concept was illustrated in the famous flow chart which put the deanery mission committee at the centre of a spider's web. This terrified most PCCs, and so effectively torpedoed a remarkable report.

Most of what Tiller says about the deanery is perfectly acceptable. He stresses that the Church as an organization needs to function at some level between diocese and parish, where it can do valuable work relating to local secular and ecumenical authorities and undertake training projects which are beyond the individual parish. He even suggests that the overlap between diocese and deanery can be circumvented, for

> matters referred for debate from diocesan synods would not be taken both to deanery synods and to PCC's. If the matter was concerned with mission, for example, it would be discussed in the deanery; if with worship, in the parish.

He continues:

> The deployment of diocesan ministry teams would take place through the deanery, and support of the stipendiary ministry would be by means of a deanery quota. In all this the essential point would be to see the local Church as variously arranged in deanery, congregation and cell, and by these means engaged in complementary rather than separate activities. (para. 237)

As this passage shows, he locates the mission committee, the deployment of clergy and the payment of quota not at parish level, but at deanery level. It is the allocation of these particular functions to the deanery which was seen by many as unacceptable.

In the view of the authors of *Church and Religion in Rural England*, Anglicanism *is* the parish system; and however important 'the cell' may have seemed to Tiller, the message that came over to readers of his report was the downgrading of the parish in favour of the deanery. Similarly, the conversion of parish priests into deanery priests was seen as a selling of the Anglican birthright. The multi-parish incumbent may be elusive, but at least he or she is 'our vicar': and 80 per cent of the church attenders questioned voted for the stipendiary in preference to a part-time, but locally resident, non-stipendiary.

Comparison with the Methodist Circuit

It is interesting to compare the Tiller deanery with the Methodist Circuit, for they are obviously very similar. The Circuit system works well in rural areas, combining local independence with strong loyalty to the centre; and encouraging invaluable mutual support between the Causes. If it works so well for Methodists, why can it not also work for Anglicans? The answer must lie in the contrast between the role of the Anglican parson and the Methodist minister as seen by rural parishioners. In the Methodist tradition local pastoral care is the responsibility of the congregation, while in the Anglican tradition it is the responsibility of the parson. It could be that if the vision recommended in this book becomes a practical reality, the Anglican benefice will begin more and more to resemble a circuit and perceptions will change; but at the moment, without local ministry groups and local non-stipendiary clergy, the Tiller/Methodist minister is felt to be alien to village tradition.

Conclusion

At the moment there is only one rural deanery which approaches the Tiller model (Pontesbury in Hereford diocese – which reports a most interesting initiative of giving a holiday to inner-city children in P. Croft (ed.), *A Workbook for Deaneries*), and it seems unlikely in the face of the lay suspicion detailed earlier that others will be proposed.

This does not deny the valuable role of the deanery in supporting clergy, relating to local authorities, and taking 'larger' initiatives (see Chapter 13); it simply suggests that it is unlikely to be a 'success' as the basic unit *for ministry*. When the clergy interviewed in the Rural Church Project were asked what they thought of the deanery, opinion was more or less divided between those who thought it was important and those who thought it was unimportant; but none of even the most enthusiastic took the opportunity to commend the Tiller recommendation that the deanery should be the principal unit of local church organization (p. 197). Nor did *Faith in the Countryside*, though the report had plenty of suggestions concering other things that could be done at deanery level.

MINSTER MINISTRY

Minster ministry takes two forms. The first, the collegiate pattern, is eloquently expounded in a paper by the Bishop of Sherborne, first presented to the Commissioners and now rewritten for the Salisbury diocesan synod: *A Pattern of Rural Ministry for the Future*. After rehearsing the problems of rural ministry today, the bishop suggests that the paramount need is for centres of spiritual power. These will be provided by the stipendiary clergy living together in a central town, worshipping together on a semi-monastic model, and supported by those laity who have a vocation to this form of the spiritual life. The focus will normally be in a market town, but could be provided by a monastic centre such as the Friary at Hillfield in Dorset. The surrounding villages will each have their own 'perpetual deacon' assisted by a local ministry group. Each Sunday the Eucharist will be celebrated at the central location, 'and the deacons from the villages would attend and take the sacrament from the Service to their people in the villages (as probably happened in the early church). This is not Holy Communion from the reserved sacrament but an extension of the Eucharist.' The stipendiaries would be available to visit and build up the spiritual life of the congregations in the villages. As the Bishop of Salisbury points out in his Green Paper, *Ministerial Resource and Deployment*, this strategy 'stands in line of development from the Tiller Report'.

This is an exciting idea, not least because it goes beyond the Tiller report in concentrating on 'spiritual centres'; and as noted in Chapter 3, such centres are already proving their value to the rural Church.

Bishops-in-little

The Bishop of Sherborne's 'vision' probably owes something to a book called *Rising from the Root* by Christopher Donaldson, published by the Beaminster Area Team in 1985 (reissued with an autobiographical introduction as *The New Springtime of the Church*, 1992). What inspired Donaldson above all was a rediscovery of the early Church as exemplified in the life of St Martin at Tours in the fourth century; and like so many of the generation which experienced the collapse of Empire and the disappearance of the old established order, he believes that the Church must return to pre-Constantinian models.

The model he commends is that of the deanery-sized diocese. In an evocative image he pictures 'the "Bishop-in-little" who walks about the central town as a citizen, and people will know him and feel free to talk with him as their known and familiar pastor'. The (stipendiary) bishop is assisted by a stipendiary deacon who is something like a parish secretary and is officially responsible for all 'diocesan' administration. The parishes of the 'diocese' are run by 24 presbyters (non-stipendiary priests) who support lay house groups in each parish. The diocese has a 'diocesan centre' (somewhere between a retreat house and a youth training centre), and its spiritual life revolves around the weekly Eucharist at the 'cathedral' concelebrated by the bishop and his presbyters. Above the 'diocese', there are area synods which serve to bring Christians together, and a General Synod which has responsibility for selecting and training bishops and presbyters. The Church Commissioners are made responsible for all church buildings, though each building is cared for locally by a board of trustees.

The French evidence

This may all seem rather visionary and impractical, but there is in fact concrete evidence of what it might look like on the ground. One of the most hopeful developments of the last decade is the way in which some English dioceses are beginning to be influenced by what is going on across the Channel. Canterbury diocese has built close links with the Roman Catholic diocese of Arras, and Salisbury with Evreux. Under the leadership of the bishop, Mgr Jacques Gaillot, the latter diocese has developed a strategy of 'minster ministry' in rural areas – similar to that suggested by the Bishop of Sherborne and Christopher Donaldson. In 1984 the steady decline in the numbers of clergy led him to set up a pilot scheme in three rural parishes which he called 'La Pastorale Rurale d'Accompagnement'. The experiment is chronicled in *Église en Marche*, no. 12, which includes a short history of the experiment, the basic documents, and reports of two surveys carried out in the parishes to try to assess the 'success' of the scheme. There is also a small descriptive leaflet, *Faire Église en Monde Rurale*.

The basic building block is the *Équipe animatrice*, which consists of fifteen or so people who take on responsibility in their parish for evangelism, and for enabling the local congregation to grow in brotherly love and spiritual depth. In this work they are assisted by a *prêtre accompagnateur* whose job is 'to encourage and accompany the initiatives of the team', to make sure that they listen to God's word and that they keep alive their links with the wider Church. He celebrates Mass for them, but he lives in Evreux. As one priest questioned about his experience of the new model puts it, 'I am less curé and more priest'. The local teams are supported by a diocesan team whose job is to listen to the local story, to mediate in cases of difficulty and conflict, and to ensure that the teams meet each other and share their insights.

It is a tribute to the authority wielded by the Roman episcopate that by 1990 there were no less than 45 such teams active in the diocese, and the literature gives the impression that the sudden emancipation of the laity is proving to be heady wine. Nevertheless, we should pause before rushing to transplant Continental seedings into English flowerbeds.

First of all, the religious culture is different. Roman Catholic laity are unused to exercising ecclesiastical authority, their worship is almost exclusively eucharistic, and their priests cost much less than an English stipendiary. Furthermore, the reason for the removal of the curé was not theological (to build a centre of spiritual excellence in Evreux), but for the good practical reason that there were not enough priests available. It was a case of experiment or close, and this is confirmed by answers quoted in the survey report which record that many of those lay people who are not members of the teams want their curé back, and do no more than tolerate the ministry of team members. The list of Masses in the September 1990 magazine for one of the parish groups is also revealing. There are only two ADAPs (*Assemblée dominicale en l'absence du prêtre* – a French version of extended communion) scheduled for the three months September–December, and yet two of the five churches only have Mass said in them on one Sunday a month. It would seem therefore that there are considerable differences between the English and the French contexts; and, without wishing to detract from an amazing experiment from which a great deal can be learned, the French grass is not necessarily all emerald green.

Conclusion

Will this imaginative strategy for the deployment of rural clergy work in the English countryside? The answer must be that, though there are elements of the plan which could be usefully adopted, introduced as a whole it would almost certainly be unacceptable to rural parishioners.

This is what the evidence from the Rural Church Project examined in detail in Chapter 8 would suggest. On the contrary, rural parishioners want a stipendiary whom they 'know' and to whom they can relate. Nor are Anglican PCCs likely to be as biddable as Roman congregations, and it is therefore doubtful whether the laity will be persuaded to support financially stipendiary priests whose main job is to live in community. This will surely be particularly so since this model deprives them of 'their vicar'.

Finally, welding on to the vision 'perpetual deacons' and a form of 'extended communion' is unlikely to commend itself to the House of Bishops, let alone to deep rural PCCs. The Acora Commissioners examined these possibilities in detail and, while recommending that the discussions about extended communion be resumed, recognized the strength of opposition from some theologians and from a number of members of the House of Bishops (*Faith in the Countryside*, 9.27).

It seems, then, that the advocates of this strategy will need to make a strong case that what sometimes works in Africa or in the French Roman Catholic Church would be an appropriate transplant for the English countryside.

MINSTER MINISTRY MARK II

The other form of 'minster ministry', of which there are many examples, links together a large centre (often a market town) with one or more small villages, and is often a team ministry under the Pastoral Measure. Sometimes there is an appeal to the 'collegiate' theory set out above, and all the clergy live in the town; sometimes assistant clergy live in the villages; sometimes there is one stipendiary who does the lot. In contrast to the 'Sherborne model', the claims for this form of minster ministry are that it has practical advantages rather than that it is theologically sound.

In theory it is an excellent idea. If there is more than one stipendiary it provides clergy with mutual support, and the small churches have the benefit of urban resources. At Market Bosworth (Leicester), for instance, the 'town' choir goes out to one of the four small villages once a month. Similarly, the choir at Grantham every so often leads a 'Praise Service' in nearby villages. A number of clergy are very enthusiastic about this strategy, and the flow chart of one such incumbent had pride of place as

Appendix I in *Faith in the Countryside*. Nevertheless, when talking to such clergy it is difficult to avoid the impression that they are at heart zealous missionaries determined to drag the villages screaming into the twenty-first century – and one cannot help suspecting that some of the villages bitterly resent it!

Unfortunately, apart from the Rural Church Project material on lay 'felt needs' already quoted, there is little evidence to go on. It would be of enormous value if funding could be found for further research on the figures of both the *Children in the Way* report and the Rural Church Project statistics to see whether the church attendance, etc. of the villages involved in such ministries is higher or lower as a percentage of population than the figures in 'normal' multi-parish benefices. Meanwhile, evidence remains 'cumulative anecdotal'.

Two of the Norfolk rural teams were centred on market towns and these have not proved the most successful examples of group ministry: and it is for this reason that a current proposal for a similar grouping is being critically examined by the diocese. A similar scheme in Hereford diocese collapsed because of local opposition:

> The original plan was that the stipendiary clergy would all live in Kington and be a collegial group, praying together, studying together and going out to the parishes to serve in their own specialist field. However there was considerable local opposition from the larger parishes who believed that they ought to have their own man living in the village. When the Team Rector, who was also Rural Dean, had a heart attack because all the pressure was too much for him the original scheme was abandoned. (Stewart, *Parson to Parson*, p. 67)

In *Church and Religion in Rural England* a Lincoln clergyman working in a team ministry based on a small country town noted in respect of the minster-model ministry that 'there is some resentment by the villages of the town. They feel they lose out, but really they get a better deal than they would otherwise.' On pp. 230–1 two incumbents whose benefices included country towns and little villages felt that united services were inappropriate because of the size differential between the two congregations.

One interesting example has been recorded in *Parson to Parson*. In

Northumberland Canon Stewart visited the team vicar of the Wooler minster ministry team:

> In 1978 the benefice of Kirknewton came vacant and when a new vicar was appointed he became a team vicar but still lived in Kirknewton and continued much as before except that he was now part of the team. However, after a few years he moved to Wooler six miles away, the idea being that the clergy of the team should all live in the same place and form a community of their own while going out to the various parishes for which they were responsible. Because Kirknewton covers a very large area and the further boundary is 17 miles from Wooler one team vicar continued to be responsible for just the one parish, while contributing in other ways to the team as a whole and helping with Sunday services elsewhere.
>
> John took up his present post in 1985. He was attracted by the idea of a 'minster'-type ministry with a team of clergy forming a kind of religious community and serving the people of the surrounding area. He has, however, since developed reservations about the appropriateness of this form of ministry and will be less inclined to join a team in the future. One reason for this is that, with the best will in the world, he finds tensions between his own priorities and those set for him by the rest of the team.
>
> He gave as an example the team policy on baptism. John feels strongly that while baptisms should, whenever possible, take place at a normal Sunday service there are occasions when this could be varied because of the needs of the particular family concerned. When, shortly after he took up his present post, he planned such a service, not knowing that there was a team policy, he found himself under considerable pressure from the rest of the team to conform to their rule of only holding baptisms at public services. This he finds difficult to accept when, as he sees it, he is responding to the particular needs of the parish for which he is responsible and it is restrictive to have to be bound by the decisions of those not directly involved.
>
> John has considerable reservation about the present approach to the ministry of the church in the Glendale Team. Although it is held up as one of the successful teams in the diocese he feels that at the moment it is neither one thing nor the other. Many of the advantages

of the old form of residential ministry of the parish priest have been lost while nothing better has been put in its place.

Another obvious corollary of the minster ministry affects the family. His wife, Judy, is not directly involved in the life of the parish of Kirknewton and as they live in Wooler her contacts tend to be mostly there.

Conclusion

We cannot commend or condemn a strategy on the strength of a couple of examples, but the sort of problems highlighted here do seem to ring true. In the absence of other documented evidence, it is on the one hand difficult to quarrel with the conclusion of the Acora report that 'the minster pattern can work well in providing mutual support for the clergy, but tends to make rural parishes feel marginalised'. On the other hand, it needs to be registered that where the local individuality of small villages is respected this model can work effectively. And there may be some small parishes which are so run down that for a few years at least they need Big Brother breathing down their neck whether they like it or not.

GROUPS AND TEAMS

Faith in the Countryside recommended that further research should be carried out regarding the effectiveness of rural groups and teams in the countryside in terms of ministry and mission. This was because, in the course of their visits, the Commissioners found that despite its potential few people now regarded this style of ministry as providing a pattern *for the future*.

There is no doubt that it has done very good service in the past. Starting from the Lincolnshire experiment of 1949, followed by no less than 17 similar schemes in Norfolk before 1970, the pastoral measure of 1968 gave some form and coherence to their structure – a form which was given further definition by the measure of 1983. Since then, many rural dioceses have established rural collaborative ministries, including Oxford, Hereford, Worcester, Bath and Wells, Exeter and Salisbury. The 1985 report *Team and Group Ministries* (GS 660) listed 333 teams and 81 groups, and the number had risen by 1990 to 430 teams and 112 groups (*Team and Group Ministries* (GS 993)). Thus no less than a tenth of the stipendiary clergy are now involved in team or group ministry.

There is of course a significant difference between teams and groups. In practical rural terms, a group leaves villages as separate units and allows them to have 'their own vicar', though the other clergy will appear every so often and villages are encouraged to work together on a number of group projects. A team creates one parish, thereby notionally downgrading the local autonomy of the individual settlements; but in practice it can take two forms. One form (as in the Beaminster Team) ensures that clergy operate evenly all over the team area so that villages no longer have their own particular parson. The other form (as in the Wexcombe Team) allocates a geographical area to each stipendiary, though there is regular interchange between members of the team. The distinction is very important, for seen through lay spectacles the latter model is really a 'group'. True it ignores the distinction in authority between team rector, team vicar and group stipendiary which is so important to the clergy, but for the parishioners the significant thing is how 'the parish' is operated in practice.

Nevertheless, there remains an important theoretical distinction between groups and teams in that teams have a much greater *potential* for close relationship and co-operative initiatives than groups. As the present Bishop of Hereford (who has worked in a team himself, and as Archdeacon of Sherborne was responsible for supporting a number of teams and groups) puts it, 'A team is a marriage: a group is shacking up together'. Stirring words – but while marriage has a potential for depth and creativity rarely achieved in other relationships, it can also lead to acrimonious divorce.

The benefits of groups and teams

The benefits claimed for rural groups and teams were persuasively set out in *Groups and Teams in the Countryside*, a collection of essays about the Norfolk experience, edited by Anthony Russell. The claimed benefits are that such collaborative ministries provide mutual clergy support, and that they offer isolated parishes both a variety of clerical ministry and a chance to co-operate with other parishes on projects which could not be otherwise undertaken.

It should of course be remembered that, as was suggested in Chapter 3, the loneliness of the rural clergy in the 1960s was often appalling, and the dereliction of rural church life almost tangible. Thoughtful bishops like Launcelot Fleming at Norwich believed that in these circumstances stipendiaries must have a network of mutual support. They needed to be able to meet other stipendiaries regularly to exchange experiences and friendship. Others went on to argue that stipendiaries should *always* work with other stipendiaries, or at least with other priests, and the team/ group model was a means of ensuring that this happened.

Groups and Teams in the Countryside gives ample evidence of how a number of rural clergy were rescued from isolation and given inspiration by the new system. It also shows that the experiment served to draw into rural ministry a number of younger clergy who would otherwise not have considered a country cure.

Turning to the other claimed benefit, there is evidence to suggest that such ministry has indeed provided new opportunity for lay people in small villages. *The Group: The Story of Eight Country Churches*, edited by J. Lathe (1986), was published in honour of 21 years of team ministry in the Hempnall group of parishes in Norfolk. Allowing for the natural tendency of such a volume to exaggerate, it is a remarkable record of successful change. The writers all bear witness to the way the group has 'made things possible'. Bob Smith remembers the summer schools and holiday camps, and Geoffrey Alexander recognizes how the attitude to stewardship of money has improved since 1965 when the average giving was one shilling and eight pence per worshipper. Eva Mainstone records how they have learned new hymns and new tunes and 'there are encouraging signs of new organists coming along'. Most exciting of all, in 1980 eight lay people became members of the team, and one of these has since been ordained. In *Groups and Teams in the Countryside*, Peter Bradshaw records that 'during the life of the Group, communicants at Easter have risen from 131 to 303, at Whitsun from 89–144 and at Christmas from 136–273' (p. 61).

In Somerset, the Camelot group of nine parishes west of Wincanton became a group ministry under the gentle guidance of an outstanding rural priest, Tony Foottit. The villages were allowed to keep their own identity and the clergy were responsible for clear geographical areas. The driving force towards united work within the group was the team council, which consisted of all the churchwardens and treasurers. Their magazine of April 1976 records a visit to the group by a presbyter of the Church of South India, a group Easter Party, a joint Lent course, joint youth fellowship, playgroup and over-60s club, and of course a joint group service on the fifth Sunday of the month. Over a decade later, John

Stewart visited the same group and recorded his findings in *Parson to Parson*. Things are still going very well, but the then rector did recognize that 'the parson is still looked on as an authority in all sorts of matters', and he felt that there was a need to convert the group into a local ministry team.

In Dorset, the Beaminster team in West Dorset has always been determinedly different. The strategy most cogently stated by Tim Biles in his submission to *Faith in the Countryside* is to encourage local autonomy in each settlement, but to deny them 'a vicar of their own'. The clergy work as a team and their major objective is to create a local ministry group in each village which will ensure that, when in the course of time two of the three stipendiaries are withdrawn, the congregations can stand on their own feet. A remarkable example of what can be achieved by such gathering together of parishes is their Waymark Parish Training Scheme. In 1983 between 60 and 80 people attended six parish days and walked the bounds on Ascension Day; while 25 adults and 25 young people went away on two Waymark weekends. Besides this, four Waymark Groups catering for four age groups met regularly. To finance this work the team were prepared to allocate a budget of £754. Clearly the possibilities for lay spiritual growth available at Beaminster go far beyond what is on offer in most rural parishes.

A changed context

Yet despite the possibilities, if groups and teams are not seen as the pattern for the future there are two fundamental reasons for this.

The first is that the context has changed. In Chapter 3 it was argued that the rural church is now faced not so much with a collapse of morale, as with a drying up of clerical resources. Certainly stipendiary clergy need support, but it is arguable that the multi-parish benefice which, used as a strategy, postdates the earliest rural teams, has itself 'solved' that particular problem – though in a different way. The benefice staff meeting, which includes on different occasions both non-stipendiary ministers and leading laity, often provides effective support for the stipendiary.

Recognizing this new state of affairs, General Synod paper GS 993 allows for both meetings of stipendiaries alone, and meetings of stipendiaries with others including laity, drawing a distinction between 'the team' – which consists of all who are authorized to minister locally by the bishop (including lay people) – and 'the team chapter', which consists of the stipendiary clergy alone. The change in contemporary practice is recorded in *Faith in the Countryside* (9.18):

> It was encouraging that a number of clergy spoke of a lay group in the benefice as their major source of spiritual support. Learning to share even this very personal part of ministry with lay people is perhaps the key to an effective spirituality for today's multi-parish incumbent.

Another way in which the context has changed is the logistics of clergy deployment. The Norfolk groups have been particularly badly affected by the decline in clergy numbers, so that a number of teams and groups which originally had three or more stipendiary clergy now have one. Similarly in Salisbury and Truro, stipendiary numbers are often down to two per group, though the General Synod report *Team and Group Ministries* (GS 660) proposes that 'no team be established with less than three members'. The decline in numbers coupled with geographical distance has made some rural groups unworkable. As early as 1983, the one stipendiary operating in the first of the rural teams, the South Ormsby Group, covered 25,000 miles ministering to a total population of 700; not surprisingly, no one now seriously suggests forming a two-, let alone a three-person stipendiary team in that sort of area.

The role of the group in encouraging 'new life' has also often been superseded. The multi-parish benefice which forced villages into partnership has often, rather to the surprise of local people, had much the same effect on encouraging new initiatives as did groups and teams in the 1960s. In many cases they are giving laity the opportunity to learn and to minister in new and imaginative ways; and with some benefices now approaching the size of mini-deaneries, co-operation on larger ventures is often becoming 'normal'.

The problems of working in groups and teams

It is also becoming increasingly apparent that groups and teams throw up as many problems for clergy as they solve. The report *Team and Group Ministries* is largely concerned not with evaluating the effectiveness of this sort of ministry, but with proposing legislation to ensure that the clergy remain on speaking terms. The 1992 paper has nine closely printed pages of suggested new 'laws' because Christian hearts are obviously not big enough to cope with this sort of collaborative ministry. In a desperate attempt to shut the stable door before any more horses escape, it showers recommendations about training for collaborative ministry on everyone in sight – from the Advisory Board for Ministry to diocesan Continuing Ministerial Education (CME) officers.

Sadly, *Church and Religion in Rural England* suggests that all this may be too late. Only 34 per cent of the clergy interviewed thought that groups and teams offered a viable pattern for the future, and of these a majority thought they would work in a group only if the clergy served separate geographical areas (pp. 176–8). The conclusion is that, apart from a few enthusiasts, the clergy are lukewarm about the idea. A senior member of staff in Salisbury diocese who was involved in a thorough review of the 30 groups and teams in 1989 believed (a) that if it was to work amicably every team should have at least three stipendiaries, and (b) that the chief cause of personality problems among the clergy was not only the autocratic team rector, but the team vicar who had taken the job as a stepping stone to 'something better' and actually wanted his own patch. A survey of archdeacons in the Lincoln, Norwich and St Edmundsbury and Ipswich dioceses carried out by Alan Pyke in 1985 ('Where are we going in rural ministry?') tells much the same tale:

> At first, this concept of ministry was thought by some to be a panacea for all the problems of the countryside. The Archdeacons with whom I have been in contact were less sanguine . . . not so much on account of any shortcomings in principle but because of the practical difficulty of making suitable appointments of Team Rectors and Vicars. One archdeacon responded: 'We have passed the "hot flush" period. . . . The main difficulty is finding good Team Rectors and Team Vicars. They have to be plural to be a Team.' All of them thought cooperative ministry was valuable, two archdeacons expressed a strong preference for informal collaboration.

There is therefore considerable evidence to show that groups and teams do not meet the felt needs of many rural clergy today in the same way as they undoubtedly did in the 1960s and 1970s.

Parishioners want their own vicar

The second reason that groups are not seen as a pattern for the future in rural areas is the determination of parishioners to have 'their own vicar', an individual stipendiary to whom they can relate. The findings of *Church and Religion in Rural England* support this view, and further evidence is provided by Salisbury's *Going with God – Together* (1990). The Bishop of Salisbury suggests that up to 6,000 church-people were consulted, and yet in a diocese which has more rural groups and teams than any other in England the only reference to this form of ministry is as follows:

> 3.4 It is clear from the balance of comment that in our diocese the ideal of a parson in each parish is still very strong. 'Churches are full where parishes have their own vicar.' Related to this is the frequent comment that 'clergy should visit more'. While some support Team Ministries, feeling that 'the Team model is particularly appropriate for this diocese', others have grave misgivings, particularly if the method of operation of the Team means that each church does not habitually have the same minister.

This is presumably why the recent Salisbury survey of groups and teams referred to above discovered that only one of their rural 'teams' was actually operating as one geographical unit: the others were geographical groups of parishes each with 'their own' priest, with joint activity depending very much on the personalities of the clergy involved. For instance, a job specification for a team vicar for the Wexcombe team in north Wiltshire (1984) states that the candidate will be allocated to a geographical area of pastoral *and liturgical* ministry.

It is no doubt because of evidence from the parishes that *Team and Group Ministries* offers as an addition to the Code of Recommended Practice (Appendix 1) a formidable list of 'preliminary steps' which have to be gone through with PCCs before there can be any question of setting up a team or group. Experience is obviously showing that this sort of ministry imposed from above often does not stand the test of time.

Conclusion

The evidence then suggests that although this initiative provided clergy support and brought new life to many rural parishes in the past, because of the tendencies to centralization it rarely fitted naturally into the rural scene. In any event there are now other possibilities, and it seems unlikely that many more rural groups or teams – as envisaged by the 1983 Pastoral Measure – will be set up except on an informal and voluntary basis.

THE MULTI-SETTLEMENT BENEFICE RUN AS ONE PARISH

The Acora Commissioners heard evidence from a number of square-jawed archdeacons and dynamic incumbents who declared in words similar to those of one Rural Church Project respondent:

> The boundaries between the parishes are lunatic and the old parochial ideas ridiculous. It would make far more sense if the three parishes were made into one single parish, particularly since there would be less duplication.

From the point of view of the stipendiary, of course it would. Mercifully, the great majority of rural incumbents recognize that the parochial system exists first and foremost for the benefit of the laity, not for the convenience of the clergy. The determination to make of many villages one parish usually centres on having one PCC and lots of united worship. The Rural Church Project has much useful material on this.

The clergy were asked whether their groups made sense geographically and socially: 66 per cent said they did so geographically, but only 50 per cent thought they made sense socially. Geographical divisions, which are after all often inevitable, included trunk roads, waterways (in the Fens) and county boundaries. (Gloucester diocese has not yet adapted to the boundary changes of *1938*, let alone of those of 1978 or the further changes proposed in 1993.) Social cohesion was more difficult to describe, but one factor mentioned was the existence of a focus such as a common school. (One three-parish benefice in Winchester diocese has, thanks to its astute incumbent, a joint church primary school set on a hill in the centre of the triangle formed by the three parishes.) Clearly, unless there is geographical and social coherence the battle for the single parish is likely to be singularly counter-productive.

Parochialism – good or bad?

The clergy were further asked whether they thought parochialism was an obstacle to the working of their multi-parish groups. Some 46 per cent said it was, and 36 per cent said it was not. Those who said it was believed that the main problem was that every parish felt threatened and was suspicious that any joint activity might be the thin end of the wedge to losing their church building. Considering the history of the rural Church over the last twenty years, who can blame them? By contrast, those who said it was not a problem said this was because the parishes within the benefice operated separately and so there was no group mentality to be obstructed by parochialism. Indeed, parochialism was often seen as an asset in such a context.

For one priest, parochialism was an obstacle to the Kingdom but also a fact of life. He advised against confrontation with parochialism as that would only lead to antagonism. Instead he advocated working with what is good in it – a sense of caring, community – and then trying to look out beyond the parish.

The moral seems to be that if clergy try to force unity on their parishes they will have a battle royal on their hands. If, on the other hand, they go along with parochialism they may be surprised to find how receptive parishioners are to the occasional joint venture. For when *parishioners* were asked whether they thought the effectiveness of the church was altered by grouping parishes, very few thought the effect was positive, but the one way it was seen to be beneficial was in bringing communities together! (*Church and Religion in Rural England*, p. 175.)

Joint worship

Turning to joint worship, there were some multi-parishes in the survey areas which had only one service a Sunday in the benefice alternating around the churches. Two-thirds of the benefices in the Rural Church Project had a united benefice service on the fifth Sunday of the month (or on some other occasion). The clergy were therefore asked whether parishioners worshipped in churches other than their own (*Church and Religion in Rural England*, p. 229). One answered 'Yes, people do – it's just part of life', but almost everyone else said that only a handful did so except on special occasions such as an induction or confirmation. A number said that some parishes were better at 'visiting' than others. When asked about the united services, the responses were similarly discouraging: 'They don't work well. People will not move. People at C are older, and not many have cars, but largely, it's because there's not the will to come here.'

Anglican attenders were asked whether they attended services in other churches in the benefice. Though their responses are not recorded in the Rural Church Project report, they in fact showed that 44 per cent said that they did so while 18 per cent said that they did not. However, when the 44 per cent were asked on what occasions they worshipped elsewhere, the response was overwhelmingly for 'specials' rather than on a regular basis.

It would be interesting to know whether those benefices which insist on only one service a Sunday in the benefice have the same percentage of the population attending church as others of a similar size. On the strength of the above evidence, it would seem doubtful. Indeed it seems likely that the more 'united worship', the fewer will be the numbers of those worshipping.

Another piece of evidence that needs to be taken into consideration is that preferences for services vary – as shown in the following table.

THE PREFERRED TYPE OF SERVICE

Type of service	No.	%
Parish communion	68	42
Evensong	39	24
Matins/morning prayer	33	20
Early said communion	20	12
Family service	22	13
Other	10	6
No preference	8	5
Refused/don't know	3	2

Note: Although there were 163 attending Anglicans, some specified more than one service.

Source: Davies, Watkins and Winter, *Church and Religion in Rural England*, p. 225.

It is difficult to see how one service a Sunday in a benefice can possibly satisfy such a range of preference.

The one piece of Rural Church Project evidence which might support the value of united worship is the fact that the percentage of those under 16 attending worship in totally rural parishes is significantly less than in the larger ones (18.4 per cent to 24.2% – *Church and Religion in Rural England*, p. 212). This could be seen as supporting the case for united family and youth services.

Conclusion

So all the statistical evidence so far at our disposal suggests that to run the multi-settlement benefice as one parish *against the will of the parishioners* is to offer a desk-top solution to a human problem, and is not likely to appeal to anyone but the stipendiary.

THE MULTI-PARISH BENEFICE

In contrast to the last model, the multi-parish benefice acknowledges the power and value of localism and allows congregations to live as independent a life as they believe to be right for themselves. In practice there are many shades between the former and the latter, with most stipendiaries hankering after some degree of co-operation between the villages, but settling in the end for the thankless role of 'vicar' in three or more places at once. In contrast to the pluralism of former generations, this model is today a last-ditch attempt to maintain the Anglican principle that every settlement should have its own stipendiary priest.

The extent of 'non-residence' is well documented. By 1987 in Hereford diocese there were nearly three and a half times as many churches as full-time parochial clergy. Francis's *Rural Anglicanism* recorded that in 1985 in another rural diocese there were 232 parishes with no resident incumbent, compared to 171 which continued to maintain an occupied parsonage.

'Pluralism' has always been considered a second-rate form of ministry because the priest can only be resident in one of the settlements, and *residence* is held to be an essential ingredient of 'identification'. Today this assertion needs detailed justification since the opposite view is now often advanced: that the *absence* of the priest is often beneficial.

The practice of the absence of the priest

The strategy adopted by many independent congregations, and particularly the United Reformed Church, is for the virtually autonomous congregation to be served by a non-resident minister.

The view is now gaining ground among Anglicans that it is often when the parson is non-resident that lay ministry begins to take off. In *New Fire* (Winter 1982), Christopher Lewis, then a lecturer at Ripon College Cuddesdon, wrote an article 'The practice of the absence of the priest', in which he reflected on his experience of being both priest-in-charge of Aston Rowant and full-time lecturer. He concluded that, provided he knew the PCC personally, and was able to be present at key village functions, his absence gave lay people the chance to spread their wings while ensuring that they did not fly too near the sun:

> The impression given by talk of 'lay ministry' is often one of unreality. There is rhetoric, but practice continues much as before. Changes in the structure of ministry in a parish may, however, enable progress to take place. The ordinary absence but occasional presence and continuous responsibility of a priest, may be one important way in which lay ministry is encouraged truly to flourish. It is commonly said that an interregnum does a parish good but that too long an interregnum does harm. What may be needed is some leadership with a structure different from that which is usual in most parishes.

He adds:

> The model of Jesus being present with his disciples must be set beside that of an absence which made his presence more acutely felt. It is, He said, to your advantage that I go away.

The same view is taken in an interesting pamphlet published by the St Hugh Missioner for the diocese of Lincoln entitled *Using the Vacancy Constructively*, though here a permanent absence is certainly not envisaged.

Faith in the Countryside reports that:

> There was also a considerable amount of evidence that some of the

most self-sufficient and forward-looking parishes were those in which the incumbent did not live. One group of parishes indicated to its parent diocese that it did not want the appointment of a new resident clergyman, but would like access to the services of a clegyman for ten hours per week.

A similar view was expressed by the diocese of York (1988) in a Ministry Council Occasional Paper on the rural Church. This report argues that sometimes the parishes where the priest does not live 'have more thriving churches than in the village where he is resident, having decided that they can no longer leave everything to the vicar. It is in these situations that lay ministry begins to be of great significance.'

There are examples to show that the 'absence' of the priest within the multi-parish benefice or the Methodist Circuit system *can* lead to a spontaneous combustion of lay ministry. For instance, the *Queen Thorne Newsletter* (August 1989) includes a letter on visiting from the rector (Claud Rutter). This records that in the six parishes of the benefice there are no less than 15 lay pastoral assistants, all of whom help with visiting (often combined with the delivery of the newsletter), and who between them also fill the jobs of adviser on health and healing, adviser on legal and social security matters, adviser on youth work, church music adviser, evangelism and art adviser, bereavement counsellor, adviser on children's work, adviser on employment and unemployment, Citizens' Advice Bureau contact, Scripture Union representative, and Brownies and Guides adviser.

Satellite parishes peopled by second-class citizens

Nevertheless, against this largely piecemeal evidence we need to set weighty statistical evidence now becoming available which suggests that the absence of the priest adversely affects the number of people con- tacted by the church in a village. In October 1976 Nigel Robertson- Glasgow, an experienced rural parish priest who had worked in the same village for most of his ministry, wrote a thoughtful paper on the prob- lems of the multi-parish benefice which was then beginning to happen all around him. He noted that the conscientious incumbent of three villages who was determined to maintain his position in the *social life* of the community was likely to have at least 70 evening meetings a year (with multiple filing cabinets to match). He argued that the removal of the rectory meant the removal of 'the door to knock on', and that this created 'satellite parishes peopled by second class citizens'. In addition to the Rural Church Project evidence already examined which shows that the vicar is less well known in those parishes in which he is not resident, his observations receive statistical support from across the Atlantic in a paper by Cantrell and Krile in *Sociology of Rural Life*, entitled 'Church activity and the yoked parish'. This shows that the community involvement of a congregation declines in those parishes where the minister is non-resident. The suspicion that 'the absence' of the priest may lead to a decline in numbers attending church was signalled by Leslie Francis in *Rural Anglicanism*. He used path analysis to explore whether multi-parish benefices are as pastorally effective as single-parish benefices which contain a similar number of inhabitants. He reports that, while multi-parish benefices maintain the same nominal membership, as reflected in the number of names on the electoral roll, they have contact with fewer active members, as shown in the numbers of people attending church on Sunday.

However, the most significant evidence is provided in 'The rural rectory: the impact of a resident priest on local church life' by Francis and Lankshear published in the *Journal of Rural Studies*. This is a reworking of the *Children in the Way* statistics (1988) on the questionnaires returned by 2,757 rural communities with populations of less than 1,250 people. The authors further subdivided from the rest those parishes with less than 250 inhabitants. They use five key statistical indicators: the number on the electoral roll, the number of adults who attend church on two consecutive Sundays, the number of Easter communicants, the number of Christmas communicants, and the number of infant baptisms. Using path analysis they show that on every count the village where there is a resident stipendiary does better than the others. Their conclusion is worth quoting in full:

> These data indicate that the presence of a rural rectory and a resident priest contribute significantly to the life of rural parishes. This is the case both for very small rural communities of fewer than 250 inhabitants and for larger rural communities of between 250 and 1,250 inhabitants. The presence of a rural rectory and a resident priest are reflected in a higher proportion of the population registering on the electoral roll, attending services on a normal Sunday, receiving com-

munion at Easter and Christmas and presenting infants for baptism. This range of outcomes suggests that rural parishes with a resident priest both build up a larger group of committed churchgoers and maintain contact with a larger proportion of the population beyond the regular churchgoers, as reflected in Christmas communicants and infant baptisms. In other words, the resident priest appears to stimulate both the associational and the community functions of the rural church.

While these findings do not invalidate the evidence reported by the Archbishops' Commission on Rural Areas (1990) that there are examples of some rural parishes flourishing better in the absence of a resident priest, they indicate that, at present, such examples are clearly less frequently encountered than examples of rural parishes performing more effectively with the support of a resident priest. While these findings do not invalidate the theological insights which commend lay ministry and local leadership, they indicate that, at present, such theory may not necessarily be working well in practice.

Conclusion

What this important paper argues is that although many multi-parish benefices are proving very effective, this is still a second-class model. It suggests that the best way of encouraging more people in villages to 'recognize God's love as real – and to respond' is to reverse the thinking processes that lay behind the amalgamation of parishes and try to ensure that there is once again a priest in each settlement.

A VICAR IN EVERY VILLAGE

The past resurrected

'Every village has a parson-shaped hole waiting to be filled.' The argument just advanced has suggested that villages want their own vicar, and that a village with a resident vicar will probably mean more church contact with more local people. Winchester diocese has taken these arguments seriously and its solution is contained in *A Church for the World*. The Ordained Ministry Review Group recommends that the diocese 'reverse the thinking processes that lay behind amalgamation of parishes. . . . So we want every parish to have a representative person who will serve as the "Parish Minister" in that place' (p. 27). It goes on to suggest that these ministers may be deacons, Readers or retired clergy who will exercise a 'presbyterate'. Should other dioceses follow this example?

It is an appealing idea, and there are a host of little villages who would love to get their hands on resident vicars for free. They would undoubtedly love them, mould them to the required shape, and imperceptibly declare UDI from the Church catholic. It is, however, the argument of this book that to secure the *long-term* vitality of the rural Church ministry should be focused not on an ordained individual, but on the whole congregation, and an authorized group within that congregation. There are enormous practical advantages in having an ordained person in each village – *provided they are part of a local ministry group*.

The past transformed

This is the view of the Working Party that produced the report *Local NSM* for the Advisory Board of Ministry. On pp. 8ff., its members describe the necessary marks of local non-stipendiary ministry as:

1. Catholic order in the service of the local church and community.
2. The collaborative ministry of the whole local church.
3. A commitment to work in teams.

The second 'mark' is expanded:

2.18. Experience suggests that LNSM cannot be planted in isolation in a traditional local church community and expected to flourish. Nor is it sufficient to say that an LNSM must be 'part of a team of people, ordained and lay'. It is recognised increasingly by a variety of dioceses with LNSM schemes that this ministry must be the fruit of a commitment by the local church to the ministry of the whole congregation. This means seeking evidence that congregation and PCC are attempting to share the work of the local church and responsibility for it, and that the incumbent works in a collaborative way. It could also mean a commissioning service for the whole congregation, committing all its members to collaborate in the work of ministry, whilst encouraging some members to act as encouragers of such ministry and to train for it.

2.19. This experience of English dioceses confirms that of the Anglican Communion and of the wider church internationally and ecumenically. The ARCIC statement describes the ministry of the whole Christian community and then notes that 'the goal of the ordained ministry is to serve this priesthood of all the faithful'. Shared ministry is a major theme of the Second Vatican Council, and of the WCC Lima Statement on Baptism, Eucharist and Ministry with its emphasis on baptismal ministry.

Robin Gill, who is in favour of 'a priest in every parish', nevertheless said in a paper presented to the House of Bishops at Manchester in 1991:

> [Lay ministries] cannot wisely be used as a substitute for trained and ordained ministry (as Methodists have discovered to their cost). Nevertheless, my own experience as an NSM has taught me that a part-time ministry is only viable if it can encourage the whole congregation to take a more central role in ministry.

Van de Weyer, another part-time non-stipendiary minister, echoes this view in the chapter on 'Ministry' in *The Country Church*.

Conclusion

What statistical evidence we have on the 'success' of 'a parson in every parish – old style' is historical, and contained in the service registers of village churches from 1945 to 1975. In Chapter 3 it was suggested that the rural Church lost heart partly because the independence and isolation of priest and congregation made it very difficult for them to adapt to changes in rural society. The lesson to be learned is surely the Pauline one – that the local church should conceive of itself as 'a body made up of many parts', rather than the property *and responsibility* of a single (human) individual. What is being recommended, then, is not an independent cleric in charge of 'his' parish, but a local ministry group of whom one is ordained.

LOCAL GROUP AND BENEFICE TEAM

Nor should the group when constituted be isolated from the rest of the local church. This chapter has concentrated on the principle of 'localism', but the principle of 'catholicity' also needs to be given practical form. This is best done by insisting that local groups and local priests are part of a benefice team served (usually) by a stipendiary. The Advisory Board for Ministry believe that in the case of local as opposed to stipendiary priests, the need for involvement in a 'benefice team' becomes imperative. The *Local NSM* report expands the third mark of local non-stipendiary ministry as follows:

III *Commitment to working in teams*

2.20. Diocesan experience again suggests that LNSM should be exercised in close relationship with other ordained and lay leaders in the local church.

2.21. The varieties of skills and needs called for in increasingly complex societies are causing churches to recognise that the isolated stipendiary minister cannot provide them all. The organised collaboration of a variety of lay and ordained ministers offers a way to develop more effective ministry and mission. Yet at the same time there is a growing recognition that Non-Stipendiary Ministers and Local Non-Stipendiary Ministers need to be part of teams which include stipendiary clergy.

Single settlements with their own vicars can be 'successful', but what we are now looking to is that local congregations with their local ministry groups and their local non-stipendiary minister should be integrated into a benefice.

The benefice may be a 'normal' multi-parish benefice with one stipendiary incumbent, or a group or team ministry, or a minster ministry, depending on the history, geography and personalities involved. This is not to deny all that has been said previously in this chapter about the various models of ministry. Rather, it is to suggest that any model can work; but if, and only if, it is founded on the principle that each settlement has a unique identity, and that the structure is there to enhance and encourage that uniqueness. It may therefore be helpful to round off this chapter – which has been critical of any tendency to centralization – by describing not a conventional multi-parish benefice, but one of the more successful minster teams: that at Leominster in Hereford diocese where, despite the size of the structure, the 'transfiguration' of local settlements is taking place.

A practical example

Leominster has a population of approximately 10,000, and has all the advantage of geography in that it is isolated from other large centres and has a natural hinterland. At the moment it is combined in a team with nine villages, while another four will join shortly. The total population in the villages is around 2,000. The team has three stipendiaries, though one of these is a youth officer and half his time is allocated to the diocese. It is a training parish, so there are also two curates: and there is a retired priest and two Readers. Each village has its own PCC, and each stipendiary has a geographical area of pastoral responsibility. Everything possible is therefore done to affirm and encourage the unique identity of the local settlement.

The team came into being at an opportune moment. Five parishes had endured a ten-year interregnum and this made bold experiment attractive. It is grounded in daily prayer: 7.00 silent prayer followed by Matins and communion at 7.30 every morning. The clergy are always joined by some of the laity, of whom half come from the villages. The team rector believes that this grounding in prayer has ensured that the team has evolved, and not become an inflexible strait-jacket.

Evidence of 'success' is of course difficult to pinpoint, though communicant numbers overall are higher than in 1970. Now that local people feel that 'their church' is secure they are beginning to move between churches on special occasions. One Sunday a month most of the villages have DIY worship, and this is often both exciting and well attended. Thirty lay people from all the parishes went on retreat recently; there is a well-attended deanery 'School for Ministry' with a three-term study course; and a ministry and worship team of 25 people meets monthly. Above all, 'morale' is generally high and worship 'has a bit of zip about it' – even when only small numbers are involved.

What I suggest this example shows is not that this is the only model to strive for and that all rural areas should be carved up into minster teams. Rather, it is evidence that, where in the context of prayer local ministry is wholeheartedly encouraged and at the same time the riches of the Church catholic are made available, there is real hope that village congregations will take heart, begin to look positively to the future, and start to grow.

10

Setting Up a Local Group

In this chapter some of the issues related to the setting up of a local ministry group are examined. First, a possible job description is offered and I consider whether candidates for such a job are likely to be available and how group members are to be selected. A further section sketches the sort of individual who is likely to be a 'good' nominee; and whether members of the group are likely to be accepted by 'the village'. Advice is offered as to how to keep the locals happy, and there is a section on training group members. This chapter ends by considering the practical issue of whether local groups should be licensed to minister only in their own settlement, or throughout the benefice; and this has implications for how the local group relates to the benefice team.

THE JOB DESCRIPTION

'Each settlement should be encouraged to grow its own local focus, its own local ministry group.' What is this group expected to do? Perhaps the simplest way to put it is to say that they will be required to fill 'the parson-shaped hole which is at the centre of each parish'. This will involve doing what the parson did – but collaboratively. Tiller says in his report that the strengths of the parochial system are that it makes available pastoral care for all, that it provides a church which is committed to a particular neighbourhood, and by its involvement with every aspect of life it demonstrates God's concern for all human activity (no. 125). The local group will be expected to pursue these objectives.

To approach it in another and more job-focused way, in *Moving Forward* (p. 28), the Bishop of Norwich identifies a list of tasks for the ministry group which it is worth expanding. The idea is that tasks are to be shared out among members of the group, and the PCC will probably nominate individuals with differing skills in order to 'cover the field'.

(1) *Ensuring regular worship in the settlement.* Worship has a special chapter to itself (Chapter 16), which concludes that the local group has a twin responsibility. First, each settlement needs a worship group to plan the weekly services, and particularly the monthly family service. It must ensure that there is maximum congregational participation; and there needs to be ample evidence in prayers, choice of music, notices and the general theme of local as well as international concerns. Secondly, if there is to be a service in each church at the same (reasonable) time every Sunday, members of the group may sometimes have to be involved in leading worship themselves. This is a task they will share with the churchwardens, and some form of training is highly desirable. Under this heading we should also include regular private prayer, for it is arguably 'holiness' – or, as Matthew Fox in *Original Blessing* would describe it, 'joyous hosting' – which is the most distinctive and respected characteristic of the Church. A major aspect of the group's prayer will be to intercede for local people and local needs.

(2) *The pastoral care of the neighbourhood.* Church growth statistics suggest that what is most likely to win people to God is their experience of his love through the mediation of another person. Bishop Hall called mission 'a pilgrimage in friendship'. This will be the aim of the visiting which the group will be called on to do. Through the Lay Pastoral Assistants Scheme, Salisbury and Winchester dioceses have considerable experience in this field, and one of the methods of pastoral care which they commend is to use the simple neighbourly act of delivering the monthly parish magazine as a means of keeping up regular contact. Nothing too frightening is therefore envisaged, but some form of basic training is virtually essential if positive 'care' is to be exercised.

(3) *The ministry to children and young people.* This has a special church component which is to establish all-age worship as a reality, and to help with baptism and confirmation training. It also has the wider aspect of involvement in local schools and youth work.

(4) *The ministry of teaching and training.* This will involve support for all forms of house-group and parish training events; also, for helping with the preparation of services – and perhaps even sermons if a local person is to preach. Clearly no one would be expected to teach or train others without receiving proper training themselves.

(5) *Helping with parish administration, parish finances and the care of the fabric.* Lay people have been doing these jobs for a generation, but the increasing complexity of faculty law and the escalating size of budgets mean that training should be available for those who want it. As *Faith in the Countryside* underlined, the size of benefices now makes a parish office and a parish secretary a necessity rather than a luxury.

(6) *Mission and unity.* Pastoral care is part of mission, but there is something more. As people who believe in salvation and judgement, the group will need to feel an urgency that more people should respond to God's love. They should also be impatient with Christian disunity, and do everything possible to make unity happen locally.

(7) *Go into all the world.* The special vocation of members of the group may be to serve God in their local settlement, but God's concern does not cease at the boundaries of the parish. Christians have a special duty in a village to show concern for the poor, whether they be local or in the Third World. They also have a duty to insist that God is concerned about what happens at work and in school and what we do with our leisure time. 'The focus and arena of the churches' work and ministry should be the world and not just the institutional church' (*Faith in the Countryside*, 8.9). This aspect of the task is described in greater detail below (p. 142) in the section entitled 'Making sure the village is happy'.

No member is expected to do everything, and members are likely to have their own specialisms for which they will receive focused training. The bishop's licence will run for three-year 'terms', so the job need not be a 'sentence for life'. Finally, none of this can happen without prayer and a moving of the heart. The local group is not called to be a skeleton, but the living, breathing exultant body of Christ. In a flight of poetry, Tiller concludes chapter 5 of *The Gospel Community and its Leadership*:

> The gospel community relates to church structures as a new building to the scaffolding that surrounds it. Reforming the structures is like reorganising the scaffolding: it may be necessary but it does not itself alter the building at all. It is not an invisible body and it does require structures to grow and express itself, but down the ages it is the Spirit and the Word of God who have continued to create the gospel community.

ARE CANDIDATES AVAILABLE?

The census material suggests that there is no dearth of talent in most villages. In 1981 the socio-economic groupings I and II in rural areas were in general higher as a percentage of total population than in urban areas, as was the percentage of retired people. It is likely that the detailed 1991 figures, beginning to be available in August 1993, will confirm these characteristics for most rural areas. It is of course imperative that local ministry groups should reflect the whole population spectrum; nevertheless, the figures do suggest that there are likely to be in most rural areas a significant number of people with time and abilities available – if only they can be motivated.

The job outlined above is a challenging one. Are there enough lay people who are likely to respond? In *Church and Religion in Rural England*, the clergy were asked in the postal questionnaire whether they believed that the development of lay ministry was important to the running of their parishes: 59 per cent said it was vital or very important, while only 4 per cent said it was unimportant. However, 25 per cent qualified their answer by pointing out the problems involved and particularly the apparent unwillingness of people to take on the job – or, in some areas, the lack of those with the time and ability to do so. Is this likely to be an insurmountable problem?

Lay ministry already happens

The first thing to note is that lay ministry already flourishes. In his Green Paper *Ministerial Resources and Deployment*, the Bishop of Salisbury describes the resources of the Church in the diocese. There are 48,000 on the electoral rolls, and 30,000 worship in the churches on most Sundays. Among these are 200 Readers, 824 lay pastoral assistants, 992 churchwardens, 990 or so PCC secretaries and treasurers, 1,147 Sunday school teachers, and 900 who have taken the Bishop's Certificate in the Christian Faith – not to mention organists, choir directors, leaders of music groups, Mothers' Union members and Young Wives. The paper states:

> At a very rough guess I would say that there are at present between 4,000 and 4,500 active lay church members in the diocese who have either been authorised for some accredited ministry or hold office or have participated in some form of training or education which has equipped them to contribute some particular ministry.

Apart from the lay ministry which is so familiar that it goes unnoticed, a new sort of authorized lay ministry is being exercised in a number of dioceses. There have been lay elders in St Edmundsbury and Ipswich since 1968, and 70 elders work in 13 parishes in Ely diocese. As noted above, there are over 800 lay pastoral assistants in Salisbury diocese, and a number of other dioceses also authorize lay pastors. Four lay ministry teams were authorized in Ripon in 1983, and the diocese produced a report on the experiment, *Two Years On – Local Ministry in 1985*. Lincoln diocese has experimented with ministry teams since 1980 and in 1993 there were 27 teams consisting of 130 lay people with another 80 in training, and 64 ready to begin training in September of that year. Clearly, then, there are some laity who are willing to accept the challenge.

Nevertheless, in other rural areas authorized lay ministry is still exceptional and there is some local opposition to the idea. *Church and Religion in Rural England* shows that rural benefices are half as likely to have any authorized lay ministry as the country towns or suburbs (p. 152) and it was the clergy with totally rural benefices who were least likely to regard the development of lay ministry as of vital importance

(p. 156). In both the Ripon and Lincoln reports it is recorded that a number of rural parishes considered lay ministry, but did not go forward to training.

Given that the experience of the Acora Commissioners was that they met enthusiastic laity wherever they went, it is worth asking why the development of local ministry in rural areas should be so patchy.

Why does lay ministry not thrive everywhere?

There is a variety of evidence which all tends to the same conclusion. *Church and Religion in Rural England* asked Anglican attenders whether they would accept lay ministry from others, whether they would be willing to take part in ministry themselves, and whether they already exercised such ministry. The table below shows that there are far more offers than are taken up.

ANGLICAN ATTENDERS: ACCEPTANCE AND EXPERIENCE OF LAY MINISTRY

	Accept other people to...		Willing to perform		Already perform	
	No.	%	No.	%	No.	%
Visiting people	123	77	91	57	26	16
Administrative assistance	152	95	76	48	25	16
Reading lessons	152	95	84	53	47	29
Leading prayers	123	77	47	29	17	11
Preaching sermons	100	63	17	11	3	2
Administering the chalice	71	44	23	14	5	3
Conducting the service	105	66	17	11	5	3

Note: Totals do not add up to 100 as only the 'yes' response for each aspect is given.

Source: Davies, Watkins and Winter, *Church and Religion in Rural England*, p. 163.

This seems to suggest that the attitude of clergy to lay ministry is important. It is only when the clergy ask them that most lay people are ready to step into the limelight.

Other evidence highlights the importance of leadership from the centre. In 'The role of the laity in the rural church', Stephen Cope contrasts the 'less accessible countryside' deanery of 'Dalesmoor' with the 'accessible countryside' deanery of 'Croppington'. The former had lost stipendiary clergy, but had not been an area of experiment. Croppington had been reorganized by the diocese into two experimental team ministries which had encouraged lay participation. Dalesmoor and Croppington follow almost identical graphs with regard to clergy allocation, electoral roll numbers, attendance, etc. – but with one exception. In Croppington deanery lay ministry was as normal and widespread as in the suburban and urban deaneries surveyed: in Dalesmoor, on the other hand, lay ministry was exceptional.

The diocese of Gloucester has over the last 15 years carried out a series of programmes designed to encourage lay people to take their part in the running of the Church. Apart from diocesan-wide training programmes there have been three Swanwick Conferences with an equal number of clergy and laity present, and over 500 people have taken a two-year certificated course on the Christian faith. On the other hand, the diocese has not encouraged authorized lay ministry by individuals or teams. One result of this is that while the Diocesan Synod and the boards and committees are extremely well served by a large number of very able laity, and a number of deanery synods exhibit a high level of debate, there are only two lay ministry groups – both of them set up on the initiative of the local incumbents.

Conclusion

What this evidence taken together seems to suggest is that three things are necessary for the emergence of local ministry groups. First, the diocese has to encourage initiatives and help to set them up. Secondly, the clergy involved have to want to set them up. Thirdly, parishes and individuals need to be presented with a clear job specification of what they are being asked to do and what training will be involved. It is not that lay people are unwilling, but that they would not dream of flying in the face of diocesan or clerical opposition: nor are they prepared, as it were, to sign a blank cheque.

INDIVIDUALS OR GROUPS

A number of earlier initiatives in lay ministry sought to train individuals. Readers, lay pastors and those taking Bishop's Certificate courses may have been recommended by the incumbent or the PCC, but they were not part of a deliberate attempt to build up a local group. This has sometimes led to problems, and those responsible for the Salisbury Lay Pastoral

Assistant programme in particular have come to recognize that unless both parish and incumbent are committed to collaborative ministry, it can cause great frustration for the lay person involved. It is where the incumbent is convinced of the value of collaborative ministry, and deliberately builds them into the ministry team, that lay pastoral assistants are most effective and feel most fulfilled (Canon Askew, evidence to Acora, 1990).

SELECTION OF GROUP MEMBERS

'It's the chap who keeps the chapel open as keeps the chapel empty' is a well-known Methodist saying. It is of course vital to guard the group against the inappropriate volunteers of this world, but this can only be done without causing unnecessary hurt if the ground rules are clear from the start.

When lay pastoral ministry in Salisbury diocese started in 1976 (in the Sherborne deanery under the inspiration of Claude Rutter), anyone could volunteer to go on the course; but in 1984, when the initiative was taken up by the diocese as a whole, it was thought necessary to lay down a set of strict rules. It was from then on open only to those who had been 'selected by the incumbent with the approval of the PCC and Rural Dean'. (The last was a long stop to veto local magnates whom the parish dare not deny!) Authorization was to be for three years only and lapsed during an interregnum. Winchester diocese stated from the start that their lay pastors training course was open to 'those nominated to be trained as lay pastors by the incumbent with the agreement of the PCC . . . Authorisation will be for a set period of say three years.'

Ripon and Lincoln dioceses have done even more to ensure that the 'right' people are selected for their local ministry training schemes, since in their case some of those selected may proceed to (local) ordination. In the first instance, it is not individuals who are selected, but the parish.

Testing the parish

In the Lincoln Local Ministry Scheme the whole parish is involved from the start by being asked to follow the course 'Exploring Local Ministry'. In the introductory session the congregation 'tell the story of their church and community, consider the achievements of the last ten years, and make a list of what might be done in the next ten years, if "the ministry" were available'. The next two sessions consider the idea of 'baptismal vocation', and the way in which teamwork has been part of the Church's ministry from New Testament times. The fourth session considers the sort of qualities and gifts that can be used in team ministry, and the last two sessions introduce the idea of the diocesan local ministry scheme and what it would involve. Only then does the local PCC make a firm decision as to whether or not it wants to proceed, and only then does the bishop decide whether or not he is going to allow it to do so. It is after this stage has been completed that the process of nominating people to be trained begins. It is difficult to envisage a more thorough way of involving the local church and testing their commitment.

The Lincoln method of nominating candidates

The process of nominating the group is carried out as follows:

> Normally PCC nominations of potential team members are received by the incumbent over the period of a couple of weeks. The nominations are then collated by the incumbent who prepares a list for each member of the PCC with the names included of all those nominated for training. It may be helpful to nominate particular people to fulfil particular aspects of ministry, but these need not be over precise. It is more important to bear in mind both the agreed local priorities of ministry development and also the list of qualities deemed necessary in local ministry team members.
>
> At a meeting called for the purpose (it may be part of a regular PCC meeting) in the context of prayer and worship, the team is chosen. This is a way of discerning God's call through the corporate mind of the local church. It necessarily demands careful and thoughtful prayer.
>
> The PCC members place a tick where they think that a certain person would be an appropriate member of such a training team, and a cross where they are not happy about the person being a member of the team. A nought may be given if the person is not known well enough. The incumbent tallies the votes which have been cast by secret ballot. The local church needs to be looking for overwhelming support for any potential team member. This means that someone

with more than two negative votes would not normally be adjudged to have been chosen as part of the training team. The incumbent's understanding and discretion is important, as is consultation with the Local Ministry Officer. It has to be emphasised that this is no simple exercise in democracy but a way of discovering God's call through the call of the local church.

The incumbent then goes in the name of the Church and asks those people who have been chosen whether they will be willing to be part of the training team. They have not been asked until this stage. Until now the local church has been making up its mind as to who should be approached. (*Exploring Local Ministry*, p. 35)

A similar scheme for selecting group members is recorded by Reg Legg in *Lay Pastorate*. After three months' prayerful consideration, PCC members were asked to make a list of those they would like to see trained. In the event, all but two nominated exactly the same five people.

Appendix 1 of *Team and Group Ministries* (GS 993) gives a series of preliminary steps which should be followed before a parish is allowed to begin an experiment in collaborative ministry, and this could form the agenda for a parish course.

The role of the bishop

The bishop representing the diocese plays a vital part in this system of selection. From a negative point of view, he must not nominate a parish as a 'lay ministry parish' unless he is absolutely sure that both the PCC and the congregation are behind the experiment. When he does feel that the parish is ready to proceed, his personal presence at a special service – when the bishop commissions the parish as a 'local ministry training parish' – underlines his commitment to the initiative. His personal interest in the training process is vital, since it gives the village the signal that the experiment has the considered approval of those in authority, and is not just the whim of a few enthusiasts. His continuing concern is also vital should personal relations in the group break down, or there be some unexpected crisis of confidence. As with any experiment, if it works its excellence will be taken for granted, but if it fails in the smallest respect in the early stages the fall-out will put back the cause of the Kingdom for a decade. The village must know that the bishop (probably via a nominated deputy) is personally involved, and personally available in a crisis.

Licensing will normally be for a three-year period only, so the bishop continues to have direct oversight of the group.

Why the process of nomination is so important

As a result of these procedures, 'those chosen for the ministry team know they have the support of the church: and the church knows that the ministry team is truly its own' (Diocese of Ripon, *Two Years On*, 2.5). It could be argued that the multi-parish benefice itself signalled the end of the old order, and that parishioners should have got used to this by now. It must, however, be recognized that authorizing a group of local people to do the vicar's job itself turns accepted practice on its head because it substitutes local people for 'the one from outside'. This is why the way members of the group are chosen is so vital, and needs to be absolutely clear to everyone. The PCC and the congregation must feel that these are 'their people'. and those chosen must know that they have the full support of the local church. If there is any suggestion of division within the congregation on this issue, the village is bound to make that an excuse for rejecting the experiment.

WHAT SORT OF PERSON IS NEEDED?

This will depend on what sort of ministry the parish decides that it needs. In the introductory session of the Lincoln 'Exploring Local Ministry' course in Lincoln diocese, the congregation 'tell the story of their church and community . . . and make a list of what might be done in the next ten years if "the ministry" were available'. It is in the light of this discussion that the PCC makes its nominations.

A cautionary tale from America

An experiment in local ministry in the American Episcopal Church is recorded in Mathieson's *Delectable Mountains*, and will help to illustrate some of the possibilities and pitfalls. Three mission parishes in the northern Appalachians were offered a 'last chance' before closure. For two years from 1974 a stipendiary was allocated to them and his job was to train a local ministry team for each of the parishes. They used the apostolic principle of going out two by two and each congregation nominated two priests, two liturgists, two preachers, two administrators, two children's workers, two pastoral assistants and so on. At the end of the two years, the priests were ordained, the teams were 'commissioned', and the stipendiary was withdrawn. In 1979 five Anglicans visited the parishes. Their impressions were mixed, for in one parish the congregation had obviously overstretched themselves and had coped with the work-load by rigid demarcation between jobs; in another, the priests had taken over as the bosses; and only in the third was there true shared ministry by a Christian team of which the priests were part, with no rigid demarcation between the responsibilities of the members.

Needed: people who will work together

The People, the Land and the Church by Lewis and Talbot-Ponsonby argues that whatever parishioners may say they want, what is really needed is a group of people who will work together collaboratively with a flexible view of how ministry can be performed:

> It was apparent from the reports, that there is a desire for clear definitions of lay and clerical roles so that each knows what to expect of the other. The suggestion being made here is that the starting point may be to look at the whole ministry spectrum to see where the gifts and skills of different people are best used rather than deciding in theory who is eligible to perform which function. (p. 82)

In other words, the most important gift of a group member is not his or her natural talent at this or that task, but the ability to work in a team. The Lincoln *Local Ministry Scheme* puts it this way:

> In looking for local ministers the parish . . . has to look for people who are able to work effectively as members of a team, who are able to receive and to give leadership, who are able to learn from others, who participate in encouraging the ministry of others, who have gained the respect of the congregation and community, who have a sense of pastoral responsibility and who can with others be a focus of the church's ministry and a sign of the Kingdom of God. (p. 8)

One wonders if the Archangel Gabriel would qualify, but the point is well made.

What these examples are saying is that the parish should try to nominate not so much the *natural* leaders as the ones they perceive to be

God's leaders. In describing who might be nominated as a lay pastoral assistant, Canon Askew of Salisbury told the Commissioners that 'they wanted people who were surprised at being asked. It was not a role suitable for people who wanted airs and titles. They had found a wide social cross-section of people coming forward.' There is an understandable assumption on the part of ministerial theoreticians and diocesan staff that a local scheme will include those who are already church officers in the village – churchwardens, treasurers, secretaries, organists, Readers and so on. Indeed, the idea is enshrined in *Faith in the Countryside* (8.87): 'The Commission feels that much more attention and support should be given to elected parish officers, and *that they should be considered first and foremost as part of a local ministerial team.*'

While heartily endorsing the first part of the sentence, what those with some experience of local ministry are telling us is that selection should start not from 'who have we got?' – let alone from 'it would be something for them to do' – but from 'what does God need done, and *who is he calling?*' Nor should parishes look first and foremost for 'doers', but for those who will 'do things together'.

WILL THE VILLAGE ACCEPT THEM?

In the Dymock and Didmarton groups in Gloucestershire lay pastors have become so well accepted that on occasion they have been asked to 'take the funeral' of people they have visited regularly during a long illness. (In Coventry diocese such requests have become so usual that there are now regulations for lay people taking funerals, and the General Synod has introduced a Canon to make such services legal.) As Reg Legg points out in *Lay Pastorate*, lay pastors are not 'parson's pets' but people who have the backing of the PCC behind them; so if the scheme has been properly set up, this new generation of lay ministers has a flying start when it comes to being accepted by local people. Nevertheless, evidence that a significant minority are likely to oppose lay ministry root and branch needs to be faced.

Opposition to lay ministry

An insight into this comes from 'The role of the laity in the rural church' by Stephen Cope. By every indication, twice as much lay ministry goes on in the urban, suburban and accessible countryside rural deanery of

Croppington as in the less accessible countryside of Dalesmoor. Yet 50 per cent of the clergy of Dalesmoor think that the laity in their area *are* sufficiently involved; while in Croppington deanery, by contrast, 81 per cent of the clergy do *not* believe that their laity are sufficiently involved (though the situation 'is improving'). This confirms the findings of the Rural Church Project already quoted: that lay ministry is least likely in totally rural parishes, and that the clergy ministering in these parishes are most likely to think the development of lay ministry 'unimportant' or 'unacceptable to local people'. If we acknowledge that stipendiary clergy have a shrewd idea of what will or will not 'work' in their patch, all of this suggests that there are likely to be significant problems in introducing local ministry into traditional villages.

Church and Religion in Rural England has important data concerning this. All parishioners were asked whether they thought it was important for the church to visit and, not surprisingly, 80 per cent of all respondents said it was. They were then asked an open-ended question as to 'who from the church would be a suitable visitor?'. With no prompt, the reply came back loud and clear: 'the vicar' (66 per cent church sample, 71 per cent parish sample). Only 28 per cent suggested that someone else might visit *if the vicar accompanied them*, and only 3 per cent did not mention the vicar at all. This simply confirms the other evidence: that the vicar is a very important figure indeed in parishioners' perception of the church.

All Anglicans (which included both church attenders and others who said they were Anglicans but who did not consider themselves to be 'church members') were then asked whether they thought lay ministry was acceptable. They were relatively positive and agreed with the theory of lay ministry (52 per cent for, 21 per cent against). (However, it is interesting that 18–24-year-olds were very unsure about the idea, with only 40 per cent for and 29 per cent against; and there were also wide diocesan variations, with Durham 66 per cent for and 16 per cent against, while Southwell was 47 per cent for, 30 per cent against.) When offered a list of tasks that might be performed by the laity (see p. 171 of *Church and Religion in Rural England*), well over half the respondents supported lay help with parish administration, lesson reading, leading prayers *and visiting*; and over 63 per cent were even agreeable to lay people preaching sermons and conducting services.

The only suggested task that did not receive the support of more than half the respondents was administering the chalice. This reaction is probably explained by later questions on belief, which show that for many parishioners the holy communion service is above all *holy*, and the sanctuary has for them something of the significance of the Holy of Holies in the Jerusalem temple. It can therefore be an affront to their deepest religious instincts if a lay person distributes the elements.

While these figures suggest that a surprisingly large proportion of Anglicans would be likely to accept local ministry groups, nevertheless the statistics also suggest that a hard core of over 20 per cent of the lay sample are likely to be opposed to anything to do with lay ministry.

The case of St Mary's, Comberton

This situation may be illuminated by reference to 'The country church – the case of St Mary's, Comberton', an anthropological-type study by T. Jenkins undertaken in 1984 and submitted to the Acora Commissioners. In 1921 there were 102 dwellings in this Cambridgeshire village, in 1951 there were 164, but by 1983 the number had risen to 780 households by the addition of a number of (mostly private) estates.

The first commandment of traditional village life is that thou shalt keep thy head down – unless you are one of the nobs, in which case it is your duty to keep your head up. Jenkins endorses this view, but suggests that in the modern village, besides the old villagers, there are now two distinct groups of newcomers who have fundamentally different views about 'village community'.

The old villagers, of whom relatively few are left, exert great influence because they 'represent the village'. They understand 'village community' as something that is hierarchical. 'We' do the work and 'they' provide an informal village welfare service free. The vicar is seen as one of 'them', and the church is seen as part of the free welfare service which goes with membership of the village. The only acceptable way of supporting the church financially is via fêtes (which are village functions), and the chief way of participating in church life is by doing certain things such as cleaning the brass lectern. They tend to be embarrassed by talk of personal religion.'Their contribution is felt, rather than perceived, as a shadow of disapproval, a weight of inertia, a lack of co-operation.'

The newcomers consist of two groups. The 'conservatives' are often urban and have an Edwardian view of village community life which is also hierarchical. They cast themselves in the role of 'them' and spend much time and money helping 'the old village', which is only too happy to receive anything offered. They see the vicar as part of 'olde village life' and believe that it is his job to visit the old villagers, and to organize village functions and be present at them. The church too, both worship and building, should be set in 1920s aspic. They are enthusiastic about raising money for the church, provided it involves fêtes and bazaars and other such 'village' occasions.

However, there is a new group of villagers who have moved into the post-1970 estates. They are also determined to foster community life, but the key difference is that for them 'community' is not 'hierarchical' but 'egalitarian'. They start village clubs and call everyone by their Christian names, and cannot understand why 'the old village' does not join in. They see religion as a matter of personal conviction, which it is the prime job of the vicar to foster. They are relatively uninterested in the church building, for to them 'the church' is 'people'. They cannot understand why church finances should not be put on 'a proper footing'. In 1983 there was a major conflict on the PCC in this Cambridgeshire village between those who wanted to give up taking collections at the services (newcomers II) and those for whom the passing round of the plate was a very important ritual (newcomers I).

Conclusion

Villages have changed since 1984, but this study confirms the other evidence quoted: that it is very unlikely that local ministry groups will be immediately acceptable to all the congregation or to the whole village. It is likely that there will be a significant minority who find the whole idea of local ministry unacceptable, and this is a fact which needs to be recognized when any proposal is made. This should not stop experiments being made, but it should warn innovators to proceed with caution if not guile. It would be wise, for instance, to package their suggestions along the lines suggested by Van der Weyer in *The Country Church*: 'Shared ministry should be seen not as a radical step, but as a conservative one, aimed at upholding the best pastoral traditions of the Church of England' (p. 87).

MAKING SURE THE VILLAGE IS HAPPY

The primary task of the local group will then be to make their number with local people. In *The People, the Land and the Church* (p. 202), Lewis and Talbot-Ponsonby state as a major conclusion of the consultation process that 'the church expects to speak, teach and lead. There was a feeling around that the church needs to be able to listen, learn and be vulnerable – in order to teach and lead.' There could hardly be a better motto for the local group in the brave new world proposed than 'Listen, learn and be vulnerable'.

In the same book, a Herefordshire farmer is quoted as saying: 'County folk always assess by results; be it seed corn, breeding ewe, their neighbours or their rector' – or, it could be said, their local ministry group. When parishioners were asked to describe the job of the vicar they put pastoral care and community involvement at the top of the list. If the local groups can win their spurs in these fields, the chances are that they will be accepted.

Pastoral care

'Lay pastoral assistants' may sound very grand and rather frightening, but, as has been suggested, they can do their visiting by means of delivering the parish magazine – and in that unostentatious way their ministry is likely to be accepted. In the early stages it will be important that the stipendiary continues to do initial visits, particularly in connection with baptisms and funerals. Church-growth booklets emphasize the importance of visiting newcomers as soon as possible; while this is an obvious job for the local group, if the stipendiary can do a follow-up visit it will help to eradicate the suspicion that he is no longer available.

The implementation of the 'Care in the Community' legislation is going to be a major concern for local Social Services and Health departments. In many rural areas they are seeking to co-operate with local voluntary groups, and the publication of *Good Neighbours* by David Clark offers an excellent introduction to the world of community-care groups. The Dymock Care Group in Gloucestershire works on the assumption that many people are too busy to help on a regular basis, but can help out on occasion; thus they have over 50 volunteers on their list, many of whom are not regular churchgoers. What the organizers (all of whom are churchgoers) provide is a central telephone number and a co-ordinator who puts volunteers in touch with those who need help. Numerous schemes in the Winchester and Portsmouth dioceses work on the same principles.

Community involvement

Pastoral visiting is an excellent way of listening and learning. It is probable that as the local group begins to be involved in pastoral work, its members will become aware of community needs. *Faith in the Countryside* records examples of church involvement in, among other things, welcoming newcomers, running mother and toddler groups, putting on summer holiday clubs, working with voluntary car schemes, and helping with village appraisals and parish maps.

Other 'community' projects which a village appreciates are social and fund-raising events – from a welcome party for newcomers to the traditional Christmas bazaar or village open day. PCCs are usually good at putting on functions which, however old-fashioned, do provide a framework in which people can meet and 'community' has a chance to 'happen'. The danger is that PCC agendas become dominated by such functions, and the fund-raising element grows to obscure their pastoral and community objectives. Because of this, it will help if one or two members of the group are given the job of praying for the 'enrichment' of the community and monitoring how the church relates to village life.

If there is a school in the village, one of the group may see it as their vocation under God to serve as a governor or to help with the Friends of the School group. All too often in the case of a church school, PCCs seem to regard the school as owing the congregation a favour, when of course the reverse is the case. An annual meeting of the PCC, when the head teacher reports on the school, will serve to focus this aspect of local mission.

Care for the disadvantaged

There are aspects of social concern which some people living in the village will wish to ignore, but which are the clear responsibility of any Christian congregation. There are disadvantaged people in every village – not just the old villagers whom everyone flocks to help, but trapped and uncouth teenagers, car-less mothers with three children at home, the young couple made redundant who are being evicted or whose house is being repossessed, the family looking after a bedridden relative, and so on. Christians are called to show practical concern for all who suffer disadvantage. It may also perhaps be the vocation of one member of the group to rescue the parish council, and even the district council, from those who are determined not to see disadvantage even when it lives next door, and who prefer to export poverty to the town 'where it belongs'; who have no vision of community beyond keeping local taxes as low as possible and excluding from the village those who are 'not like us'. Christians have an understanding of 'community', focused in the sharing of bread and wine, which could revitalize not only congregations, but villages.

Nor are rural people always very good at looking beyond the village boundary. *Faith in the Countryside* insists on more than one occasion that for most Christians their primary field of mission will be their place of work rather than the village. Charity may begin at home, but it does not finish there – and one way of keeping this in mind will be for members of the group to work with others on behalf of local charitable organizations situated in the neighbouring towns, and with charitable organizations working overseas – of which the most obvious is Christian Aid.

Care for the natural environment and buildings

'Concern' should not stop short at people, for 'the earth is the Lord's and all the fullness thereof'. Arguably the most important debate in villages today is about conservation and the environment, focused on planning regulations about buildings on the one hand, and farming methods on the other. Here it must surely be the calling of the church – which has a practical knowledge of, and concern for, everyone living in the village – to get people to talk to each other face to face. A number of congregations visited by the Commissioners had helped to carry out surveys of local housing needs which had led to the building of low-cost property; another congregation helped form a group to rescue the village pond; yet another led a campaign to reorganize the footpath network around the village and then wrote a guide for visiting walkers; and one diocese sponsored the idea of 'a farm walk in every parish' (June is the best time) to bring together the farmers and their critics. Concern for these less popular causes is unlikely to win easy friends for the local ministry group, but when the dust has settled it will surely earn respect for the Church.

The Rural Church Project showed that popular Christianity focuses not only on the vicar, but also on the church building. The local ministry group is also likely to win the respect of parishioners if the church building and the churchyard are cared for and kept open; and if the church can in some sense become the unofficial village cultural centre, this will be an appreciated bonus. A number of villages display art work done in the local school or area; others have a village scrapbook on display; some have a book of remembrance; others encourage local arts and crafts – not least in the form of locally embroidered kneelers – and many provide the venue for music and drama.

If the local ministry group can begin to show God's love and concern in some of these ways, there is a good chance that it will begin to be accepted as 'the collaborative local vicar'.

Relations between the group and the congregation

The local group also has to ensure that it does not lose touch with the congregation. Elections can sometimes create a 'them and us' situation, and there is some danger that the local group will be seen as a charmed circle or cabal. Its relationship to the rest of the congregation, and particularly to the PCC and churchwardens, therefore needs to be sensitively handled. First, it needs to be emphasized that the rights of the PCC to decide policy issues remain intact, as do the rights of the church-wardens to represent the parish to the bishop and archdeacon. Secondly, local ministry is about implementing what the church decides it wants to be done; it is not about deciding policy. Clearly it would be foolish to pretend that a group which meets regularly with the stipendiary is not powerful and does not take decisions; but this is no different from what happens today when either the stipendiary by himself, or the stipendiary with his 'official' staff, take many decisions without reference to the PCC. In the early days it would obviously ease the situation if one of the churchwardens was a member of the local group, and it would be difficult to have a member of the group who was not on the PCC.

The opposite danger is that, having nominated the group, the congregation will then leave everything to the group – in the same way that the congregation was happy to leave the vicar and his wife to do everything in the past. In fact, in two of the interviews in Stewart's *Parson to Parson* there is some evidence of this happening. One of the ways of ensuring that this does not happen is for the stipendiary to make a point of asking non-group members to serve on the committees which local ministry will undoubtedly spawn. Pastoral care, for instance, will be the responsibility of the stipendiary and the local ministry group, but they must enlist the support of all sorts of allies: from the milkman to the one member of the congregation who lives in 'the outlying-hamlet-which-no-one-ever-thinks-of-as-part-of-the-village'. It will be helpful if one member of the group is specifically responsible for co-ordinating pastoral work; efficient co-ordination will be especially important if 'pastoral care' widens to a 'community care' system involving non-churchgoing volunteers.

The stipendiary clergy exist to 'resource' the 'people of God'. In just the same way, the local ministry group is not called to rule the congregation, and certainly not to impose its own model of the Church. It is called, both by God and by the rest of the congregation, *to serve*.

TRAINING THE LOCAL MINISTRY GROUP

Does the local group need training; and, if so, who should do it and how should it be done? In Ely diocese elders receive no training 'on the grounds that they do whatever any other lay Christian should be doing anyway' (*Ministry: A Report to the Bishop of Ely*, 3.52). In the Didmarton and Dymock groups in Gloucestershire, the local vicars trained their own lay pastors – in the former case using a Bishop's Certificate course as a basis for training, while in the latter the rector used his own material. Other dioceses have come to the conclusion that if lay ministers need to be trained and if courses are to have credibility, the training must be supervised by a diocesan tutor. This is the case in Ripon, York (the East Riding Lay Ministry School), Bath and Wells, and Lincoln. Similarly, in Salisbury and Winchester the lay pastors courses are now prepared and supervised by the diocesan training officer. One pattern is for a number of local tutors to be trained by the diocese and assigned to work with particular parishes; but since this is obviously a very demanding job, it is not always easy to find people who have both the expertise and the time to do the job effectively.

The training of lay ministry groups is increasingly being associated with training for the local non-stipendiary ministry, and this involves submitting the course for approval to a national body, the Advisory Board for Ministry. This is a healthy process for any course, and it is to be hoped that in future all lay training courses can receive national as well as diocesan approval.

Training as a group

The lay pastor training schemes mentioned draw together a number of individuals from a series of parishes, and Salisbury note that this sharing with other parishes is appreciated by the lay pastors. The training of a local group, however, has to be different, since it is of the essence that practical work is locally based and that the individuals learn to work together. If there are enough members, the group would normally be trained in their own parish – though sometimes it will be necessary to link with another benefice.

The bonding of the group is a very important part of the training, and it is for this reason that Readers, NSMs and retired clergy who are going to be part of the group should be trained with the group – even though they have already been 'trained' before.

In the Ripon and Bath and Wells schemes, the incumbent is also part of the training group, while the Lincoln scheme distinguishes between study meetings run by an outside tutor and the monthly benefice team meeting presided over by the incumbent. Clearly it is vital that the incumbent is closely involved with the training of the group, and interestingly Lincoln has recently taken steps to ensure that incumbents receive further help in how to use the benefice team meeting as a training exercise.

Unfortunately, the corollary of a strong bonding in the group is the problem (a) of what happens when one member goes or a new member comes, and (b) of how a new generation of members are trained. Even in the short time that the Lincoln scheme has been in operation, there have been problems. In Stewart's *Parson to Parson* (p. 52), we are told that 'one member died two months after the commissioning, and another has left the area. This means that the group is now down to three and the rector wants to add new members.' These people are in fact being trained with another group, but inevitably their full integration into the old group will need sensitive handling.

A possible curriculum

Granted that most dioceses will want to ensure that local ministry groups are trained under their own direction, what sort of curriculum is needed?

Winchester and Salisbury run a similar lay pastoral assistant course and the Winchester Leader's Guide is well produced and clear to follow. The course begins with an introductory day conference which includes units on 'Listening', 'What do I want from the course?' and 'The practicalities of making a visit'. This is followed by six two-hour evening sessions, covering visiting the sick, pastoral care for the elderly, baptism, marriage and bereavement visits, and visiting newcomers. There is a final day course which concentrates on evangelism and 'dealing with the difficult questions'. There are a maximum of twelve people on each course. In-service training is regarded as essential, and in some deaneries this will involve three evening meetings a year.

If this course seems rather 'thin', it must be remembered that both dioceses also run a Bishop's Certificate course on the Christian faith which many of the lay pastors also take; and that this 'first generation' lay ministry was conceived with the limited objective of training people to help the vicar with visiting. Our understanding of collaborative ministry has developed since those days, and the present generation of lay ministers will be expected not only to visit, but also to understand something about worship and the Bible, and will be called on to tell in a straightforward way their own Christian story. Not surprisingly, therefore, the courses proposed for the training of local ministry groups (as opposed to lay pastoral assistants) are longer and more demanding.

Training takes place within the context of parish life, and from the start members will be expected to 'learn by doing' under the supervision of the stipendiary. So, as well as the tutorial sessions, the group members join their local team meeting once a month, during which the practical assignments for each group member are planned and evaluated.

During the first two years of the Lincoln course there are 20 two-hour tutorial meetings in each academic year, with an extra session each year given over to assessment. In the third year there are just ten tutorial sessions, but each group member opts for two specialist modules of five sessions each. During each of the three years there are two one-day courses and one short weekend course.

The course begins with the theme of the 'Faith Journey', in terms of both the individual and the community of which the student is part. During the initial weekend, introduced by one of the bishops, they reflect on Abraham and what his faith journey has to say to them about the three-year journey on which they are setting out. This theme is picked up in the yearly self-assessments and during the final weekend when 'stories' are retold and preparations made for the next stage. During the first year two modules are studied. The first, 'Caring for People', has some similarity to the Winchester lay pastors programme. The second, 'Worship', aims to develop the understanding of and responsibility for worship, and to make life in the Spirit 'real' for the individual. There is one session on intercession, and another on the place of children in the church.

During the second year of the course students explore the Bible – first St Mark's Gospel, and then a selection from the Old Testament. The two study days are devoted to 'The Use and Authority of the Bible' and 'Communicating with Corinth: Using an Epistle'. In the final year the ten sessions are devoted to aspects of Christian doctrine, concentrating on how what has been learned so far – along with students' own personal experience – can be articulated as a statement of faith. The study days are on 'Anglicanism' and 'Ecumenism', and the specialist modules are on such practical topics such as 'Bereavement Counselling' and 'Youth Work'.

It is worth describing the course at length because it is so excellently presented. Each module has its own study booklet which is attractively printed, includes photographs and supplementary material such as poems and letters, and is eminently user-friendly. Many of those who have studied the Lincoln presentation to the Advisory Board for Ministry, the introductory course for parishes and the study booklets have been enormously impressed, and question whether it is really necessary for other dioceses to reinvent the wheel, so to speak. In the Methodist Church one central body prepares a syllabus for local preachers' training which is used throughout the country. (It was revised in 1992 and, thanks to the advice of the Church in Rural Life Committee, it now contains a number of 'alternatives' to make it more suitable for use in rural areas.) Inevitably, 42 training officers in 42 dioceses will think that they can improve on the Lincoln scheme. It is to be hoped that those who hold the purse strings, at least in rural dioceses, will advise caution before yet more courses are churned out. The Lincoln scheme is ready and tested and it is an outstanding product.

Nevertheless, even the Lincoln scheme is not perfect and needs to be flexible enough to accommodate change. These are some of the concerns that have been expressed recently:

(1) It was felt that tutorial sessions needed to be more explicitly linked to the team meeting, and that incumbents needed more advice on how to train group members.
(2) LNSM deacons and priests were not felt to be receiving adequate CME (Continuing Ministerial Education) for their particular job.
(3) Local tutors have a key role in developing local ministry, and Nottingham University has now agreed to help train the tutors to do their job more effectively.

All of these concerns are being met by changes to the training scheme, and they illustrate how important it is for any course to be constantly monitored and adapted.

THE GEOGRAPHICAL BOUNDARIES OF LOCAL MINISTRY

There is some debate as to whether the basic unit for local ministry should be the settlement or the benefice. The Advisory Board for Ministry's *Local NSM* explicitly allows for the possibility of a local non-stipendiary minister (LNSM) in one specified church or one specified parish:

> Perhaps the mark that most distinguishes LNSM from other ordained ministries is its concentration on a particular locality and church. . . . In relation to this style of ministry, 'local' may be used to refer to a geographical area not greater than a parish or group of parishes. (2. 12)

It is not therefore even assumed that the LNSM will always be licensed to operate throughout a benefice. What is true for an LNSM would clearly also be true for a lay pastor or other members of a local group.

A group in each settlement

The idea of a local group *in each settlement* has great imaginative attraction and is forcefully expressed in Bishop Baker's *Salisbury Diocese: Ministerial Resources and Deployment*.

> 5.2. We have to start from the basic reality of the local congregation. This is where Christians offer their worship, do their praying, grow in

understanding, join in showing care, reach out to others and build up a Kingdom community. Theologically, we are told, the whole church is present in each place and congregation. The word is there, the sacraments are there, Christ and the Spirit are there. . . .

5.7. Taking our terminology from the New Testament, I want to say that in the local church we need a structure based on *presbyteral leadership*. Each congregation needs its own ministerial team to facilitate the work on as many as possible of the tasks.

A group in each benefice

However, not everyone is persuaded by this argument. Two dioceses which have significant practical experience of establishing local ministry groups both prefer to see the group as operating *within the benefice, rather than within the settlement. Two Years On* describes the setting up of an experimental ministry which covers 70 square miles to the west of Ripon. While admitting that 'there was evidence that the idea of a "parish" (benefice) was something peculiar to a number of church members and clergy, and "the village" was the community concept held by most people', nevertheless the general body of the report argues for local ministry being based on the benefice rather than the village:

2.44. Progress with country groups has been slow, in spite of some promising starts, and undoubtedly one reason for this lies in the multiplicity of PCC's, even when they have met jointly. It has always been envisaged that where there is one incumbent there would be a single team, and that where a single team is serving several churches, some members of it would work mainly or only in one small area, while others with different responsibilities would work more generally. There seem to be no particular difficulties in this, except for that of being responsible to more than one PCC. On the whole we should like to see country groups becoming single parishes.

Lincoln diocese is even more definite that members of the local group must be able to operate throughout the benefice. It is clear that underlying much of its strategy is a determination to ensure that local ministry does not lead to congregationalism. One of the fears is that, given half a chance, parishioners will raise their local NSM on to a pedestal and venerate him as 'our own vicar'. One of the strategies for containing this tendency is to insist that he or she does not minister in only one church (or parish). Lincoln diocese further urges that while village autonomy makes good poetry it does not make good sense. The Church would in the long run be foolish to ground its ministry on a romantic fantasy. Furthermore, if stipendiaries are to play the significant role which everyone agrees they will have to play, their unit of responsibility (the benefice) will in practice become the operational unit of local ministry. Lincoln's only concession to 'pure' localism is that in some benefices *pastoral and community ministry* may be localized in particular villages (for instance, pastoral oversight is exercised by one person delivering magazines in his or her own hamlet); but even so, these local ministers will on occasion be involved *in worship* in all the churches of the benefice. Finally, Lincoln diocese reports that so far local ministers have been accepted in those parishes of the benefice which have not supplied a person for training.

Conclusion

There is so little practical evidence that it is perhaps dangerous to question the few who do have experience of running local ministry groups. On the other hand, a 'benefice' is a strange unit which has no natural 'reality' apart from being the area of responsibility of a stipendiary minister. It is not difficult to think of a dozen benefices which are not homogeneous units, but straddle a geographical divide or a social chasm: and it is very rare for all the parishes in a benefice to be at the same 'spiritual stage' of development. Are all such benefices to be debarred from experimenting with local ministry groups because of one village which does not feel able to co-operate?

In the circumstances, then, it is perhaps wise to urge caution on those who would plunge headlong down the road of 'pure localism', but at the same time plead for maximum flexibility so that any parish which sincerely wishes to experiment may be allowed to do so.

WELDING THE LOCAL GROUP ON TO THE BENEFICE TEAM

Chapter 5 stated that the local group must be welded on to a benefice team so that it remains part of the Church catholic. In Chapter 8, the theological and practical reasons for this were set out. A few things now need to be said about how to put the theory into practice.

The discussion in the last section about 'the geographical boundaries of local ministry' noted that in Lincoln and Ripon dioceses there are no local groups, only benefice teams. But whether the 'local' or the 'benefice' option is adopted, certain common factors will need to be born in mind.

The wide literature on group dynamics and the organization of groups and teams is referred to in *The Gospel Community and Its Leadership* by Tiller and Birchall; it is only necessary here to underline those principles which have special relevance to the rural situation.

The first principle is that the relationship between group members and the incumbent and other members of 'staff' has to be clearly defined. Coventry diocese publishes *Guidelines for the Establishment of Pastoral Teams* and *Guidelines for the Establishment of Leadership Teams*. Furthermore, there needs to be clarity about what is the precise nature and function of the benefice team.

The second is that the relationship between ministry group members and the parish 'officers' has to be constantly examined, since the local team draws its strength from its authorization by the PCC. The church-wardens in particular have an official role which is as important as that of members of the ministry group, and they therefore have the right to be consulted on all policy issues.

A few examples of existing teams will show what a wide variety of models are available. In the paper mentioned above, Coventry diocese identifies three broad types of leadership teams:

(1) An informal eldership model (as used in Styvechale parish).
(2) A 'sub-groups of PCC' model (as used at Potter's Green).
(3) An 'ex-officio' team (as used in the multi-parish benefice centred on Hunningham).

The united parish of Wolverton treats its PCC standing committee as a team; Birdingbury has both a standing committee and PCC sub-groups; and the North Ferncumbe group have a ministerial (staff) team which meets monthly, and a benefice team (including lay pastors) which meets quarterly. The Brothertoft team in Lincolnshire (*Parson to Parson*, p. 52) 'meets every Tuesday morning for communion and a staff meeting which includes study, diary business, training, and is conducted in a fairly free and easy atmosphere'. At Eythorne and Elvington in Kent the team revolves around the daily saying of the offices in the parish church. In the Beaminster area in Dorset, the *Team Handbook* outlines with admirable clarity the relationship between the team council (consisting of 'staff' plus up to three members of each PCC) and the individual parishes:

> In its early meetings the Team Council received four Policy Papers concerning Worship, Finance, Lay Ministry and Pastoral Care. These form the basis of an accepted policy. Circumstances change and there is no wish to create an inflexible structure. However, changes should only be made at the request of a member Church Council and should be agreed by the Team Council. This will prevent any church large or small from making unilateral decisions which are not in the wider interests of the Team of Churches.

In case this sounds too autocratic, the document goes on to say: 'We believe each PCC should retain complete sovereignty over all income, expenditure and budgeting.' In this case every PCC member is regarded as a 'lay minister', and PCCs are expected to meet once a month – sometimes, but not always, with a stipendiary minister.

There are then as many different ways of running a benefice team as there are stipendiaries to run them. Every situation varies and it would be wrong for a diocese at this stage of knowledge to impose one team pattern rather than another. The job of the diocese is to ensure that local people recognize what the problems are likely to be; and that they have a chance to view and assess other teams within and outside their own diocese before making firm plans.

To this end it would be extremely valuable for the Church at large if dioceses could monitor such schemes, assess their 'success', and try to come to some understanding of why one model is more or less 'successful' than the others.

11

Local Non-stipendiary Ministry

'The vision' suggests that within the local group there *may* be a priest, Reader or other church official. In Chapter 9 evidence was presented to suggest that the village with a resident priest was likely to be more 'successful' than one which had no parsonage, and therefore that there was a prima facie case for encouraging 'local priesthood' in its various forms (provided that settlements served in this way were welded into a benefice team). This section goes back a step and examines the theology which undergirds the idea of local ministry, and the concept of 'vocation' within local ministry. The practical implications of this are then examined for members of the local group, Readers, local non-stipendiary ministers, non-stipendiary ministers and retired clergy.

A THEOLOGY OF LOCAL MINISTRY

There are obvious practical advantages if one of the group is ordained. The 'parson-shaped hole' will be filled and there can be 'regular services when we want them'. It could also be argued that the traditionalists are right in recognizing instinctively that it is the priesthood which sets the seal on the catholicity of the local church. Nevertheless, just as the practical argument for villages needing local ministry groups was built on a sound theological foundation, so any consideration of 'multiple local priesthood' needs to be based on an acceptable theology of ministry.

Canon Royle on local ministry

In a paper presented to Salisbury Diocesan Synod in January 1992, Canon Stanley Royle argued that our understanding of ministry begins with God's choosing of Israel to be his agent to the nations, and is focused in the incarnation and the purpose of Christ to bring all humankind into a relationship with the Father. It is the genius of St Paul that he helps us to recognize that all of God's chosen people (the New Israel) share in his continuing ministry to the world. Within the early Church the highest value was placed on spiritual gifts which were severally available through the Holy Spirit, but officers were also appointed:

> It appears that officers were of two distinctive types. There were those who appeared to hold office within a particular community such as the elders at Ephesus (Acts 20) or in the churches which were the recipients of 1 Peter. There are also office holders who appear to have a wider responsibility e.g. Paul himself as an Apostle, and those whom he sent as delegates to other Churches e.g. Tychicus and others Eph 6:21, Col 4:7, Rom 16:1ff.

Today we have come to take it for granted that Anglican stipendiaries should all be trained to be 'apostolic delegates', and indeed they are not encouraged to serve in the parishes in which they grew up.

In the same way, while discernment of a vocation to an office in the Church tends in our tradition to be based on a parson's sense of inner calling, this was not always the case. H. J. M. Turner argues in 'Ordination and vocation' in *Sobornost* that while in pre-Reformation times an inner sense of calling was confirmed to those wishing to follow a monastic way of life, the office of bishop or presbyter was taken on – sometimes reluctantly – in response to the call of the community (e.g. Ambrose of Milan and Martin of Tours). The Greek Orthodox Church has retained the tradition of both apostolic priests and local priest/ presbyters who are often nominated by the local community, and Royle argues that it is therefore perfectly legitimate for the Anglican Church to revive the practice of training and ordaining *local* priests:

> The selection and training of stipendiary clergy is deliberately geared in such a way that the person trained may be capable of serving anywhere in the Church of England. . . . Local Non Stipendiary Ministers would be based on the more static model of the elders of Ephesus.

Finally, it is essential, he argues, that LNSMs should function as part of a ministry team.

Bishop Baker on local ministry

Royle is making such an important point that it is worth seeing how his insight is carried forward in diocesan thinking as illustrated in *Salisbury Diocese: Ministerial Resources and Deployment* by Bishop Baker:

> 5.5. The other method of relating the local to the universal is through *authorised ministers*. The bishop is the chief of these, but in practice all ordained ministers have come to be representatives of the wider Church in the local situation. They are selected, trained and deployed by or through the Church as a whole. They stay, mostly, only for limited periods in any one place. They may move anywhere within their Church. They are consecrated to minister the Word and Sacraments within the Church as a whole.

> 5.6. This has resulted in an *imbalance* within the authorised ministry which our Church is only now trying to correct. It has meant that for many generations the parish clergy have not normally been members of the local community and congregation. Some have felt this, and deliberately stayed long enough to become such. Some have been sons of local families which had the right of presentation. The parson's freehold could also help to ally him with his parish against the hierarchy. But by and large the clergy have identified with the wider Church, leaving the laity to stand for the local community – with results often only too predictable. When this was combined with little lay involvement in or responsibility for authorised ministry, contribution to spiritual leadership by the local church was virtually

impossible. Another result was to concentrate ecclesiastical power in the hands of those identified with the centre, and so further to deprive the local church of any authority. The struggle to break this pattern of centuries is inevitably hard and painful. The campaign for lay ministry and the slow growth of parochially sponsored NSMs are doing something to erode it, but it is a slow business. Once, however, we see clearly that we need a structural balance between the local church and the wider church, and that this is where the heart of the problem lies, we should find the courage to make the necessary changes in the pattern of ministry.

5.7. Taking our terminology from the New Testament, I want to say that in the local church we need a structure based on *presbyteral leadership* (from the Greek word englished as 'presbyter', meaning 'elder'). Each congregation needs its own ministerial team to facilitate the work on as many as possible of the tasks described above. In our present situation this team might comprise, e.g. the Churchwardens, PCC officers, Parish Secretary (if there is one), Reader(s), LPA(s), group leaders, Sunday School teachers – and someone to be their president. The natural and I believe, desirable course would be for that person, called and sponsored by the congregation, to be ordained.

5.8. Similarly, for the relationship of the local to the wider Church we need what, again following the New Testament, I would call the *apostolic team*. Their primary responsibility would be to help make the resources of the wider Church available to the local congregation as local needs required; to keep the local Church spiritually in touch with the life, faith and mission of the Church as a whole; to represent the wider Church in the worship and activities of the local congregation and community. They could also play their part with representatives of the local Church in ensuring, through whatever structures might be in place for the purpose, i.e. Synods, etc., that the local congregations made their essential contribution to the thinking and practice of the Church as a whole. But it is essential that they also take their share of the general ministerial duties in their area.

5.9. A pattern such as this would be, I believe, very much *healthier* and *more effective* than the one we have now. It would also be *more scriptural*. As regards *vocation*, this pattern offers another approach to supplement the one that prevails at present. It has always been true that some have become ordained because fellow-Christians challenged them to consider it seriously or simply put the idea in their heads. Perhaps a majority of lay people engaged in ministry have been invited to take it up by the Vicar or a friend. But the majority of clergy are those who have felt an inward call, and have then offered themselves to the Church. Today there is a growing emphasis on the need to balance this with the Church itself putting a call to people it considers fitted for ordination.

IMPLICATIONS FOR THE LOCAL GROUP

Not everyone will endorse the 'Salisbury' theology of local priesthood, but 'the vision' assumes that in the rural context the distinction between 'local' and 'apostolic' ministry offers a pattern which makes sense in understanding the current situation. It has implications for the vocation of everyone within the local group, both lay members as well as clergy.

Local ministry is grounded in the worshipping congregation whom God has called to be his people in that particular place. It is a high and glorious calling and involves members in prayer, teamwork and commitment, so that 'God's love may be experienced as real' by more and more people in their village. God will also be calling some in the congregation to be his people in their places of work and influence, and it is particularly important that local worship should focus and re-fuel their Christian lives not only in the settlement, but also outside it.

So that ministry should be more effective the congregation call on a number of their members to be trained as a local ministry group. Since the Reformation, vocation has typically been understood as the call of God to an individual which the Church then tests. This model revives an older tradition whereby vocation is initiated by the congregation. Nevertheless, once called, individuals will have to make this vocation their own. To act as a minister on behalf of the congregation is an awesome responsibility, and one of the chief purposes of the three-year training must be to give trainees a chance to test their own vocation.

In some ways this testing will be all the more difficult because they will not have 'received' local ministry themselves – they have no role model to follow. It is not even as if they have a clearly defined job, for some will be pastors, some evangelists, some teachers, some workers of miracles; some good organizers and some good at editing magazines, some good with a typewriter and some good with a scythe. The two charisms they should – hopefully – all have in common are 'love' and the ability to function as 'the body'. Nor will they have that universally respected badge, the dog collar, to get them over every doorstep. They will not even have special robes at services, where they will usually be just 'ordinary' members of the congregation. Yet gradually, if their ministry becomes effective, they will in the eyes of parishioners become something a little different. This is bound to affect their families too, because with local ministry goes a commitment to God, to the Church, and to the local area. These factors will certainly affect the family diary, and might well have a bearing on such critical decisions as changing job or moving house.

IMPLICATIONS FOR READERS AND LAY PASTORS

If ministry is to have its roots in the settlement, and if that ministry is to be collaborative, there will be implications for those who are already Readers or lay pastors. If, as *Faith in the Countryside* suggests, it is desirable that services of worship should be taken by local people, we will be asking Readers to become 'local' for the sake of the village. This will not mean that Readers cannot take services in other parishes, nor even that they have to live in the village: but it will mean that they need to identify with the village by regular worship, joining in village events, and local visiting. The best way of doing this will be to join the local ministry group as they train and learn together, and indeed they could play a key part in helping the group to develop. Lay pastoral assistants, elders, lay liturgical assistants – and others with different titles but similar functions – are already local people, but they too will need to become part of the ministry group: and again the best way they can do this is to join in the three-year course. Obviously this requires humility and commitment beyond the normal, but it is to be hoped that the process of preparation already described will convince them that it is well worth it for the sake of the parish.

IMPLICATIONS FOR LOCAL NON-STIPENDIARY MINISTERS

Like the other members of the group, local non-stipendiary ministers are called initially by the congregation. Because theirs will be an especially representative role on behalf of the Church, their vocation will be tested according to the Bishops' Guidelines in the Advisory Board for Ministry report *Local NSM*. The vocation to priesthood must obviously become their own, and all the more so since they are called to a particularly exposed and spiritually demanding office. Most of their training is done with the rest of the group and is not essentially academic: it will not for instance require the writing of essays. Unless they receive further 'Reader-style' training they will not be authorized to preach, nor will they probably be encouraged to wear robes or sit in the clergy stalls unless they are actually taking part in the service. An LNSM will not necessarily be the chairman of the PCC or group meetings, any more than these days the stipendiary is always chairman of the various parish committees. They will contribute their natural gifts (whatever they may be) to the group, but their special vocation is simply to be the local priest ministering the sacraments of the Church. In this sense they will be not unlike the bishop, who has ultimate authority under God in the diocese, who represents Christianity in the area to those 'outside', and can do whatever he chooses 'within', but who actually chooses to work collaboratively with the other members of the body. Like the bishop, LNSMs will have the outward trappings of office, but will not in practice be autocrats in command of puppets. At the same time, though, they will often have to take responsibility in public for what is done by others in the name of the Church.

Clearly such a calling is one which demands great spiritual resilience and maturity. This is why LNSMs need to know that the congregation has chosen them and supports them, that the wider Church represented by the stipendiary and the diocese have endorsed this choice, and to know in their hearts that it is indeed a call of God. All Christians are called to holiness, but perhaps in a special way the local ministry group will look to their local priest for devotion, and wisdom born of much prayer, and to a theology grounded in experience rather than in books.

Local non-stipendiary ministry – training and selection

Local NSM has regulations about selection and conditions of service, and among these is a rule that selection for ordination may be during or prior to a training course. Naturally, not everyone agrees with all of the regulations, but at least everyone now knows what the rules are. In the light of the report, two of the 'open-ended' regulations need to be discussed.

First, there is the question of how the training for local priests should be done. There are two lines of argument. Lincoln argues that it is of paramount importance that *ordained* local ministers should not act as old-style incumbents, but should recognize that they share their ministry with the local group. It will be only too easy for them to drift into the role of 'vicar' unless 'collaborative' is written on their hearts. To this end Lincoln suggests that all training should be done with the local group until the last year before ordination. At this stage they will for six months join other ordinands for training in priestly functions, and to make them aware of the wider Anglican Communion. After ordination they will, if not taking part in a service, sit in the congregation: and rural deans and diocesan officials are especially instructed to negotiate with the *group*, not simply the LNSM, even when arranging services during an interregnum.

In 1985 Ripon diocese was planning to follow a similar scheme. Ripon, however, wanted to train LNSMs for an extra year to the same standard as Readers, so that they would be able to preach, as well as to celebrate the sacraments. (It was, however, recognized that some local priests would not be naturally academic and therefore might not be suitable for such an additional course.) Truro and Salisbury dioceses, however, tend to see the ordained person as the automatic 'president' of the local ministry group. To them, it seems of the utmost importance that priests should not be considered second-class just because they are 'local' rather than 'apostolic'. It is therefore necessary that they receive a full, thorough and special training, even if the method used is 'experience-based pastoral theology' rather than 'systematic theology of academic descent'. Truro and Salisbury dioceses believe that local priests in training should therefore be primarily attached to a local School for Ministry, while at the same time doing some training with their local group.

Secondly, there is debate, along the same lines, as to when people should test their vocation to the local priesthood. Lincoln diocese believes that this should take place after candidates have completed a year of the local ministry course, while Truro and Salisbury dioceses believe that, ideally, local priests should be selected before training of the local ministry group begins.

Which course is the right one to follow? The way in which both cases are argued is so unrealistically neat that it betrays how little experience we have on which to make judgements. To return to a now familiar plea, this subject is of such vital importance to the future of rural ministry that experiments *must* be monitored. Of the bandying around of ministerial theories there is no end, but what is desperately needed is sound research based on experience.

In the circumstances, therefore, it is not as yet possible to say which is the 'right' way to train local priests. Two principles which are not necessarily in conflict need to be considered. Local priests must feel themselves to be, and act as, members of the local ministry group; but though their vocation is to local priesthood, neither they nor anyone else must be allowed to look down on their priesthood as second-class.

IMPLICATIONS FOR NON-STIPENDIARY MINISTERS

Non-stipendiary clergy, both male priests and women deacons, are already making an enormous contribution to the rural Church. In the diocese of Oxford for instance, there are already over 130 non-stipendiary clergy working in villages, of whom 5 are priest-in-charge of the parish, with a further 35 in training. As we have seen, Robin Gill and Robert Van der Weyer urge eloquently that the rural Church should be run by non-stipendiary clergy: in other words, the old system (as in the good old days), but at no charge to the quota. As we have persistently argued, it is not just that there are not at the moment enough non-stipendiaries to plug the gaps, but that the old system is itself flawed: for ministry should be collaborative, not individual. It is to be hoped therefore that those non-stipendiaries who are at the moment incumbents of rural benefices will set about introducing local ministry in exactly the same way as their stipendiary colleagues. In doing this, they are taking on the 'apostolic' rather than the 'local' priestly role.

Ministry in the Countryside: Testing the Vision

The choice – local or apostolic?

The non-stipendiaries who could be most affected by 'the vision' are those who operate as *de facto* curates to stipendiary clergy. If their parish becomes a local ministry parish, their role will change – and in some ways their most significant and difficult decision will be whether their future ministry should be essentially 'local' or 'apostolic'. Some will live locally and be retired from secular employment; their ministry will obviously be local. Some will have a full-time secular job, but still see their ministry as focused in the village where they live; still others will exercise their main ministry at work, but give a hand in the parish on Sundays. For the last group, the initial stages of local ministry with the inevitable concentration on the local will probably be particularly difficult, though in the long run a local ministry benefice could be an excellent base for a non-stipendiary working in, for instance, the local large factory or comprehensive school.

Whether they are 'local' or 'apostolic', non-stipendiaries already in post will find that their role changes. Before, the staff meeting was probably a cosy huddle over a pint of beer with the stipendiary and the Reader. Now, though, there will be seven or eight at the meeting and the proceedings will have to be more formal. Previously, they ran their own services, did the visiting, and automatically chaired sub-committees of the PCC. In contrast, the congregation is now being asked to recognize a group of people as the 'corporate curate', and that must mean a sharing of jobs with others.

Involvement in group training

The non-stipendiaries will also have to consider their involvement in the group training. The theological position set out at the beginning of this section argued that the local priesthood is unashamedly of a different order from apostolic priesthood. It is not a second-class priesthood, but a different form of priesthood; and therefore all who are to serve as local priests need training which is appropriate to the context – whether or not they are already trained 'apostolic' priests. In the same way as a minister trained exclusively in urban ministry who moves to a rural station needs appropriate extra training, so a non-stipendiary minister, or a retired priest, or a Reader who is going to become a local priest, will need appropriate extra training. We have seen that the essential basis of local ministry is that it should be collaborative; consequently, everyone who is to minister locally needs to be bonded into the local group and to experience collaborative ministry.

Those theological colleges which take collaborative ministry seriously (e.g. Salisbury and Wells) themselves run on collaborative principles, on the grounds that in this field two pennyworth of practice is worth a gross of lectures. It is for this reason that bishops and incumbents will need to insist that only those who have experienced collaborative ministry (or are prepared to undergo training), and are prepared to become members of the group, should be ordained (or licensed) to local priesthood. An example of one of the less obvious sorts of personal problem such a stand might involve is given in Stewart's *Parson to Parson* (p. 52): 'The locally ordained member of the Group was originally a reader, and as such was authorised to lead worship anywhere in the diocese. Now his licence is local to the Group, and he is unable to accept invitations to function as a reader (or priest) beyond its boundaries.' Nevertheless, in the early days of establishing what is for the Church of England a new form of ministry, it will surely be necessary to stick to the rules to establish the principle.

IMPLICATIONS FOR RETIRED CLERGY

Another group who have for over a decade kept rural ministry going are the retired clergy. Some retire to villages largely because they want to help in the parish, others are actually offered a free house in return for 'occasional duty'. Some adopt a particular benefice and become 'honorary curates', while others take services as and when they are needed. It would be churlish to undervalue the splendid service that they give. Nevertheless, 'the vision' implies that they too need to collaborate with the local group and become in some sense 'local'. Retired clergy who are in post when a parish becomes a 'local ministry parish' are likely to have the same transitional problems as non-stipendiary clergy. Their particular strength will be their experience and spiritual maturity; their weakness will be that, for the most part, they have had enough of PCCs and committees, and may well feel that they want to sit light to the demands of 'community involvement' and 'localism'. Because of their experience and spiritual charisma, it is vital that they should work with 'the strategy' and not at an angle to it, but being a member of a group could involve a commitment of time and spiritual energy they are not prepared to make. For many retired clergy and rural parishes, this will be a hard decision – but it is one which must be honestly faced.

LOCAL NON-STIPENDIARY MINISTRY – A FIRST-CLASS MINISTRY

Thus local ordained ministers may come in many different forms, and could make a vital contribution to the development of the local ministry group. Inevitably they will be seen by some as second-class priests. What we need to do to counter this tendency is to highlight what local priests are being asked to do. Every survey of the clergy carried out in recent years shows an extraordinarily high level of job satisfaction. The job which they find so fulfilling is in most cases precisely what we have called 'local ministry', and they are happy to work long hours for a relatively small reward because they believe they are doing something worthwhile and ultimately purposeful. They believe that God has called them and anointed them to minister to everyone living in a certain geographical area so that more and more people 'may experience God's love as real and respond'. It is exactly this ministry which we believe now has to be exercised in rural areas, not by the stipendiary alone, but by the local ministry group. As we have seen in this section, it will demand great sacrifices of those involved. It will be that much harder than what went before because it will be seen as a new ministry, even though it is actually the old ministry in a new guise. There will be no financial reward, and so no financial incentive. Nevertheless, a reading of George Herbert's *A Priest to the Temple*, or more recently Vere Hodge's handbook *The Newly Ordained and Other Clergy* (given a re-review in *Modern Churchman*, New Series, vol. XXXIII, No. 2 (1991)), conveys something of the deep attraction of such a ministry. It is a ministry which is now available to members of rural congregations; I believe that many will respond to the call and find the challenge both exhilarating and ultimately rewarding.

12

The Role of the Stipendiary

In this chapter the role of stipendiaries in implementing 'the vision' is described, and the conclusion is drawn that they will need to be holy, learned, local and apostolic. I then ask whether the existing rural clergy are likely to rise to the challenge of pioneering this new form of ministry; and whether the added burden will be more than they can cope with emotionally. Finally, in a postscript I draw on personal experience to suggest how fulfilling this new model of ministry can be.

Collaborative ministry should have obvious attractions for modern rural clergy because one of their most frustrating problems is trying to meet conflicting expectations. Parishioners expect of them the same care that they received from their predecessors who were incumbents of only one village. The diocese expects stipendiaries to minister to and 'be responsible for' not one settlement, but perhaps five. Theological training probably inculcated personal expectations grounded in veneration of the Curé d'Ars, Charles de Foucauld and David Watson. Where expectations conflict, there is bound to be spiritual turmoil. A collaborative team ought to be able to help the stipendiary cope with this, for many hands should make lighter work.

Nevertheless, if collaborative ministry has certain obvious advantages it also raises the fear that it could make the stipendiary priest redundant; and the way in which local ministry is inevitably being 'pushed', alongside the cutting down (for financial reasons) of stipendiary posts, hardly encourages confidence. It is therefore important at this stage to establish that there is still going to be a job for the stipendiary under the new dispensation.

A NEW JOB DESCRIPTION

The answer given by all the dioceses who have so far published papers on local ministry is a resounding 'yes' but it will be a different kind of job. Rather than being a father of dependent children, clergy are being called to accept the role of midwife for the future leadership of the rural Church (see Nicholas Bradbury, 'The minister as midwife'). It will be the job of stipendiaries to catch hold of 'the vision' so that they can see where their benefice should be going, and to follow 'the vision' with resolution and enthusiasm. It will be the job of stipendiaries to ensure that others in the parish understand; yet not to force decisions on them, but to come to a consensus about what precisely the local context needs. It will be the job of the stipendiary to ensure that suitable people are chosen to form a local ministry group; to be involved in their training and to stand beside them and hold their hands as they take their first faltering steps in ministry. It will be the responsibility of the stipendiary to ensure that after the first flush of success, the group and the team settle down in a stable relationship; and it will be the responsibility of the stipendiary to see that unexpected events, such as the coming of a retired priest or the departure of a member of the group, are not allowed to divert the local churches from their original vision. It is an awesome challenge, and for most, it will be a full-time job.

In a particularly helpful passage, *Faith in the Countryside* sets out the new role of the stipendiary in this way:

8.18. Ordained ministers, like lay people, have their own particular gifts and abilities, so it would not make sense to create a restrictive list of the priest's tasks. Each priest will be able to offer particular skills just as each lay person is able to offer theirs. But the key role of the priest is to bring into focus and enable the total mission and ministry of the Church. The priest should be the one who is trained to hold the breadth of the vision and to share in it with the whole body committed to his charge. This is particularly vital when the corporate nature of mission and ministry has to be worked out in a multi-parish situation, where the priest cannot feasibly be present in all parishes at all times.

8.19. The role of the priest in relation to the parish is:

(1) To be aware of the full breadth of the mission of the Church in its priestly, pastoral and prophetic aspects.

(2) To share in this vision with the corporate body of the people of God in the parish, coming together in worship.

(3) To focus with others on what can and should be done in ministry, using the gifts of all members of the body.

8.20. In practical terms, this points to guiding and enabling people to minister within the broad vision of mission, without falling into the trap of feeling responsible for doing everything themselves. A large part of the priest's task will be reaffirming the vision and helping others to focus on it.

Anthony Russell analyses the new job in *The Country Parish* (pp. 270ff.). He identifies four roles:

(1) Local ministry is not going to happen anywhere unless stipendiaries have themselves seen 'the vision' and can communicate their insight to the congregation. It will be the stipendiaries who together with diocesan advisers work out how to put 'the vision' into practice, and who take an essential part in the process of training.

(2) Having set clear goals for their parishes, it will be the responsibilty of stipendiaries to see that the enthusiasm and energy of the group are 'directed aright', and that in the excitement of doing things together they do not lose sight of where they are going.

(3) They are the theologians for that parish, they are in daily touch with the wider catholic church, it is their vocation and profession to pray, and it is part of their work to study the Word of God so that their ministry can be not only pastoral but also prophetic.

(4) In the tight sociological context of the village they have to free lay people to take on responsibility, by themselves taking full public responsibility if things go wrong.

HOLY

To begin to fulfil this new role, stipendiaries will first need to be 'holy'. It is difficult to see how the job can be done unless they have a regular prayer time, a regular time for study, a regular time each year for spiritual refreshment, and unless the advice of a 'spiritual director' in some shape or form is readily available.

Traditional holiness is described in *A Priest to the Temple* by George Herbert as a devotion to prayer and the study of the Bible, an awareness of the awesomeness of worship, a compassion for all, and a zeal for souls. In *Original Blessing*, Matthew Fox identifies another aspect of holiness. The holy person is, he says, one not 'perfect', but mature, adult and fulfilled:

> In nature imperfection is not a sign of the absence of God. It is a sign that the ongoing creation is no easy thing. We all bear scars from this rugged process. We can – and must – celebrate the scars. (p. 111)

Another sign of holiness is 'hospitality' as God shows 'hospitality', who is host and guest and the banquet all in one.

LEARNED

Stipendiaries will need to be 'people of God' not just because that is the only way they will survive, but also because they will be the 'theological resource people' for the team. A frequent regret of stipendiaries is that their hard-earned skills in theology are rarely used. As noted in Chapter 10, the stipendiary is called on to play an extremely important part in the training of the local group. This is bound to continue, because it is as people begin to minister that theological questions come alive. Respondents to the Salisbury Consultation believed that 'the role of the clergy is to reflect theologically upon the raw material of life and to facilitate growth in spiritual awareness'. Mark Birchall visited collaborative ministries all over the country, and he tells us in *The Gospel Community* that wherever there is collaborative ministry the theological skills of the stipendiary are in constant demand. The Methodist Church in Singapore includes in its ordination service the following charge, which seems particularly apt as a description of the theological role of the rural stipendiary who is to lead a local ministry group.

Called to something smaller

We are not ordaining you to ministry; that happened at your baptism.

We are not ordaining you to be a caring person; you are already called to that.

We are not ordaining you to serve the Church in committees, activities, organisation; that is already implied in your membership.

We are not ordaining you to become involved in social issues, ecology, race, politics, revolution, for that is laid upon every Christian.

We are ordaining you to something smaller and less spectacular:

to read and interpret those sacred stories of our community, so that they speak a word to people today; to remember and practise those rituals and rights of meaning that in their poetry address man at the level where change operates; to foster in community through word and sacrament that encounter with truth which will set men and women free to minister as the body of Christ.

We are ordaining you to the ministry of the word and sacraments and pastoral care.

God grant you grace not to betray but uphold it, not to deny but affirm it, through Jesus Christ our Lord.

LOCAL

Tim Biles of the Beaminster team concluded his charge to the parishes in 1989:

[By the year 2000] the Rector will have made peace with the environment and will have no car. He will walk everywhere, meeting the people and hearing their story as he journeys. Freed from correspondence, administration, finances and buildings he will walk in the villages daily, the one who knows and is known.

He will be like the 'Bishop-in-little' of Donaldson's *The New Springtime of the Church* who 'walks about the central town as a citizen, and people will know him and feel free to talk with him as their known and familiar pastor'.

This beatific vision of the future envisages a stipendiary who is not only 'apostolic' but also 'local', for in one sense the stipendiary remains 'our rector'. *Church and Religion in Rural England* stresses the enormous importance of the vicar whom everyone wants and everyone wants to know and this is endorsed by the Salisbury Diocese Consultation: 'There is a clear desire for clergy and people to belong to each other, and to have time for a deeper relationship to develop. We need continuity of clergy.' Certainly from the point of view of developing local ministry, stipendiaries who are known and loved and trusted have the great advantage that they will have personal influence with the congregation. If incumbents not only love the parishes and people, but also believe with all their heart that God wants local ministry to develop, local ministry will almost certainly happen.

New strategies for keeping in touch will have to be devised because benefices are so much larger, but it is to be hoped that the stipendiary will find it easier to know and be known just because the weight of pastoral responsibility is shared with the rest of the group. In a submission to Acora, the Bishop of Stafford pointed out that many rural clergy do find it possible to keep in touch with their parishioners by such means as delivering a Christmas and/or Easter card to every house, visiting in each village on a regular basis, saying the weekday office in different villages on different days, and so on; and it is interesting that the Beaminster team have the intention that 'one of the priests will regularly spend several days at a time in each of the villages in turn'.

APOSTOLIC

The 'local' stipendiary must also be 'the person from outside', for it is the stipendiary who represents the 'catholicity' of the Church in the local context. Jonathan Thacker, interviewed in Stewart's *Parson to Parson*, views leadership as very much his role as vicar.

He is very aware of the peculiarities that have developed in all denominations when the locals have been left to get on with it, and so he would not be happy with a purely local leadership. He thinks that there must be a strong link between the individual church and the wider church and that is the vicar's job. (p. 58)

Robert Van der Weyer, who argues strongly for this role for the rural incumbent, puts it slightly differently. He quotes a PCC chairman as saying: 'Within the parish we can care for each other . . . but we look to you as the outsider who can help our mutual ministry.'

He continues:

The ministry of the incumbent depends on his being an outsider, sent by and responsible to the Bishop. In the proper sense of the word the incumbent is an apostle – an ambassador – who is outside the complex web of the rural community . . . and for this reason he can exercise a vital prophetic and pastoral ministry. (*Church Times*, 10 February 1991)

PROFILE OF THE RURAL CLERGY

Rural parishes thus need stipendiaries who are 'visionary', 'inspirational leaders', 'holy', 'local' and yet 'from outside'. Are the rural clergy in office today likely to respond to the challenge? There is important material on the rural clergy in *Church and Religion in Rural England*, chapters 4 and 6. The rural parishes in the five dioceses surveyed have a higher proportion of older clergy, a significant number of whom were late entrants to the ministry and came via a training course rather than college. Some 20 per cent of rural clergy in totally rural benefices in the five dioceses were ordained after the age of 40 compared to 5 per cent in urban benefices; and while 90 per cent of all respondents were college trained, in totally rural benefices the figure drops to 84 per cent. In totally rural benefices 25 per cent of the clergy are aged over 60 compared to 15 per cent in urban areas. Interestingly, the figure is even higher for small country towns, but 'partly rural' incumbents have much the same age profile as suburban incumbents. (This corresponds with the findings of Cope's 'The role of the laity in the rural Church', where the deanery of 'Dalesmoor' has a higher clergy age profile than 'Croppington' deanery.) In suburban benefices, 29 per cent of clergy are 'Evangelical', but only 1 per cent in rural benefices, while 29 per cent of suburban incumbents are 'central' compared to 40 per cent in rural benefices.

THEIR ATTITUDE TO LAY MINISTRY

As was noted in Chapter 9, when the clergy were asked in the general questionnaire about the importance of developing lay ministry in their own parishes, 59 per cent said it was vital or very important with no qualification; and although many of the others had reservations which they took the trouble to record in some detail, only 4 per cent said it was unimportant. There are variations, for while Evangelicals welcomed the idea with open arms (80 per cent), Catholics have more reservations (50 per cent); and the bigger and the more suburban the parish, the more likely the incumbent is to approve of lay ministry unreservedly. What the responses show conclusively is that the *idea* that 'lay ministry is a good thing' has got firmly into the consciousness of Anglican clergy, a fact confirmed by all the other surveys so far referred to. However, not everyone means the same thing by 'lay ministry'. From the general questionnaire answers recorded in detail (*Rural Church Project*, vol. 3, pp. 60–6), it is clear that some clergy mean full-scale collaborative ministry: 'I have five lay pastors, each of whom shares in the whole ministry'; while others see lay ministry as giving the vicar a hand: 'all these aspects of lay ministry are supplements to the ordained ministry and not substitutes for it'. When the rural clergy sample were asked about lay ministry, some concentrated on what was involved, some on who was involved, and some on the relationship of lay ministry to the role of the clergy.

To try to get behind what attitudes to lay ministry might mean in practice, the rural clergy sample were also asked 'what particular attribute they possessed as a priest which non-ordained people lacked'. As many as 23 per cent said they believed there was no essential difference, while 19 per cent instanced their training, and 16 per cent the authority of the Church and bishop. Only 9 per cent mentioned the eucharistic role, and only 7 per cent the grace of orders. These responses suggest that many stipendiaries may at a deep level be very unsure about their role, and it certainly suggests why there are differing views about lay ministry.

The clergy questioned seemed more at home when asked about the 'new' ministry they knew from personal experience. Most of them had worked with non-stipendiary ministers and Readers, and though approximately 40 per cent thought there were some problems about those forms of ministry, only 8 per cent thought they were 'a bad thing'. When it came to their views on *local* non-stipendiary ministers, fewer had personal experience, and while 44 per cent were in favour, 32 per cent were (theoretically) against it.

If this evidence seems perplexing it is because attitudes to lay ministry among the clergy are undoubtedly changing. The evidence suggests that the battle for the *minds* of the clergy has been more or less won, and it can be assumed that at least 50 per cent of them are likely to be enthusiastic about 'lay ministry' because they are convinced that it is vital for the future of the rural Church – but the evidence also suggests that the battle for their *hearts* is only just beginning. Many have major reservations about full-scale collaborative ministry on theological grounds – because of their churchmanship; on practical grounds – because they have had bad experiences of lay ministry themselves; and on personal grounds – because they are unsure whether they have the stamina and the temperament to cope with the challenge.

CAN THEY COPE TEMPERAMENTALLY?

The last section asked whether the rural clergy themselves are likely to want to develop local ministry. This section turns the question round and asks whether the job is likely to be too great a burden for them: or, to put it bluntly, it asks whether they are up to it. One approach to this question is to consider the age profile of the rural clergy and to ask what the implications of this are for local ministry.

The relevance of the age of the rural clergy

It is unfortunate that the Rural Church Project did not explore the significance of the age variable in relation to lay ministry, for, as we have seen, extreme rural benefices and market towns have significantly older clergy than other benefices. Leslie Francis, in *Rural Anglicanism* and with David Lankshear in 'Ageing clergy and the rural church', argues that clergy aged 60 or over tend to have contact with a smaller number of active church members – as indicated by attendance on a normal Sunday – than younger clergy working within comparable parishes; but they maintain contact with the same number of nominal church members, as indicated by the electoral roll and festival communicants. They suggest that the older rural clergy, judged by the above criteria, are likely to be less 'effective' than younger ones.

On the other hand, there is a growing body of research in the USA which suggests that older clergy are better than younger clergy when it comes to relating to people and working collaboratively (Carroll *et al.*, 1983). Coming at it from this angle, the *Rural Church Project* (vol. 2, p. 112) shows that those clergy over the age of 40 feel they have fewer problems connected with lay involvement than their younger colleagues and this may be a significant factor. Bearing in mind that a large number of rural clergy were ordained after the age of 40 (and therefore have previous work experience), it would be valuable to know whether their responses on lay ministry support the idea that older rural clergy might be particularly suited to the challenge of setting up local ministry groups; it is hoped that further research might throw light on the age factor in relation to this aspect of rural ministry.

The relevance of temperament

Another way into this issue is to ask whether individual clergy are suited to working in teams by (natural) temperament. This is a very important question which is *mentioned* in all the literature, but only to be skated over and left to pious exhortation. It is therefore worth noting that research in this area has been carried out and personality characteristics can be tested if people are prepared to face the consequences. In 1990 Leslie Francis delivered a paper, 'The personality characteristics of Anglican ordinands', published in *Personality and Individual Differences* (1991), which sets out the literature on the subject and 'explores the relationship between religion and the Eysenckian account of personality'. Literature on the Myers–Briggs Type Indicator is now becoming available in this country and, though this 'test' has less support from professionals than the Eysenckian one, it has been used extensively in American churches. Professional psychologists would of course argue that the purpose of such tests is not to determine appointments, but to enable clergy (and others) to know themselves better and so help them to face up to the particular challenges that teamwork might involve for them as individuals.

Clergy stress

A related topic which has been more openly discussed over the last few years has been 'clergy stress', and unpublished studies have shown that a number of rural clergy find running a multi-parish benefice 'stressful'. In asking clergy to add yet another challenging job to the one they already have, are we asking too much of them? In a paper delivered in September 1990, 'Stress and the parochial clergy', Ben Fletcher of Hatfield Polytechnic (now the University of Hertfordshire) gave an overview of the literature on the subject. He described his own research of 1988 which involved sending a detailed questionnaire to a random sample of 372 Anglican clergy. He discovered that clergy worked long hours, were frequently 'rushed off their feet', '60% had had the feeling that they could not cope with the thought of a life spent in the parochial ministry', and 'job demands and job disillusionment seemed to play a role in depression and general anxiety'. Nevertheless, by objective measures of strain, very few clergy indeed were in the danger zone. 'It seems that parochial clergy are being stretched in a demanding job, but not one which is overtaxing the vast majority.' In answer to questions, Fletcher said that he believed they were in much better shape than most professionals, and he attributed this to the very high level of job satisfaction that they experience.

Problems perceived

This is good news, but it remains true that if a number of rural clergy do feel that their job is stressful, it is unlikely that they will be willing to take on extra work. It is illuminating to see what they see as the 'problems' and 'rewards' of their job in relation to the record of how they actually spend their time. The problems are contained in *Rural Church Project*, vol. 2, pp. 84–112, particularly pp. 88–106; rewards, pp. 62–84, particularly pp. 66–73; success and failures in present parish, pp. 113–17; which together make fascinating and moving reading. The allocation of time formed the core of the questionnaire sent to all incumbents in the five dioceses.

The areas of concern noted by clergy both in the Rural Church Project and in evidence to the Commissioners are familiar:

(1) The weight of administration.

(2) Buildings and finance.
(3) The Sunday morning 'rush around'.
(4) Trying to fulfil all the expectations in a group of villages.
(5) A failure with youth, children and young families.
(6) The feeling that those who run the diocese (and also the urban clergy) do not understand how different and demanding the rural job is.

What the general questionnaire shows is that in fact a number of these concerns are groundless. In an average 56-hour week, clergy spend 19 per cent of their time on administration *and* fundraising, 29 per cent on pastoral work, and 12 per cent on private study and devotion. What is even more remarkable is that the variations between rural clergy and urban clergy *on allocation of their time* is minimal. Furthermore, on average rural clergy take less time conducting services on a Sunday than their market town and suburban colleagues, though the editors argue that 'there is a world of difference beween conducting three services in one place and attending three or four different churches' (pp. 82–3). These findings partly confirm those of Francis and Lankshear in 'The rural factor: a comparative survey of village churches and the liturgical work of rural clergy in the diocese of Chelmsford', which shows that although rural clergy have to take more services than their urban colleagues on a Sunday, they have fewer services to take on weekdays – and thus their liturgical work load is more or less similar. The evidence does not of course prove that the rural clergy are making a fuss about nothing, nor does it prove that rural ministry does not have its particular problems, but it does offer some objective facts to set beside emotionally charged 'hunches'.

Rewards enjoyed

If we come on to the 'rewards' and 'successes' experienced by the rural clergy, we find first that everyone questioned regarded at least part of the job as rewarding. A distinction is commonly drawn between 'instrumental' satisfaction (to do with financial rewards or satisfaction from being in control of the work process) and 'expressive' satisfaction (to do with non-pecuniary benefits resulting from the intrinsic nature and worth of the job). Most workers combine the two categories, but for clergy it is entirely a matter of 'expressive' satisfaction; none, for instance, identified administration or organization as a source of satisfaction. This remarkable response is worth remembering when listening to discussions in clergy chapters, and it indicates once again the positive potential resource that the rural stipendiary clergy represent for the Church. The editors found it difficult to categorize the 'reward' responses, but there are two areas of satisfaction which seem to stand out: first, pastoral work (43 per cent), and second, 'getting the church going better' (24 per cent):

'The steady care of all within the parishes.'

'No matter how crazy it all is the people are quite inexplicably well disposed towards Church and rector, and one feels very loved.'

'Participating in a close-knit community.'

'Helping people struggle on in the Christian way of life.'

'Signs of spiritual growth, a return of hope, the grasping of vision.'

'Development of Lay Ministry.'

'Seeing a parish which for many years has thought small beginning to think big, and awakened from sleep.'

'Having a number of people in both parishes with whom I can be quite open and honest, and who love me and I them.'

Conclusion

This section began by asking whether the rural clergy are up to the 'new' job. Awkward questions have not been avoided, nor have they been dismissed as groundless. Nevertheless, the final picture is essentially optimistic. The fact that the rural clergy are older than their urban colleagues could be an advantage, and if they lack confidence in their own ability professional advice is widely available. They may *feel* under stress, but actually most of them are in good psychological shape. Above all, they love their job; and though this could be a problem, because they are being asked to convert from one model to another, it could be argued that local ministry is tailor-made to help with what they consider to be 'problems', and to offer them the chance to concentrate on doing precisely what they find most 'rewarding'. It will be up to the diocese to identify stipendiaries to set up local ministry, to persuade them, to encourage them, to train them and to support them. The evidence suggests that there should be no lack of suitable candidates.

POSTSCRIPT

There is still a job to be done

Some enthusiastic advocates of lay ministry in the last few years have tended to give the impression that the chief problem with the Anglican Church is the stipendiary clergy, and that when they are removed from the scene congregations will rise to the challenge and mission will once again flourish. The fact that this sort of thinking has infected the clergy is highlighted by the finding of the Rural Church Project that half the rural clergy saw little difference between the clergy and the laity and would not encourage others to enter the stipendiary ministry. In such an atmosphere, it is hardly surprising that vocations have declined.

The argument of this chapter has been that, on the contrary, the job of the stipendiary in rural areas is as vital and challenging as it ever was. This particular ministry will be to call out and establish local ministry, and to maintain that ministry once it is established. The job description has certainly changed, but no one is sending out redundancy notices.

On the other hand, the role of rural stipendiaries must change and, although they must be 'local' enough to be known, from now on they are essentially to be the 'apostolic' priest of the area. It is precisely this realignment of roles, which seems to deprive stipendiaries of their 'local' birthright, which troubles many clergy. Though their head embraces the new challenge, their heart hankers after the old familiar pattern which no doubt first inspired their own vocation. It may be helpful here if I lapse into biography.

Autobiographical

Back in the 1970s, I was asked to speak in the USA about my ministry in the Northampton village of Byfield. I told them how I was on the parish council, the board of school governors, the village hall committee, and the executive of the (not yet Royal) British Legion. I told them how our rectory (seventeenth-century) was used by the local playgroup and our three-acre garden let out as the village allotments. I told them of the Byfield village fête and exhibition, when church and rectory provided the setting for what would now be called a village open day. I told them of our local ecumenical agreement, which was to all intents an LEP before its time. I no doubt gave the impression that nothing moved in Byfield without my knowing it and without my support – an exaggeration may be, but not without a grain of truth! Afterwards a senior Episcopalian commented: 'Son, you're a lucky fellow: what wouldn't I have given to have the chance to exercise a ministry like that.' I must admit that I hadn't seen it in quite that light before, but in retrospect of course he was right: it was a *great* privilege. But I was the last to enjoy the privilege. The present rector of Byfield lives in a sensible modern rectory and, in addition to Byfield, is responsible for Upper Boddington, Lower Boddington and Aston-le-Walls.

Besides being Rural Adviser to the diocese, I am now rector of three Gloucestershire parishes which cover seven separate settlements with five churches and a chapel. I cannot be on any of the three parish councils because I have to spread myself evenly over the area. There are two small schools, both of which would welcome me as chairman of the governors, except that such a demanding job is way beyond the bounds of reasonable possibility. There are no fewer than eight pubs, which makes it difficult to carry out sustained pastoral work in 'the local'; and the five village halls, all built through clerical inspiration and energy, now all have to survive without the benefit of clergy. Mercifully, there are only two cricket teams, one WI, one gardening club and no football team; but inevitably all three parishes manage to fix their jumble sales or 'Friends of the School barn dances' on the same date, and it is only by dictatorial edict that I ensure that harvest festivals and carol services do not clash. Thanks to my wife, I just about keep abreast of the social goings-on in Coates where we live, but I visit Culkerton (population 60) briefly perhaps once a month, and Hazleton (population 20) once a quarter. Since the total population of all the parishes together is only a little over 1,000, the diocese is unlikely to suggest giving me a stipendiary curate, and yet it will never be possible for me to do a 'Byfield' in any of these parishes. A visiting anthropologist would undoubtedly conclude that the effective priest of Sapperton is the verger Frank Cook, and the priestess of Culkerton is the lovely lady who runs the chapel, Hazel Boulton.

It would be foolish to pretend that I have found the transition from parish to multi-parish easy, but I do now find this job exhilarating and affirming. The fears that loss of glebe and loss of freehold would reduce my independence and ability to take an unpopular stance on a local issue seem irrelevant to a situation where the parishes are desperate to keep a stipendiary, and where the diocese is keen to maintain any stipendiary who is willing to plan coherently for the future. Undoubtedly, one of the attractions of Byfield was that it was my own empire – and it took some time to get used to the idea that if anything was going to happen in seven villages, I would have to appoint vice-regents. Nevertheless, everyone still looks on this as 'my empire' and, though autocratic government is no longer possible (even if I wished to work that way), my influence as professional and stipendiary is in practice paramount. The greatest loss is undoubtedly the ability to know everyone well, and to play a leading part in community life. Nevertheless, by judicious attendance at large social events, by targeting newcomers for personal visits, and by regular annual delivery of Christmas and Easter cards to every house, I can keep some sort of tabs on the area and 'be known' – even if I do not altogether 'know'. I also discover that there is a need for someone who can relate to district and county authorities, so that if I cannot be on the various parish councils I can at least be useful to them when they need contacts. The benefice, comprising as it does parts of five civil parishes, ensures that my concern can never be exclusively parochial – and that too is often valuable.

Rural clergy often used to complain that their theological training never seemed to be put into practice. I find the reverse. If our parishes are to plan for the future, as opposed to just 'carrying on somehow', I need to convince a number of key lay people that there is an alternative strategy which requires their involvement. This has led not to my giving a series of lectures on evangelistic theory, but to meetings where lay people have begun to understand life theologically for the first time, and to interviews when I have been able to help them plan a regular prayer life for the first time. More and more I find that one of my most important jobs is to identify those individuals who will be future leaders and to help them to test their vocation.

A number of talented teachers who become head teachers bewail the fact that they no longer have time to teach in the classroom: a sentiment endorsed by many other professionals promoted to positions of leadership – including bishops! So too a number of clergy will bewail a change which tends to take them away from the 'coalface'. What I want to urge is that in my experience the new job can have its own very considerable rewards, not least the knowledge that in the multi-parish benefice we are in a pioneering ministry where there are no set strategies, no easy answers, and where everything therefore depends on God – and God through us. I remember vividly the weight of exhaustion and disillusion and bewilderment of the rural clergy conferences of the early 1970s. The courses for multi-parish clergy today are not like that: they are by and large vibrant, cheerful and purposeful, and indicate as powerfully as any amount of statistical evidence that the new system can be both rewarding and fun.

13

Diocese and Deanery

'The vision' suggests that, without diocesan support, local ministry will not happen; and in this chapter an outline is given of the particular jobs that the diocese needs to do. Every diocese needs a rural strategy, a framework within which parishes can develop their own version of local ministry. The stipendiary will need support and will need to be trained for rural ministry. The diocese will also need to support and train lay people. Finally, there is a section in this chapter on the antagonism that so often exists between diocese and village, and a discussion of how relationships might be mended. There is a final section on the relevance of the deanery to local ministry.

THE NEED FOR A RURAL STRATEGY

If the stipendiary is vital for the development of local ministry groups, so is the diocese. If the diocese is to play its part effectively, it must first hammer out a rural strategy in which both the bishop and his colleagues believe. What has too often happened in the past is that the multi-parish has been commended as a temporary measure which could be reversed if only there were enough clergy (and yet when by some miracle the village produced its own ordinand, he or she was promptly sent to work in the inner city). Alternatively, the multi-parish solution has been sold as a pastoral second-best, with no real attempt to link legal pastoral reorganization with the introduction of collaborative ministry.

Local congregations will look to the diocese for a range of policy decisions and practical guidelines. The most important will be a clear policy on the deployment of stipendiary clergy in rural areas; and guidance on what the overall aim of the stipendiary clergy should be. Congregations will also want to have simple practical suggestions as to how local ministry groups can come into being. There is in most dioceses an urgent need for guidance about how small congregations can become ecumenical – or 'Christian'; and there also needs to be advice on how 'God is to be worshipped in every settlement every Sunday'.

It does now seem that more and more dioceses are trying to develop strategies, and Coventry, Salisbury, Gloucester, Lincoln and Winchester have all produced policy discussion papers. There emerge from them a variety of approaches. Some put the stipendiary at the centre of the scene and are in essence schemes for spreading stipendiaries ever more thinly over the diocese, bolstered by NSMs, Readers and laity who will take on some of the jobs. In a sense they are a continuation of the pastoral reorganization strategies put together in the wake of the Sheffield Report. A number of dioceses have already invested heavily in one or more forms of ministry and are loath to take on yet another experiment with the attendant training and administrative staff involved. Lichfield, for instance, has chosen to develop local ministry under the umbrella of Reader training: while Oxford, with 130 NSMs in post, is anxious to ensure that these are not 'downgraded' by the introduction of a Lincoln-type scheme.

Other consultation papers start from the settlement and ask what ministry is needed there. Not surprisingly, these documents recommend that there needs to be a radical change of emphasis and that the diocese must concentrate on establishing local ministry groups. This latter approach is the heir to the radical strategies put in place in the Norwich and Salisbury dioceses during the 1960s and 1970s. All of the documents have about them an air of discovery and excitement, but few suggest that the authors are aware that other people in other dioceses are doing the same thing. It is hoped that this book may help to facilitate the sharing of experiences so that the wheel is not too often reinvented.

Having produced policy and guidelines, it will be the job of local people to give them 'local flesh'. It will however be the continuing job of the diocese, exercised especially through its local representative the stipendiary, to encourage the setting of local aims and objectives and to ensure that these are kept before local eyes.

So the first job of the diocese is to weigh the evidence, decide on a strategy, make sure it is expressed clearly and understandably, and then present it to clergy and laity.

SUPPORTING STIPENDIARIES

If stipendiaries are to be 'apostolic priests' or 'the diocesan representatives', they will need to have colleagues who are also stipendiaries with whom they can talk frankly. This has been the great strength of formal group and team ministry where it has worked well; but, as was suggested in Chapter 9, this form of ministry is unlikely to develop much further in the rural areas. Partly because of this, a number of dioceses are taking very seriously the role of the deanery chapter in this respect (*Faith in the Countryside* notes evidence received from Ripon and Liverpool dioceses). *Church and Religion in Rural England* (p. 195) records that 31 per cent of clergy felt that the deanery was important and that by far the most valuable thing it did was to 'enable support and fellowship among the constituent clergy'. Other organizations which some rural clergy have found to serve a similar function are local Rural Theology Association groups and clerical societies.

Nevertheless, if stipendiaries are to 'represent the international face of the Church' and to implement a diocesan strategy, the diocese must also provide direct advice and support for the job. It would be unthinkable for a commercial firm to leave a paid representative in post without head office requiring regular reports and making regular visits. Some clergy still cling to the theory that the diocese should not interfere except in emergency, but far more stipendiaries told the Commissioners that they want the diocese to take some notice of what they were doing. In *Parson to Parson*, Stewart writes of Nicholas (a first incumbent):

> no one asks him to write a report as he had to when he was a university chaplain. . . . He would like someone to talk to about his job, and to ask their advice. This sort of thing would be a good role for a diocesan rural official.

Faith in the Countryside quotes with approval the diocese of Truro, which has set up a triennial visit to each parish in the diocese by one of the bishops; and since the publication of the report most dioceses have instituted consultancy and review systems for clergy. The book *Holding in Trust* by Michael Jacobs has helped clergy to see that the process of assessment is not so much interference from the centre as a way of helping them to have a coherent ministry.

THE TRAINING OF STIPENDIARIES

A major responsibility of the diocese is the training of stipendiaries for rural ministry. *Faith in the Countryside* devoted no less than seven pages to the need for such training. There were a number of recommendations directed to theological colleges and institutes, but the main message was for dioceses. Specific training for rural ministry was, it believed, the clear responsibility of the diocese, a responsibility which, at least in 1990, every diocese in England seemed to ignore. The truth of this was confirmed by *Church and Religion in Rural England* (pp. 69ff.):

> The postal survey respondents were asked to furnish details of up to four previous ministerial appointments. . . . It showed that nearly a third of clergy currently working in rural benefices had had no previous rural experience. . . . By contrast 86% of all clergy had had some urban experience compared to 57% who had had rural experience. Urban clergy would appear to be considerably better prepared for their current posts than rural clergy – nearly all had prior urban experience.

This reinforces a survey done in Glouceser diocese in 1986 of 21 incumbents who had recently moved to rural benefices. No less than one-third had never slept in a village before the night on which they moved to their first rural incumbency. Some 98 per cent felt that they had not received appropriate training for their present job.

The reason for making the diocese responsible for rural training is as follows. Theological courses have a responsibility to introduce all students to collaborative ministry, and in all probability they will also expose students to inner-city ministry in the course of pastoral training: but it is the responsibility of the training diocese to train priests for practical ministry. However, since all but a handful of training parishes are urban or suburban, there is a strong chance that by the time a stipendiary finishes post-ordination training he or she will still not have had any experience of rural ministry. Some dioceses argue that if they are to train all curates for rural ministry they should also train them for hospital chaplaincy, prison chaplaincy, the armed services, etc. This ignores both the fact that these other agencies always give chaplains extensive specialist training before they take up posts, and also the relatively small number of chaplaincy jobs available (approx. 1,500 in all forms of chaplaincy as compared to approx. 3,700 in rural ministry – *Church Statistics 1991*). If there are very roughly three forms of parochial ministry, urban, suburban and rural, stipendiaries should have some experience of all three by the time they end their training. The argument of *Faith in the Countryside* is that it is the responsibility of the training diocese to see that they do so, and that this can be very simply achieved by a system of placements in selected parishes.

Continuing Ministerial Education

Nor does the responsibility of the diocese end there. Continuing Ministerial Education (CME) needs to include preparation for and induction into new fields of work, including rural ministry. Up till now the dearth in induction courses in rural ministry has been filled by the Arthur Rank centre which runs two such courses a year. These are valuable, and are now being supplemented by follow-up days. Some dioceses, among them Canterbury, Rochester, Southall, Truro and Lincoln, have developed rural induction courses and the Rural Theology Association and other groups also run courses in rural ministry. However, it is evident that even now fewer than 20 per cent of those taking over rural benefices for the first time actually get any induction training. One of the more imaginative initiatives in this area has been taken by St Edmundsbury and Ipswich in appointing an experienced rural clergyman to offer his services as adviser or visitor to stipendiaries taking over rural benefices. Ideally, a prospective rural incumbent (who has had no previous rural experience) needs a short (a week?) placement before induction, a course on rural ministry six months after his induction, and an experienced adviser whom he or she can call on when in need. At the moment no diocese offers this, let alone insists upon it.

THE DIOCESE AND MEMBERS OF THE GROUP

The role of the diocese in the training of lay ministry was outlined in Chapter 10. Training for local ministry must be done by the diocese, since this is the only way in which such ministry can be accorded the status needed if it is to be effective. As was shown, the diocese has an essential part to play in the setting up of local ministry and it does this by authorizing parishes, training the group and providing continuing ministerial training for them. In one sense the diocese provides continuing support for the group via its local representative, the stipendiary – but obviously diocesan staff will need to form personal relationships with members of the group just as they do with churchwardens. This personal support becomes particularly important during an interregnum and during holiday periods, and when the licence of the group comes up for renewal (at the end of three years). The diocesan office and the deanery secretary need to be aware of the sensitivities of the situation so that information is passed to the right person and gets properly distributed.

THE DIOCESAN STRATEGIC RESERVE

The idea of a 'strategic reserve' for use in small run-down parishes (mentioned in Chapter 5) is indeed a 'visionary' ideal. The case for such an experiment is well made in various books, including *Reform of the Ministry: A Study of the Works of Roland Allen* by David Paton.

Reference was made in Chapter 11 to the use of a 'strategic reserve' in the American Episcopal Church which is recorded in Mathieson's *Delectable Mountains: The Story of the Washington County Mission Program*. Three neighbouring parishes had failed to pay their way for many years and were given notice by the diocese that they would have to close. After consultation, the bishop decided instead to second a full-time stipendiary to work with the parishes for a limited period of two years. His job was to prepare three local non-stipendiary ministry groups to take over the running of the parishes, and he used a system not unlike that now commended in the Lincoln scheme. An English group visited the parishes a year after the stipendiary had been withdrawn and, though there were some problems, the congregations as a whole were alive and flourishing.

It should of course be noted that the parishes had been threatened with closure and *the diocese meant it*. A number of rural stipendiaries have found that the threat to close a village church can have an electrifying effect on church life, and it is difficult to see how a diocesan reserve could operate effectively unless the diocese was prepared to close down those parishes which failed to respond. This is obviously a very difficult policy decision, though total closure might be mitigated by putting a building into mothballs in the hope that newcomers might bring a change of attitude. Granted that the English church has minimal experience of operating such a 'strategic reserve', its proved value in other parts of the world should perhaps suggest that a group of rural dioceses agree to set up such an experiment and monitor progress. It would at least be a positive initiative to offer to those rural parishes which are too depressed and tired to respond to the challenge of setting up a local ministry group themselves.

BRIDGING THE GULF BETWEEN DIOCESE AND VILLAGE

Faith in the Countryside believed that the first challenge for the diocese was to help rural parishes (and clergy) feel less isolated. The Commissioners were constantly told 'no one bothers about us', 'no one understands', 'no one listens when we do say anything'. They recommended that bishops engineered some way in which they could visit the rural parishes, and that diocesan officers overhauled their communications with rural areas. The Rural Church Project asked selected rural clergy about diocese, deanery and synodical government, and though half of them said that the diocese was helpful to them as individuals, a large number felt that the diocese, and particularly synodical government, seemed irrelevant to rural parishioners.

Various ways of bridging the gulf are currently used. The system of area bishops seems to work well in some dioceses. A number of bishops have carried out a 'walkabout' of the area, and two have circumnavigated the periphery of their dioceses. Diocesan officers have run open days for deaneries, and some diocesan secretaries have a policy of visiting every deanery once a year; and, as was noted in Chapter 8, some dioceses take special trouble to explain to small parishes the quota and its relation to the stipend. Yet still 'small villages with small congregations feel threatened and exposed and need encouragement and help' (Diocese of Salisbury, *Going with God – Together*, p. 25). Perhaps the most important thing is for the diocese to recognize how great the gulf is between the centre and the rural periphery, and why this should be so. It can then take the action which it thinks is most appropriate in that particular situation.

The problems of synodical government

Synodical government has perversely made matters worse rather than better by inserting the deanery between the parish and the diocese. As has been pointed out before, people tend to participate in local organizations and identify with big ones. Just as it is natural for people to play for Rodmarton Cricket Club and support the Gloucestershire county team, so it is natural for them to 'participate in' Rodmarton church and 'identify with' Gloucester diocese. Cirencester deanery may make sense to Cirencester parishioners, but it is not of natural concern to the parishioners of Rodmarton who shop in Tetbury. As a result, many rural parishes have a tradition of electing as their deanery synod representatives those PCC members who fail to turn up to the AGM, and the attempts of the diocese to force the deanery to allocate the quota are simply viewed by small rural parishes as further evidence of the determination of the centre to ignore the periphery.

The fact that neither the benefice nor the parish is automatically represented on the Diocesan Synod rubs salt into the wound. Seen through the eyes of rural parishioners, the sensible way to make important decisions is either to have a referendum of all on the electoral roll, or for each congregation (or perhaps benefice) to send a representative to a diocesan meeting. To discuss an issue in the parish study group, hear about it in a sermon, vote on it at the PCC, debate it at the deanery and then yet again at diocesan level, seems not only a gross waste of busy people's time, but is still ultimately felt to be unfair because the little parish is not directly represented at the decisive vote. It is of course unlikely that the Church will unscramble synodical government simply to suit small rural parishes, but the diocesan staff do need to appreciate what the system looks like through the front window of the village churchwarden.

In rural as opposed to suburban areas, the unit (apart from the parish) which does now have natural significance is not the deanery but the benefice; and one of the advantages of introducing local ministry in the way suggested is that it would both strengthen co-operation within the benefice and strengthen links between the benefice and the diocese. In this way the Church could, if it chose, move to a structure similar to that of the Methodists. Methodists 'participate' in their local congregation and in the life of the Circuit, while they 'identify' with the district. Both 'tiers of collaboration' make 'natural' sense. If the diocese abandons its attempts to work through the deanery and instead gets to know and relate to the key personnel in the benefice, there is some chance that mutual trust will revive.

Money, appointments and buildings

There are three major problem areas: money, appointments and buildings. The money problems were set out at length in Chapter 8; and the moral was drawn that with quotas increasing at twice the rate of inflation, it must be a priority for the diocesan staff to make personal contact with parish treasurers and churchwardens to explain why this should be so. It is surely likely that those dioceses which make a real effort to build a bridge of understanding about money between the centre and benefices are much more likely to weather the economic storm than those which go on in the old centralist way.

Recent legislation on appointing stipendiaries has ensured that local views are now heard, and in some multi-parish benefices the process is so cumbersome that it involves a disproportionate amount of diocesan staff time. A social anthropologist would no doubt suggest that the reason why rural PCCs are sometimes so choosy and awkward about appointments is a perfectly understandable reaction to their being given new rights which they are exercising for the first time. The obvious way through this difficult stage is for the diocese to build close personal relationships with the benefice *before* the interregnum. The form of local ministry we envisage could only help such a process, for if both the diocese and the parishes are committed to collaborative ministry both will be determined to appoint a stipendiary who will continue what a predecessor has begun.

The church building has a central place in village Christianity. It is a potent symbol of history, community and identity, and as such local people regard it as 'theirs' in a very special way. Clearly the diocese has to represent a wider vision, and has a duty to act as legal custodian of the national heritage as well as to give encouragement to locals; but once again, the closer the personal links between the diocese and the benefice the better. Parishes who want to beautify their church or to adapt it must be encouraged, not slapped down; and parishes must know that if they call in members of the advisory committee at an early stage the reaction will be positive. Similarly, parishes who try to be businesslike in raising funds for fabric maintenance (such as perpetual fabric fund trusts) need to be encouraged in their forward-looking initiative, not criticized from the standpoint of suburban stewardship principles – and certainly not taxed at supertax levels.

WHAT THEN OF THE DEANERY?

If in rural areas the two key tiers of organization are the diocese and the benefice, the diocese will need to put less emphasis on the deanery and give a greater priority to building up personal contacts in the benefices.

Nevertheless, the deanery can have a significant role in supporting local ministry. In particular, the deanery chapter is extremely important as a forum for stipendiaries to air their grievances and talk 'trade union shop' with their colleagues; for while it is no doubt important that 'local' ministers, such as Readers, LNSMs and retired clergy, join the chapter on a regular basis, at this stage of rural ministry the chapter essentially needs to be the meeting place for the 'apostolic' ministers. A number of dioceses are seeking to improve the pastoral care offered to the clergy by giving a special role to the rural dean. Norwich diocese envisages creating larger deaneries and making the new rural deans pastorally responsible for the clergy in the area.

The second function of the deanery is to relate to the local secular world at a district council level. It is a waste of the stipendiaries' valuable time if every incumbent makes and keeps alive personal contacts in every walk of life; but at a deanery level one stipendiary can relate to the district council, one to the local hospital, one to the comprehensive school, one to the community centre, one to the social services, one to the voluntary sector, one to local industry, and so on – all of which are likely to be centred on the local market town. Not all deaneries will be geographically homogeneous (and perhaps boundaries will need to be redrawn), nor will all sectors be covered, but such a role for the deanery would make common sense to most rural congregations.

Finally, there are times when benefices need to link with others to do together what they cannot do alone. The deanery can be a good unit for co-operation, as is well illustrated in P. Croft's *A Workbook for Deaneries* and in chapter 9 of *Desert Harvest* by Arthur Dodds, provided that it is not seen as a geographical strait-jacket. Co-operative ventures need to be planned by those benefices which feel the need for co-operation, rather than (as all too often happens) dreamed up by the deanery synod and imposed on benefices, with predictable results.

These are all valuable functions, but they do not constitute using the deanery as the basic unit of ministry. Those who would give to it any greater importance in rural areas still need to answer the arguments against the deanery as an effective unit put by Anthony Russell in 'The countryside and its church'. People naturally 'participate' in the local unit (the parish) and 'belong' to the area unit (the diocese), but intermediate units (the deanery) are neither one thing nor the other, and they therefore tend to 'atrophy'.

14

The Ecumenical Dimension

Chapter 5 suggests that every local group should, if possible, be ecumenical from the start. This chapter goes back a step and asks hard questions about the apparent 'collapse' of the chapel in many villages. The current involvement of the Free Churches in rural areas is surveyed, and evidence about ecumenical co-operation is examined. Examples are given of what the churches are already doing together; and the particular problems for ecumenism in those villages which have only one place of worship is examined in some detail.

THE DECLINE OF THE FREE CHURCHES IN RURAL AREAS

As was noted in Chapter 8, most rural Free Churches in this country have always been 'local ministry groups'. The fact that in recent years so many of them have closed their doors inevitably poses difficult questions. Does their failure mean that the whole concept of local ministry is flawed? And do they have anything useful to say to Anglicans who seem, on the face of it, to have kept the show on the road where the Free Churches have shut up shop? These are important questions and need to be answered honestly.

The decline of the Baptist Church in Wales was referred to in Chapter

8. Membership has fallen from 81,600 in 1950 to 26,465 in 1991, though it has to be remembered that 'when the Consolidated Budget was introduced churches immediately began to prune membership'. The number of ministers has fallen from 330 in 1950 and 161 in 1978 to 119 in 1991, of whom 22 are over the age of 65 and 22 others are non-stipendiary. In 1991 there were 557 churches, but the figures for earlier years are not available. None of these figures is broken down by 'rural-ity'. In 1970 the Methodist Church in Rural Life Committee published a report, *Country Pattern*, which began with a statistical section based on a survey of 2,477 rural societies. This revealed that between 1958 and 1968 only 18 of the 110 completely rural Circuits had shown an increase in membership: 'that circuits centred around a town of 3,000 or more population are holding their own, but most others are declining in membership'. There is no reference in the report to the number of chapels closed.

In England, membership figures for each denomination are available in Brierley's *Christian England*, but they also are not broken down by 'rurality'. The figures for numbers of ministers are available from the denominational handbooks. What is not available, though they must be retrievable from the records, are figures for the number of village chapels which have closed since 1945. Presumably, one must therefore accept provisionally the widespread perception that a great many village chapels have closed since the Second World War.

What went wrong?

Methodism has survived in many villages, and the other denominations in most market towns; but it would be foolish not to admit that all the Free Churches are very worried about the future of their small rural congregations and much of their 'rural' literature offers suggestions as to how small 'societies' can try to recoup numbers. What is perhaps lacking is a serious statistical and sociological analysis as to why the great days of expansion have given way to decline. Such analysis would help Anglicans to avoid the same mistakes, and some of the hypotheses that need testing are as follows.

Theology

No one could accuse most modern Free Church members of being exclusive and dismissive of the community model of the Church. Nevertheless, historically theirs is a demanding creed. The Methodist minister of Amberley, Gloucestershire, was asked what is distinctive about a Methodist. He replied: 'historically Methodists have put emphasis on four aspects of Christian theology:

All need to be saved
All can be saved
All can know they are saved
All can be saved to the uttermost.'

One can recognize at once how such a distinctiveness sits uneasily with 'village religion', and it suggests that part of the reason for the decline in village Non-conformity is that at heart its theology is 'associational'.

Political context

Rural Anglicanism has always been accused of being the Conservative Party at prayer, and we discover that the archetype of the rural clergyman, George Herbert, accepts without question a hierarchical society in which the good parson is part of the establishment: for instance, he shows 'courtesy' by entertaining the well-to-do at his table, but he shows 'courtesy' to the poor by giving them money, for they will no doubt appreciate that more! (*A Priest to the Temple*, chapter XI). By contrast, Non-conformity has strong links with Liberalism, and Methodism played an important part in the rise of the Labour movement. It would seem that in many cases chapels flourished in the hierarchical society of pre-1939 village life as either the church of the tradesmen or the working man's church, and became just as culturally 'fixed' as rural Anglicanism. That society has gone or is fast going, and in particular farming no longer dominates either villages or the rural labour market. As a result, the rural chapel now often finds itself 'a rebel without a cause'.

Worship

Anglicanism has now more or less broken the shackles which chained its worship to the Prayer Book, whereas the rural Free Churches are only just beginning to break the bonds of the inherited preaching service. In the 1960s when the gap between Church and secular culture became suddenly so apparent, the Free Churches – which had traditionally championed freedom of worship – seemed liturgically paralysed, and it was left to Anglicanism and Roman Catholicism to forge a new liturgical language.

From the rural perspective this was particularly important when it came to dealing with young children at services. Anglicans have developed family services which make use of the hymns and songs sung at assembly in the local school, while the chapel tradition (which may work in the suburbs, but is unworkable in villages) is to banish the children to Sunday school while the adults enjoy their 20-minute sermon. Furthermore, despite the power of the laity within the Free Churches to make decisions for themselves, they have traditionally left the conduct of the service to the preacher (even if he is not a local person). As a result, until recently many Free Church acts of worship seemed to ignore the local context almost entirely; while Anglican services, for all their formality, often had that inner spark of localism which made them relevant and human. This problem over worship has surely been one of the reasons why (urban) newcomers to villages have tended to gravitate to the parish church rather than to the chapel.

The need for a trusted stipendiary to make difficult decisions

We have already noted the significance of the two models of Free Church organization when it comes to making changes. Those Free Churches which have tackled the problems of inherited tradition are beginning to grow again. They tend to be the larger societies and many of them are in market towns where the minister is resident. Where a stipendiary with vision is resident, trusted and loved, changes can be made. The problem of the small village Cause remains for they also need someone who is trusted, loved and preferably resident if changes are to be made and closure averted. John Bradley, vice-chairman of the Rural Theology Association, and himself minister of a large rural Circuit in Devon, recognizes the problem, but with six such societies all needing his undivided attention he cannot see an immediate solution.

Conclusion

What the evidence seems to suggest is that the closure of the village chapel is at least in part a historical and cultural phenomenon. The moral to be learned is not that lay ministry is a blind alley, but that even locally rooted lay ministry must respond to change if the doors are to stay open.

THE RURAL FREE CHURCHES TODAY

Church and Religion in Rural England contains a section on ecumenical co-operation, and the table below gives a useful comparison of their religious allegiance statistics with those of other comparable surveys.

The denominational allegiance of parishioners surveyed is given in the following table.

RELIGIOUS ALLEGIANCE – COMPARISON OF DIFFERENT SURVEYS

| Religious allegiance | Rural Church Project | | Bible Society/ Gallup | | Forster (Hull) | |
	No.	%	Villages %	Cities %	No.	%
Church of England	212	62	68	59	160	77
Roman Catholic	19	6	9	16	19	9
Methodist	28	8			10	5
Baptists	3	1	} 12	} 7	2	1
United Reformed	2	1			3	2
Other denomination	15	5	6	9	1	0
Christianity	26	7	–	–	2	1
Other religions	2	1	–	–	1	0
Don't know	2	1	6	8	2	1
No allegiance	37	10	–	–	7	4
Total	341	100	101	99	207	100

Source: Davies, Watkins and Winter, *Church and Religion in Rural England*, p. 243, Table 52.

The figures of three separate surveys are shown and it can be seen that those relating to villages are relatively similar. The Hull survey asked a different question. Respondents were asked what denomination they declared on entering hospital, and this probably accounts for the higher Anglican rating.

Brierley's *Christian England* helps us to see the present situation in more general terms. The URC has approximately 1,800 congregations, and 28 per cent of them are located in settlements of less than 10,000 population. The Baptists have 770 churches in the countryside, but only 440 of these are outside the 'metropolitan shadow'. There are 618 'Independent' churches in rural areas, and 490 Roman Catholic churches. The Methodist Church has much the largest Free Church presence with 3,430 churches, many of them in villages of under 1,000 population.

Though there are no precise statistics on the size of settlements served it is generally accepted that, with the exception of the Methodist Church, most 'rural' chapels are in fact located in market towns or villages with a population over 2,000. It also needs to be recognized that denominational allegiance varies geographically. The Methodists are particularly strong in the North and in Cornwall, the Baptists in East Anglia and Devon, the URC in Northumberland, the Roman Catholics in the urban North and in rural Yorkshire and Lancashire.

In total, *Christian England* reports that there are approximately 5,700 Anglican churches in 'rural' areas as against approximately 5,000 churches/congregations of other denominations. This is a very different picture from that often painted, and it certainly calls in question the often voiced Anglican assumption that in the rural areas 'we alone are left'.

The Free Church contribution to the rural ministry debate

There are plenty of signs that the Free Churches are just as aware of the needs of rural ministry as the Anglicans, and are already contributing valuable insights to the rural debate. The Arthur Rank Centre is an ecumenical foundation. The Rural Theology Association has many Free Church members, and the Federation for Rural Evangelism has from the start been inter-denominational. Some of the most influential publications on rural ministry in recent years are ecumenical: I. Calvert's two *Workbooks in Rural Evangelism*, E. Bailey's *Workbook in Popular Religion*, the Baptist Church's *Half the Denomination*, J. Richardson's *Ten Rural Churches*, the Methodist Church's *Mission Alongside the Poor*, J. Salsbury's *And Is There Honey Still?* and now the magazine *Country Way*. At a national level rural issues are today dealt with ecumenically as a matter of course; and it seemed quite natural to those involved that among the Acora Commissioners were a Methodist, a Baptist, a Roman Catholic and a member of the URC.

All the Churches are concerned about how to maintain adequate ministry in rural areas; and co-operation between the churches in rural areas is increasingly a necessity rather than a luxury. The next section in this chapter describes what is already happening in a number of areas.

ECUMENICAL CO-OPERATION

Councils of churches

In 1945 the British Council of Churches report *The Land, the People and the Churches* found that ecumenical co-operation in villages was then very rare: 'Some of the clergy are getting to know each other, but this increased understanding is not passed on to the laity who are as aloof as ever.' Today, the reverse is true.

An important report gives a snapshot of what is happening at 'council of churches' level. In a survey of local councils of churches in England (*Churches in Fellowship* by Francis and Williams), the secretaries of councils of churches were asked questions about what they did and how effective they felt the influence of their council was.

In rural areas, all the councils include Anglican churches, 95 per cent include Methodist churches, and another 95 per cent included Roman Catholic churches. The URC with 69 per cent, the Baptists with 46 per cent, the Salvation Army with 37 per cent, and the Society of Friends with 37 per cent lead the rest. Some 88 per cent of the rural councils have ecumenical Lent Groups, 89 per cent collect for Christian Aid, and 67 per cent have ecumenical services apart from those during the Week of Prayer for Christian Unity. Some 68 per cent of the rural secretaries believed that the work of their council had increased during the last five years, and 81 per cent said that both Anglicans and Free Church people in their area were interested in ecumenical activity.

Churches in Fellowship shows that on almost every count rural councils of churches are more active, more confident, and give greater job satisfaction than their equivalents in the towns. *Church and Religion in Rural England* corroborates this evidence in so far as it shows that by every criterion (except, interestingly, that of clergy fraternals) the small country town scores high in comparison with all other parishes.

Ecumenical co-operation in small villages

Ecumenism in small villages is more difficult to evaluate, as is shown by the following table from *Church and Religion in Rural England*.

NATURE OF ECUMENICAL CO-OPERATION BY RURALITY

Co-operation	Totally rural %	Partly rural %	Small country town %	Part urban non-rural %	Urban %
United services	33	39	33	35	34
Seasonal services	22	10	22	19	14
Church council	5	14	27	27	21
Clergy fraternals	6	13	13	21	24
Yearly/occasional	5	14	17	12	12
Lent	6	13	11	13	11
Prayer/study groups	7	10	12	9	7
Children/youth	10	8	4	7	5
Shared buildings	4	4	9	7	5
Other specified	18	21	12	24	20
Other unspecified	7	13	8	9	12

Source: Davies, Watkins and Winter, *Church and Religion in Rural England*, Table 51.

The totally rural benefices score so poorly in the above table because the factors taken into account are all 'official ecumenical occasions' which are more or less impossible in small settlements. As one respondent commented: 'These are all country parishes with no other denominational buildings, therefore we regularly have Methodist, United Reformed, Presbyterians, Roman Catholics and sometimes Jews as part of the congregation' – a pattern which is replicated in rural congregations all over the country. (In the diocese of Chelmsford, Francis found that it was also a feature of urban and suburban congregations. Indeed, 'informal' ecumenical worship was even more prevalent in the suburbs than in the villages.) There is thus no reason to suppose that totally rural benefices are anti-ecumenical – simply that there are problems about *formal* ecumenism (which we will examine shortly).

Rural Church Project has further material on ecumenical co-operation (vol. 3, pp. 78–110) which is discussed in *Church and Religion in Rural England* (pp. 237ff.). This shows that 81 per cent of all incumbents in the five dioceses are involved in some form of ecumenical co-operation, though the nature of this co-operation varies from the occasional ecumenical service through to an official Local Ecumenical Project (LEP) or Shared Building Agreement (as is shown in the table above).

Examples of co-operation

When considering ecumenical co-operation it is useful to divide settlements into three categories: the market town, the village which has more than one worship centre, and the settlement with only one place of worship. Some examples of co-operation are included in Anthony Russell's simple and attractive booklet *Christian Unity in the Village*, though the time is surely ripe for another publication detailing further examples.

The classic example of market town co-operation is in Loddon in Norfolk which involves Anglicans and Methodists in a Shared Building Agreement. An account of this, along with the 'Loddon Ten Guidelines', is given in *Faith in the Countryside* (11.49). A more frequent level of co-operation is noted in Stewart's *Parson to Parson* in the account of Skelmanthorpe, in Yorkshire (p. 42), where there is a clergy fraternal and there are several united services annually.

When there is more than one worship centre in a village there is the opportunity for co-operation in the use of buildings. This may consist of sharing one building – as at Belthorn in Lancashire (Anglican and URC), Wilton in Wiltshire (Roman Catholic, Methodist and URC), Much Hadham in Hertfordshire (Anglican and Roman Catholic) and Hamstreet in Kent (Anglican and Methodist); or it may involve using one building for services and another for other activities – as at Pilning in Avon (Anglican and Methodist) and Amberley in Gloucestershire (Anglican and Methodist). On the other hand, the denominations may keep their buildings and different traditions of worship, but unite for almost everything else. At Byfield in Northamptonshire, the Anglicans, Methodists and URC have a council of churches and do all fund-raising (including collecting for Third World and missionary work) together, while pastoral responsibility is shared between the three ministers involved. Similar examples are Tytherington and Oakridge (both in Gloucestershire) and Whixall in Shropshire.

THE VILLAGE WITH ONLY ONE CHURCH

In one sense, as Robert Van der Weyer points out in *The Country Church*, the small village which has only one church building is often, without knowing it, thoroughly ecumenical:

Without any deliberate intention, and often without being aware, our village churches have for many decades been in the forefront of the ecumenical movement. Many old non-conformists have started attending the parish church: and newcomers with a non-anglican background often prefer to worship in the parish church with their neighbours. (pp. 30–1)

He goes on to point out that this has historical precedent in the 'occasional conformity' of dissenters after the Restoration. It was also a common practice for Methodists to bring their children to the parish church for baptism. Nevertheless, this 'ecumenism by erosion' is not generally regarded as satisfactory. In particular, it is not felt to be fair to other denominations, who in most cases simply lose money and members to the Anglicans.

Faith in the Countryside outlines some of the problems of Anglican canon law as to who may or may not receive communion, be on the PCC, and serve as a deanery synod representative (11.45–47). Clergy worries about ecumenism in the small village were examined in the Rural Church Project when they were asked 'whether they thought rural circumstances encouraged or inhibited ecumenical developments'. Of those questioned, 27 per cent said they inhibited them, 20 per cent said they encouraged them, and 12 per cent said they *ought* to encourage them, but generally they did not do so (*Rural Church Project*, Table 5.3.14). Problems identified were the difficulty of doing anything official if there are no 'official' buildings or ministers *in situ*, small numbers, distances involved, and deep historical loyalties; and to these might be added the 'pressure of things to be done'. With a congregation of ten, even if two are Methodists and three Baptists, it is difficult to see that 'ecumenical activity' is the top priority.

Shared oversight and the village Local Ecumenical Project

Two possible ways forward are being pioneered for such small villages. There are a few examples in sparsely populated areas of a division of pastoral responsibility among the ministers, none of whom are resident in the area: examples are Nidderdale in Yorkshire, the Three Dales scheme (also in Yorkshire), a rural area in Shropshire (see Russell's *Christian Unity in the Village*, p. 17), and Culkerton in Gloucestershire.

The second possibility is that each village should become a 'Local

Ecumenical Project' (LEP). Details of how this can be done and what is involved are set out in *Anglicans and Worship in Local Ecumenical Projects* by Colin Buchanan. If followed through this would mean that the local church would not be Anglican or Methodist, but the *Christian* Church in the settlement – indeed, it would once again be the *parish church* in a meaningful sense. Some 5 per cent of the rural benefices in the five dioceses surveyed by the Rural Church Project already involve LEPs, as do 11 per cent of churches in small country towns. This is a remarkably high figure, for the received wisdom in Rural Theology Association circles, and repeated in *Faith in the Countryside*, is that the complexity and paperwork involved in setting up an LEP makes it very unattractive indeed for small villages.

It is because this is perceived by many to be a problem, that the Group for Local Unity of Churches Together in England asked Peter Poulter (URC) and Geoff Towell (formerly ecumenical officer in Lincolnshire) to write a paper setting out the issues which needed to be faced. They identified the following:

a) Agreement whereby regularly, with specified frequency, the normal worship service of the local church reflects the liturgical practice of the minority/guest members of the congregation.

   Is this a matter of right or at the discretion of the 'incumbent'?

   Is this just to do with comprehension across denominational lines or could it extend to affirmation of diverse theology/worship style within one denomination?

b) Patterns of collaborative leadership
   - where ordained ministers plan and operate as a team, albeit some have only notional pastoral responsibility.
   - where the single local minister works with a team of lay leaders of different traditions
     either i) gathered by him/herself
     or   ii) identified and authorised by other denominational authorities
   - who has the right/responsibility for appointment, training, setting parameters, including timescales, discipline?

c) The possibility of isolated Roman Catholics fulfilling their obligations by attendance at other forms of service than the Mass

- rights, expectations and safeguards.
d) Matters of membership
 i) how to affirm the belonging of those of other traditions within the local, nominally single-denomination church;
 ii) ecclesiological implications of local effective 'membership' of a church of another tradition for a person's actual membership of a local church of his/her own denomination: cutting edge and significance of whole matter under consideration is somewhat lost if the 'guest' members are not 'members in good standing' of their own denomination.
 iii) practical implications of ii) above for quota/assessment purposes if a market town free church has a significant number of technical members whose real life and commitment of personal and other resources is to their local single-congregation village church.

Certainly it is to be hoped that diocesan ecumenical officers can simplify the procedure so far as is possible, and can highlight local examples so that others can see that it is not after all impossible.

Conclusion

The evidence suggests that there is overwhelming support for ecumenical co-operation in theory, though in practice the co-operation does not always go very far; and one of the reasons for this is that, unlike the market town, the small village is not naturally geared to organized ecumenism. A simple guide on how to set up a single-church LEP would help ecumenical co-operation, but even if this is not immediately available no parish should embark on local ministry without doing everything possible to ensure that it is 'Christian' rather than 'denominational'.

Chapter 5 suggests that 'church buildings should be cherished rather than complained about'. This chapter describes the significance of buildings for rural spirituality, and their capacity to attract support from those who rarely attend services. The problems of maintenance are recognized, but a strong plea is made for the adaptation of buildings for modern liturgical and secular use. The problems of doing so in the face of the conservationist lobby is noted.

THE SIGNIFICANCE OF BUILDINGS

The Rural Church Project contains important material on the significance of church buildings. Incumbents were asked whether it was important to have a church in each settlement. Some 83 per cent said yes, and 10 per cent said no. Many stressed that the parish church was an essential focus for community – particularly in scattered villages: 'In this Celtic spread it's the one thing, the only thing, that gives the community a centre; without it the raison d'être of a place is lost.'

A significant number of clergy would actually like to have fewer churches, but they are swayed by the views of their parishioners. That their parishioners do want to keep their churches is dramatically confirmed by the lay response to the question 'How important is it for a parish to have its own church?' The replies are shown in the following table.

Importance of church	General sample		Church roll sample		Total sample	
	No.	%	No.	%	No.	%
Very important	112	33	87	59	199	41
Important	170	50	54	36	224	46
Unimportant	42	12	3	2	45	9
Don't know	16	5	4	3	20	4
Not answered	1	0	–	–	1	0
Total	341	100	148	100	489	100

Source: Davies, Watkins and Winter, *Church and Religion in Rural England*, p. 186.

Both clergy and laity were then questioned as to whether they were 'in favour of redundancy'. A fifth were in favour and a quarter against, but most opted for 'it all depends'. An interesting comment was:

'Some people felt we should pull down St J—. But, although it's only used for half the year, it's very popular. It's a standing witness even when services are not held. It would be a terrible witness if redundant.'

One of the arguments most frequently used against redundancy was that rural populations are rising, or may rise, a trend confirmed by the 1991 census:

'Only in 1968 the archdeacon wanted to make T— redundant. Now it is thriving. Villages are growing [now] and I think we have to think very carefully about redundancy.' (p. 187)

'I don't agree with redundancy on the whole . . . nor with new uses . . . neglected decay I support . . . churches are hallowed places. If they had closed down all the redundant churches in Cornwall 200 years ago we would have no churches in 90% of the villages today.' (pp. 186–7)

When asked 'How many regulars are needed to keep a church open?'

the answers varied from two to 60! When parishioners were asked whether a parish church should be closed if the numbers attending it became 'very small', 31 per cent agreed, but 54 per cent said 'no'. Interestingly, the youngest age group (34 and under) were the most opposed to closure, while the oldest group were least opposed.

Trying to probe the importance of the aesthetic beauty of the building, clergy were asked whether they thought it was important that the church should be 'old'. Some 52 per cent said yes, but a large minority said 'no'. Parishioners were asked whether they themselves had visited a church to look around it during the previous year. A very high 63 per cent of the general sample, and 78 per cent of the church sample, had done so. Obviously church buildings do have their own charisma.

Such findings would not surprise Robert Van de Weyer, whose book *The Country Church* contains what amounts to an extended prose poem in praise of church buildings (pp. 104–38). Among other things, he thinks money is better spent on keeping up churches than in paying stipends to clergy. A particularly attractive touch is that he sees the working of kneelers (brighter still and brighter) as an example of the church patronizing the local arts and crafts movement. In the same vein, the Bishop of Norwich writes in *Moving Forward*:

We use the same English word 'church' to denote both a building and a community, and that has significance. A church is not just bricks and mortar, not just plant to be used or discarded. These stones, especially these ancient stones we have, mean something sacred, and though it may sound sentimental, if we understand them and love them, we may find they become our friends in ways we have not dreamed of. As far as mission is concerned, it is curious the things that can sometimes happen through, for example, an appeal for a roof or a tower or crumbling porch. I had the problem once, when I was an inexperienced Vicar, and I grumbled because it diverted me from what I regarded as the real work of the Church in that place. My wife amongst others told me to stop moaning and identify with the money raising and get involved in bricks and mortar. When I came to myself and joined the fun, I found that people right outside the conventional life of the Church were interested in our building, that it drew the community together in a curious way, and in the end it proved to be itself a missionary activity. Through the enterprise people felt needed, their help was asked for, and a few, just a few, found their involvement in the bricks and mortar led them into the heart of what those bricks and mortar stood for. (pp. 23–4)

If the Bishop of Norwich, who is responsible for 642 churches, can write that, we may wonder what the rest of us are complaining about.

In conclusion, we may say that church buildings in villages play a special part in the spirituality of many rural people. They can enhance community life (as was noted in Chapter 10, p. 145) and they can also be effective instruments for the evangelization of visitors (a point elaborated in Chapter 17). They are 'the city set on a hill', the finger pointing to heaven, the pillar of cloud by day reminding people of God's presence. They need to be embraced rather than discarded.

COPING WITH MAINTENANCE

In Chapter 9 it was suggested that the pressure from 'the centre' to close rural churches had declined. Stipendiaries may be withdrawn over the horizon, but the branch surgery will be kept open. In the future, responsibility for closure (and maintenance) of village churches will more and more rest fair and square on the shoulders of local people; and though everyone wants these churches to remain open, hard facts will have to be faced for 'building upkeep is a constant problem' (comment from Rural Church Project).

There are churches that have lost their villages, and there are villages that could more or less fit inside their churches. A young (and very dispirited) cleric described it as 'the rabbit and ferret syndrome'. The congregation look at the building and are so terrified that they can do nothing. There are other buildings which are either so cold or so impractical that they cry out for reordering. So it is worth making two further points.

Fabric funds which work

We first need to commend the Rochester scheme quoted in detail in *Faith in the Countryside* (p. 297). Essentially it is a savings scheme whereby a church pays so much to an interest-bearing fund every six months (the repair rate) so that at the end of five years there is something in the kitty to pay for the quinquennial. (A fabric fund which is not part of the PCC accounts has the added virtue that it cannot be 'raided' to pay current bills.) A variation on this which has great appeal to those with a special love for 'their' church is the perpetual fabric fund. This is a trust fund, with the incumbent, the churchwardens and the archdeacon as managing trustees, which is dedicated to the fabric of a particular church. The fund is invested for growth and income, but only the interest may be used. A number of small churches in Gloucestershire have established such funds and they have attracted legacies and large donations. As a result, regular maintenance is no longer a significant drain on the budget.

Reordering village churches

Secondly, it is important to note that small village churches *can* be reordered. One of the most unexpectedly revealing occasions of the Acora process was a slide show given by Michael Ward, Rector of Gunthorpe with Bale (Norwich), of photographs that he had taken of reorderings of village churches up and down the country. There were many hundreds of them and far more than the Commissioners had expected. They ranged from the magnificent (and costly) reordering at Chislet, Isle of Thanet, where the nave has been turned into a mediaeval-banquet-style village hall, to the glassing-in of a screen at Wistanstow, Hereford, so that the congregation can keep warm in February. Every Advisory Committee should keep a list of 'examples of good practice' which they can share with other dioceses.

Faith in the Countryside warmly commends the adaptation of church buildings for secular as well as religious use:

11.13. A growing number of church people are actively trying to rearrange their church building through some process of re-ordering. We were impressed by those churches which did not leave this at the worship level but reviewed the use of the church building in broader community terms. Where re-ordering for worship involves an attempt to make the church structure and furniture more helpful for the needs of worship today, the altar is frequently brought forward and obstacles separating priest from people removed. We have seen parts of larger churches partitioned off to enable the worship to be more intimate and warmer, while carpeting, moveable seating, as well as modern heating, lighting and toilets have all been added in an attempt to create a contemporary setting within an ancient building. When reordering has only the purpose of allowing for modern styles of worship it may be that due regard should be paid to the possible transitoriness of such approaches. We warmed to the advice given by the Provost of Bury St Edmunds, as Chairman of the St Edmundsbury and Ipswich Diocesan Advisory Committee, that this type of re-ordering should be of a reversible nature.

11.14. Some of the most successful schemes we saw had clearly been designed so that the church could be used for a number of more secular activities. The best took into account the fact that the needs of the young, aged and handicapped are the same in social activities as well as in worship. This approach is particularly important where a community lacks other adequate public meeting places. Successful arrangements have been seen on our visits, which allow for youth work, meetings in comfort, a playgroup area, kitchen facilities and a church office. For all of these, the provision of toilets is crucial.

Examples are given:

The Victorian church at Neston near Chippenham in the Diocese of Bristol was adapted by building a two-storey suite of rooms at the west end of the church providing a large meeting room used by the school assembly for 120 children, Churchmen's Dinners with speaker, and, for festival occasions, the screen is folded back and the gallery provides overflow for the nave seating. Downstairs the parish has a kitchen, toilets and office.

The church at Flax Bourton in the Diocese of Bath and Wells solved their dry rot problem, and the absence of a community building in the village, by creating an open space in the nave, with moveable seating for use throughout the week. The atmosphere of the ancient church was not adversely affected at all.

In the diocese of St Edmundsbury and Ipswich there are several examples of adaptation of churches to provide for social purposes: Ixworth, St Mary and Sutton, St Peter (where the north aisle now serves as a parish room) are particularly noteworthy.

The parish church at Riseley in the Diocese of St Albans has had the chancel converted into a soundproof room for the junior church, coffee etc. Further consideration is being given to expansion of the church building to provide more meeting rooms since there is nothing suitable near the village.

The conservation lobby

It is increasingly the case that some people see village churches as museums and want them preserved in aspic. One of the jobs of the local ministry group is to oppose such conservation and to ensure that the group members' own church is adapted for the needs of the present generation, just as it has been adapted for the needs of past generations. One of the factors that has given rise to antiquarian lobbyists is that over the last 20 years enthusiastic vicars have turned churches upside down in favour of the parish communion movement; but, as Van der Weyer noted in *The Country Church*, there is no need to cause mayhem in order to achieve the desired effect. Taking the two parts of the communion service in two different parts of the church, or using a movable nave altar, makes the point without forcing through a major reordering which inevitably enrages 'the village'. *Faith in the Countryside* counsels 'resolute conciliation':

> 11.15 In the end an agreement has to be made, and we urge churches to discuss their objectives with conservationists at an early stage; equally we remind conservationists that the church building needs to fulfil its original purpose and therefore must not become fossilised. The whole question of re-ordering is a sensitive and important matter, but we urge local churches to reflect on their buildings, using imagination to see how they can best serve the community at large.

OTHER CHURCH PROPERTY IN VILLAGES

This chapter has concentrated on church buildings. In planning for the future, local groups should also consider other church property in their village. *Faith in the Countryside* included a major section (11.12–11.26) on the potential importance of this property for any missionary strategy, and they drew the attention of glebe committees to the opportunities available for the 'constructive' use of local assets.

Leslie Francis has for some years underlined the importance of the parsonage as a base for Christian mission in rural areas, and his views are summarized in *The Rural Church Towards 2000* (pp. 75–7). He has conducted a survey in conjunction with the Rural Theology Association of the use made of parsonage houses, 'The parsonage today'. The results were presented at a national conference at Ecton House, Northants, 20–23 October 1993, with a subsequent report in the *Church Times*. This has had the desired effect of opening up serious discussion on a subject which is important for the future of the rural Church.

Regular Sunday Worship

Chapter 5 suggests that the local ministry group should meet for worship in their church every Sunday at the same (convenient) time. This chapter asks first whether there are in fact many rural churches with no service on a Sunday, and then goes on to look at the implications of putting the above recommendation into practice. Issues raised include the use of the stipendiary, the frequency of communion services, and whether lay people are likely to go to lay-led worship. The implications of attendance at 'occasional' services for mission will be considered in Chapter 17.

WORSHIP IN EVERY CHURCH EVERY SUNDAY

Faith in the Countryside argued that the 'clerical steeplechase' of the multi-parish benefice was a travesty of true worship and must stop. It further urged that there was positive virtue in Sunday worship being taken by local people in preference to someone with no roots in the village. It is difficult now to discover who coined the recommendation that 'there should be a service in every church every Sunday at a reasonable time', since those precise words are neither in the report nor in *Moving Forward*, from which the concept was drawn. Nevertheless, this is the single idea which has most fired the imagination of PCC members. Lay people's theology may be flawed, and not a little tinged with veneration for 'the earthly temple which is our house of God', but, for many, a church where there is no Sunday worship seems to be a contradiction in terms.

Parishioners and visitors also seem to value the intercessory role of the local church – a fact which those congregations who invite visitors to record prayer requests (on a notepad provided) can endorse. While the best way of praying for the village is for the bell to be rung and the office said in 'our' church each day (as in Eyethorne in Kent and Childswickham in Gloucestershire), if that is impossible it is expected at the very least that local prayers should be offered up on Sunday. Nor perhaps is it spiritually healthy for the church to give official blessing to the idea that once-a-month worship is 'reasonable if that's all you can manage': for that is what the once-a-month pattern of Sunday services implies, even if only subconsciously.

It is, however, necessary to turn from exhortation to fact and ask how widespread the problem is, whether the recommendation could be put into practice, and whether it is likely to bring more people to recognize the reality of God's love, and so encourage the process of 'transfiguration'.

How many churches have no Sunday service?

The fact that there is a problem was first pointed out with his usual stark clarity by Leslie Francis in *Rural Anglicanism*. He noted (p. 51) that 20 per cent of the churches in Suffolk offered no service at all on any one Sunday, 57 per cent offered one service only, and in only 11 per cent were the 'traditional' three Sunday services maintained. This, as he pointed out, was markedly different from the situation in 1956 when his records started, and meant among other things that the variety of services on offer in villages was greatly curtailed. The statistics of the General Synod Board of Education's *Children in the Way* questionnaire, conducted by Francis and Lankshear and covering 24 dioceses, confirmed the trend. One in six churches in villages with a population of 500 or less have no service on any given Sunday, and the figure falls to one in four in villages of less than 250. Clearly, then, this is not just an East Anglian phenomenon.

Will people worship elsewhere?

The practical importance of this change is that it has implications for mission and evangelism. *Faith in the Countryside* suggests that by denying local people the opportunity to worship in 'their church' we are cutting down the number of church attenders, because in practice Anglican parishioners are often not prepared to travel to church. As was seen in Chapter 9 on pp. 114–16, the evidence on joint-benefice services tends to confirm this. It is given in full in *Church and Religion in Rural England* (pp. 229ff.):

> The vast majority of rural clergy did say there was some movement between parishes for services, but nearly all answered in very guarded terms, saying that the amount of movement was very small and infrequent, and often restricted to certain services.

The main reasons given for attending elsewhere were 'if the particular time or type of services suited them' and 'for formal united benefice services'. Two-thirds of the benefices have some sort of united service at least once a year, and in some cases that is the only service in the benefice held on that day. When asked whether they went well, a third said yes, a third said no, and a third that they were reasonable. Both those who do not have a united service and those whose united services do not go well gave as a reason for this that 'people were not prepared to move to attend services at other churches'. The section concludes: 'Despite the efforts of some incumbents, the loyalty of parishioners would seem to be very much to the parish, and to the parish church, rather than to the wider benefice.' This evidence would seem to support the contention that if there were a service in each settlement every Sunday, then the number of those attending church would increase.

SHOULD SERVICES BE AT A REGULAR AND CONVENIENT TIME?

At the moment the service rota in multi-parish benefices is designed for the convenience of the stipendiary. If this is turned on its head and a service rota is designed for the convenience (and encouragement) of the laity, the programme would of course be different. Most rural people would like to do what their brethren in towns and suburbs do and have morning worship at 10.00 a.m. or thereabouts. If this aspiration is linked with the hope that the person taking the service should be 'locally grounded', a number of important changes would evidently have to be made to make this possible:

(1) The stipendiary would probably be able to take only one service each Sunday morning.
(2) The number of communion services would probably have to be reduced.
(3) Local people would regularly have to take the service themselves and, unless they were trained as Readers, they would not be authorized to preach; so the service on these occasions would be 'thinner' than usual.

These potential problems need to be considered in more detail.

Stipendiary availability

The Rural Church Project emphasized how important it is that the vicar should be 'known', and it is partly because the vicar cannot stay to coffee after the service that the mad Sunday rush has to stop. In principle, a case could be made for adopting the semi-episcopal model of Methodist ministers in the early days – that is, of visiting only one place each Sunday. In that tradition, morning service was followed by visits, meetings, and lunch with one of the members, and concluded with evening service – all in the same village. Nevertheless, most congregations will probably feel that this is not the best use of a very expensive 'resource'; furthermore, they will consider that in the initial stages of 'ministerial evolution' the stipendiary is such a key figure that he or she needs to be 'there on a Sunday' as often as possible. This need should of course decrease as the local ministry group becomes established and is accepted locally as 'the collaborative vicar' – and particularly if one of their number is ordained.

It is probable, then, that at this stage most rural benefices will adopt a compromise whereby one village has a service at 9.30 a.m. and another at 11.00 a.m. or thereabouts, thus allowing the stipendiary to visit two villages each Sunday morning.

Fewer communion services

Faith in the Countryside argued that the '*parish* communion' was exactly the opposite in that it excluded half the parish; there was also significant evidence that in the 'semi-unofficial inter-denominational' situation of many rural congregations, some believed that a communion service every Sunday was inappropriate. The Rural Church Project and the *Children in the Way* statistics show that there is indeed a potential problem for Free Church parishioners since the communion has now become the main service in villages as in towns. Some 83 per cent of all *morning* acts of worship in rural benefices in the five dioceses were a form of communion service, as were 72 per cent of all services on a Sunday (morning and evening) in villages of up to 2,000 population.

If we compare this with the preferences of parishioners as indicated in the table on p. 115, we find that the management is not providing the menu that the customer wants. The Rural Church Project records that 112 attending Anglicans expressed a preference for a service other than communion, as against 88 who wanted either a said or sung communion. Nor will the Liturgical Commission perhaps be pleased to know that the preferred form of communion service was: 45 per cent BCP, 26 per cent no preference, 22 per cent ASB.

Looking at the same statistics from the other direction, it becomes clear that (as Francis pointed out in *Rural Anglicanism*) the variety of services on offer in rural churches has contracted drastically since 1956. *Church and Religion in Rural England* (p. 223) shows that in rural benefices BCP communion is available on average only every other week, BCP or ASB morning prayer only once a month, and BCP or ASB evening prayer only three weeks in four. Unfortunately, the Rural Church Project did not distinguish between Rite A and Rite B communion, but the *Children in the Way* statistics suggest that in rural parishes over 50 per cent of ASB services are Rite B, so that probably many parishes do not offer the option of Rite A (and vice versa). Thus the table of parishioners' 'preferences' shows a wide range of significant demand which is certainly not being met in every parish – and not even being met very adequately in many benefices.

The conclusive point is surely that the major growth area identified is not in traditional parish communions, but in family services (though some of these are family communions). The Rural Church Project recorded the comments of the rural clergy, many of whom had introduced some form of family service 'so that there would be some non-eucharistic services for non-confirmed people'. Opinion among the clergy about the importance of a Eucharist every Sunday was of course divided along churchmanship lines, but there was a general impression among the responses that family services do attract new people. This is reinforced by the statistics, which show that 22 per cent of all morning services in rural benefices are now billed as 'family services' and this suggests that well over 80 per cent of all rural benefices now have a family service once a month. This is over twice as many 'family' acts of worship as Leslie Francis found in Suffolk in 1983, when he pointed out that, even then, family services provided the major means of contact between the Church and young people in rural areas.

No one who has been involved in the parish communion movement would doubt its value. It has given to ministry a sense of coherence and direction, and has provided a meaningful spirituality for many individuals. Nevertheless, in the rural context, where the model of the future Church is 'community ecumenical', the principles propounded by A. G. Hebert in the 1950s need – at the very least – to be reformulated.

The evidence shows that lay pressure for weekly communion services in small villages is not so great as is sometimes suggested. On the contrary, it could be argued that the greatest need shown by the statistics is for a greater variety of services, some of which will be non-eucharistic.

Lay-led short services

The surveys quoted all suggest that only a small number of Anglican parishioners are prepared to 'travel' to worship. The logical corollary of this is that if there were a service at the same convenient time in every church every Sunday, more people in a benefice would attend worship each week. Would this really be the case if there was neither music nor sermon, if the congregation numbered ten or less, and if the service were taken not by 'our vicar' but by the members of the local ministry group?

The available statistics about the 'attractiveness' of small congregations are not encouraging. *Rural Church Project* (vol. 3, 5.1.19) notes that in parishes of under 1,000 population the number of those under 16 who attend is only 15 per cent as compared to 22 per cent in parishes with 5,000+ population: a finding which is endorsed by Francis and

Lankshear in 'Do small churches hold a future for children and young people' in *Modern Churchman*, who conclude that 'small churches experience special difficulty in maintaining an effective ministry among children and young people'. A similar difficulty is noted in the literature about 'the small congregation' produced by the Free Churches, and it is linked by them to the problem of providing 'child-worthy' worship with a congregation of 15 or less.

So are small acts of worship taken by local people doomed from the start? A lot will depend, first, whether there are at least two 'bigger' services each month with music and sermon (in other words, the short said service is not the exclusive spiritual diet provided), and secondly, how good the local ministry group is at making worship 'real'. That it is possible to do so is shown by the local group in the Gloucestershire village of Elkstone (population 200), which has a highly informal monthly 'Songs of Praise' service which is attended by 20 per cent of the population and a monthly family service which regularly draws over 30 people. Such events, though, require commitment, confidence and flair on the part of the ministry group, which in its turn will require extensive help and support from the diocese.

It needs, however, to be stressed that the problem is the smallness of the congregation, not the fact that it is lay-led. Anecdotal evidence from all over the country indicates that a significant number of the family services which attract large congregations are taken by lay people. Trained teachers are much more likely to be able to relate to children in a liturgical or 'gathered together' context than many clergy, and a number of clergy are sensible enough to realize this and to call in lay assistance. Another reason for such use of lay people to take family services was put to the Commissioners by a stipendiary in Ely diocese who bewailed the fact that, as the only available priest in the area, he had to celebrate communion for eight people in one church, while two miles up the road an unlicensed lay person was taking a family service for 80.

Conclusion

As has been pointed out before, the available statistics have not yet been 'banded' to allow comparison between one parish 'strategy' and another. It should for instance be possible to discover from the *Children in the Way* statistics whether a benefice which has a service on Sunday in every church at the same 'reasonable' time has comparatively more adults,

children and teenagers worshipping regularly than another similar benefice which gathers everyone into one church – or another benefice which
has a variable range of service times. Unfortunately, the Rural Church
Project aggregates Sunday attendances rather than separating out attendances for individual services, but even in that case important information
could be gained by 'banding' parishes according to 'ministerial strategy'. Such research would cost money, but it could be invaluable in
making a balanced judgement about which liturgical strategy to pursue.

What the available evidence seems to show is that while 'the vision'
of 'a service in every church every Sunday at a regular convenient time'
is not impractical, there are potential problems which have to be faced
squarely. Nevertheless, providing opportunities for worship that suit the
people, rather than a rota of services that suit the parson, must be a vital
symbolic part of the 'local ministry' package.

17

Mission and Evangelism

The previous chapters have shown that the rural Church has real problems which need to be faced, and it has been suggested that if more
people in villages are to 'experience God's love as real' the structures of
rural ministry need to develop. Principles for development have been
set out and have been tested against current experience and statistical
evidence. Much of the discussion has been academic and involved, and
at times the impression has no doubt been given that if the structures are
right, everything else will follow. So at the beginning of this last chapter
it is worth restating that the aim of all structures and all ministry is 'that
transfiguration may happen from glory to glory'.

This chapter is about the strategy of mission and evangelism which is
most likely to encourage 'transfiguration'. The particular constraints of
evangelism in rural areas are set out, and it is suggested that as village
life changes, so our strategy needs to change with it. The 'vision' of
local ministry that has been outlined in this book at least starts where
people are, and a strategy for rural evangelism is suggested which will
take the local group beyond 'keeping the locals happy' (see Chapter 10)
to 'feeding the locals spiritually'.

CONSTRAINTS ON EVANGELISM IN RURAL AREAS

The last section of Chapter 5 suggests that since the most effective evangelism is local and personal, a 'local' strategy is likely to be 'successful'. The difficulty is that 'evangelism' is a word rural PCCs tend to shy away from.

The Measure of Mission (BMU, 1987) seeks to clarify the vocabulary of evangelism, and points out that in the New Testament the word 'witness' is as significant as the word 'proclamation': and John Poulton's classic distinction between evangelism as 'light' and evangelism as 'yeast' has proved particularly helpful in understanding the rural situation. The conclusion usually drawn today is that evangelism in villages is best seen in terms of 'witness' and 'yeast'. An example of this way of thinking is the chapter in *Faith in the Countryside* entitled 'Mission, evangelism and community', which devotes nine pages to the community use of church plant, six pages to the social gospel, and two pages to evangelism. No one who lives in a village would want to deny that Christian mission in the village context implies meeting human need, seeking to enhance for God local community life, and caring for the local environment; but it does also surely need to extend to touching the hearts of individuals.

The reason why the call to evangelism falls on deaf ears in the traditional village was well expressed in my article in *Partners* (Summer issue, 1985):

> The urban visitor tends to think that life in a small village is peaceful and secluded. Far from it. A small village is the one place on earth where you cannot remain anonymous. Everyone knows everyone else – at least by sight. In a village everyone knows that the lesson reader on Sunday kicked the cat on Monday, beat his wife on Tuesday, and went hunting on Saturday. This is true for a newcomer (or even a second home owner) as for a local resident. A person who was born and brought up in the immediate neighbourhood faces the added publicity that everyone knows a great deal about his family, and there are recorded in the community memory facts about him from the cradle. He was pigeonholed by the neighbourhood during his first week in infant school, if not before. It is scarcely surprising then that

the first commandment of village life is – 'Thou shalt keep thy head down' – and that 'word' evangelists are in short supply where the retort will so inevitably be – 'Preacher heal thyself'.

In his amusing yet highly academic study of Gosforth in Cumbria, Williams showed how important the pigeon-hole system is. While it gives a security, a place, to each person, it also confines him, and makes it very difficult indeed for him to step from one pigeon-hole to another. Jim, who left the choir at 10 and has been for 12 years 'one of the lads', is pigeon-holed as a no-nonsense chap who only goes to church for funerals. To ask him to step out of the mould and enter church on an ordinary Sunday is tantamount to asking him to deny his innermost self (that is the self which is given him by the village). It is only when he moves out of his village to put down new roots that he has the 'freedom' to take up a new stance. In an interesting study of small Norfolk villages in the 1960's it was found that 90% of the regular congregation were born out of the village (even if only five miles away), and moved there by marriage, retirement, employment etc. . . . Or put it another way. In London a person can be a churchgoer and keep it a secret from his neighbours and his workmates – (and even from his family if he goes to a weekday service). In Sapperton he can't. This puts considerable pressure on the village churchman.

Evangelism in a small settlement will always be difficult and, although the village world described in the above extract is changing fast, many of the constraints on direct 'word' evangelism will remain. Nevertheless, 'witness' and 'yeast' are as appropriate weapons for mission in the new village as they were in the old, and so evangelization can with sensitivity and guile happen if the congregation wants it to happen. What is in a way a more intractable problem is what has been called 'village religion'.

It has been the traditional Anglican view that every member of the parish should be considered as a member of the church, and that it is unwise to draw a clear distinction between 'the congregation'; and 'the village'. An analogy has been drawn with the tribes of Israel, who were all members of the one holy family, but who seconded the Levites to do the priestly job on behalf of the others: and on this model 'the village' are seen as members of the chosen race, while the congregation or 'good church workers' are seen as the modern Levites.

The fact that this model is now being questioned is illustrated in *Church and Religion in Rural England* (pp. 111ff.). Clergy were asked 'Do you see your ministry primarily in terms of serving all who live in the parish, or serving the members of your congregation?', and this theme was taken up again in the detailed interviews. 43 per cent said they served all the parishioners (the traditional community model), 23 per cent stated that they served only their congregations (the traditional associational model), but as many as 27 per cent recognized that they served both – and that in practice the congregation had more of their attention than the rest. Lay people were asked 'For which group does the church in your parish exist in practice?' As many as 22 per cent of the general sample and 18 per cent of the church sample believed that it existed for churchgoers only. Perceptions are certainly changing.

Popular religion

At root, much of the debate revolves around whether the occasional attenders are really Christians – or, put another way, whether 'popular religion' inoculates people against catching the gospel, or prepares them to receive it.

For practical purposes, 'popular village religion' may be divided into religious observance or experience which is articulated, and observance which appears to an objective outsider to be 'religious' but which is not articulated or even recognized as such.

'Articulated' popular religion includes occasional ceremonies of a national character (such as Remembrance Day), rites of passage, local traditions such as well-dressing ceremonies, and occasional church attendance of which the most obvious example is the annual visit to the Christmas carol service. The latest 'growth area' in articulated popular religion has been the development of 'festivals of creation' and 'animal blessing services' which seek to express 'green' theology in liturgical terms. Opinion is divided as to whether to regard such occasions as a debasing of true religion or as a welcome opportunity for evangelism; but what is an undercurrent of dissatisfaction usually erupts into open conflict over baptism policy. Some clergy (and PCCs) want to make regular church attendance by the parents a prerequisite of baptism for the child, while at the other extreme grandparents cannot see why their grandchildren cannot be baptized in the village where they themselves live rather than in some anonymous town parish where their children happen to have taken up temporary residence. It is interesting that even the Movement for the Reform of Infant Baptism (MORIB), in their evidence to the Commissioners, admitted that a 'strict' baptism policy applied in a village could often be counter-productive.

Implicit religion

'Non-articulated' or 'implicit' religion is a concept which has been developed in this country by Canon Edward Bailey, Rector of Winterbourne, Avon, and has proved a useful neutral term for opening up discussion between theologians, sociologists and anthropologists. The basic insight of implicit religion is that humankind is naturally religious and that 'orthodoxy defeats its own ends if it de-religionises those who are less articulate' (evidence of Canon Bailey to Acora). Statistical data to support the contention that 'humankind is naturally religious' are being provided by the Religious Experience Research Unit based in Oxford, who claim as a result of many years' research, that at least a third (and possibly as many as two-thirds) of the population will admit to having had some sort of religious or transcendent experience.

In *A Workbook in Popular Religion*, Edward Bailey argues that people often venerate without being able to put their veneration into words. Contributions to the book on such diverse topics as the veneration of home and garden, the village hall, the business corporation, the school ethos, the Lewes Bonfire celebrations and the rituals of bereavement help the reader to see well-known phenomena in a new light. Readers are also forced to examine their own religious practices and to recognize how much of their own spirituality is 'popular', irrational and inarticulate.

Many of the studies are anthropological in nature, and this method of approach has been used by Noel Baker in his unpublished Advanced Diploma dissertation for Trinity College, Bristol, entitled 'Eastington: A living theodicy?' Baker had an extended conversation with 30 parishioners of Eastington, a village near Stroud, Gloucestershire, with the aim of understanding what 'the village' and 'the locality' meant to them. He discovered that their attitudes to the locality and home surroundings could be understood in terms of natural religion; and he goes on to show how their 'religious' understanding of their locality helped the interviewees to integrate their understanding of life, and particularly helped them to make sense of pain, misfortune and injustice (theodicy).

Popular beliefs

The Rural Church Project used the tools of sociological research to try to illuminate popular belief, and the results are reported in a closely argued chapter, 'Belief and theology' (pp. 248ff.), in *Church and Religion in Rural England*. They begin by recalling the data already referred to which show that for many parishioners 'religion' is not so much a matter of explicit beliefs as a matter of attendance at church rituals, and a sincere feeling of belonging to a family institution.

They go on to analyse the answers to questions put to lay people about their personal beliefs. Not surprisingly, the responses to questions about belief in an afterlife, ghosts, Friday the 13th, etc. are disconcerting and sometimes contradictory. Though 92 per cent said they were 'Christians', only 42 per cent of the general sample and 69 per cent of the church sample said they believed in life after death; and yet when asked if in the context of death we must 'Trust in God and put everything in his hands', 60 per cent of the general sample and 85 per cent of the church sample agreed. In fact, 'Trust in God' is the most generally accepted of all the theological ideas mentioned.

Parishioners were then given a number of statements about religion and life and asked whether they agreed, disagreed or were unsure. On the basis of their response they were divided into a number of groups, as constructed by Towler in his book *The Need for Certainty* (pp. 269–70). The point about this rather complicated argument is that it gives a clue as to the sort of religious and philosophical presuppositions which are likely to guide parishioners' lives. The results were as follows:

'You only live once'	18%
'Search for Truth'	16%
'Everything will be all right in the end'	4%
'Keeping the faith'	10%
'God is creator of everything'	10%
'Jesus is an example to follow'	10%
'Each person must receive Jesus into their lives'	5%

This reinforces the view that however unorthodox their views as expressed in words, nearly half of the parishioners interviewed guide their lives on 'religious' presuppositions, and that, for many more, 'belonging to the church' means more than just a formality on the census form.

At the very least, this material illustrates in statistical form why so many experienced rural clergy are sympathetic to popular religion (*Church and Religion in Rural England*, pp. 262–5), and why so many rural people prefer 'witness' and 'yeast' to 'proclamation' and 'light' when it comes to evangelistic strategy.

Community church Mark II

Nevertheless, evangelism in villages can perhaps 'expand' little by little – if the topic is examined from a new perspective. In *The Country Parish*, Russell argues that the village church today is in practice both 'communal' and 'associational' on different occasions. On Maundy Thursday and Good Friday, for instance, it is 'associational' and the services are designed exclusively for 'the committed'; but on Easter Day the church, with all its spring decorations, becomes a village focus and the services are unashamedly 'communal'. Other writers have helpfully suggested that within the village congregation there will be both 'Old Testament' and 'New Testament' Christians; and that since in the course of their pilgrimage most people have at different stages belonged to both 'camps', coexistence should be possible. These insights make it possible for the rural congregation to remain true to its calling to be the church of the community while at the same time helping individuals to grow spiritually towards 'transfiguration'. Such an adaptation of the traditional model might be described as 'community church Mark II'.

WHAT STRATEGY FOR EVANGELISM IS LIKELY TO WORK?

Communal not associational

Christian England produced evidence that the congregations which were most likely to have grown over the four years 1985–89 were those which adopted an associational model. Similarly, *Church and Religion in Rural England* (p. 21) 'found that evangelical incumbents were likely to attract considerably greater attendances than catholics'. However, these figures do not tell us how many *local* people attended the associational churches, and therefore how effective they were at primary evangelism. As against the associational model, both the Federation for Rural Evangelism and the Evangelical Council in their submissions to the Commissioners recommended that the rural Church should adopt the community rather than (or at least as well as) the associational model. The Grove booklet *Strategies for Rural Evangelism* by Chris Edmondson agrees.

Local and personal

Church growth statistics tell us that the most effective evangelism is local and personal. Preaching, Bible study and missions reinforce a process which is begun in a local context. The Salisbury Consultation (7.6) records that there is general agreement that faith is best shared in small groups and in one-to-one friendships. The Bishop of Norwich's *Moving Forward* and B. Osborne's *The Key to Effective Rural Evangelism* make the same point. D. Simpson's *Team Missions* constantly returns to the theme that the whole point of the exercise is not mission from outside, but the support of local evangelism. Not surprisingly, a number of modern evangelical writers recommend the formation of lay ministry groups. *Strategies for Rural Evangelism* names as the first key area 'There needs to be the development of a ministerial team, lay and ordained, with scope for the work of evangelism to be central in the team's task' (p. 26); and Tiller and Birchall, in *The Gospel Community and Its Leadership*, also lay great stress on the ministry team as the focus for growth. *Half the Denomination*, the Baptist handbook on small-church ministry, is equally positive about local ministry, as is a very attractive resource handbook, *Sharing Faith in the Countryside*, published in 1993 by the Council for Mission and Unity in the diocese of Chelmsford.

Starting where people are

If community model Mark II is to be adopted, it will be essential to begin where local people are – and the findings of the Rural Church Project help us to do this. They suggest that most rural people value their church building and want the services of a vicar whom they 'know'. This is where rural people 'are' spiritually, and this is where any agenda for evangelism must begin. In Chapter 10 (p. 142) it was suggested that the local group would be accepted by local people if they concentrated on pastoral care and community involvement; and this is where the agenda for evangelism in a village should also start.

AN AGENDA FOR RURAL EVANGELISM

Pastoral care

It is through the adventure of friendship that the gospel must be preached, and the stipendiary needs local help if this is to be done. Perhaps the greatest tribute to the potential of lay ministry in small villages was the occasion when parishioners requested that a particular female lay pastor (in preference to the vicar himself) take the funeral of someone whom she had regularly visited.

A particularly important area of pastoral responsibility is the care of children and young people. The *Children in the Way* statistics showed how few of this group now have any contact with the stipendiary clergy. *Faith in the Countryside* reported how a number of URC congregations have accepted the challenge of doing something themselves to 'bridge the gulf', and the URC scheme *Stepping Forward* was particularly commended.

Care for community life

The second item on the agenda for rural evangelism is likely to be involvement in the life of the whole community. Suggestions for implementation are offered in Chapter 10 on pp. 142–5.

Vibrant worship

The third item on the agenda will be worship. In Chapter 16 we have discussed at length why it is to be hoped that there will be a service in each church every Sunday at a set time.

As important for evangelism as regular Sunday worship are 'occasional' services and this is highlighted in an important section in *Church and Religion in Rural England* on 'occasional attendance'. Parishioners were asked whether they had attended any specific church services in the last year. The table overleaf shows that an astonishingly high percentage claimed to have done so.

If this is the case, it underlines the enormous importance of keeping the local church clean and available for the occasional offices; and it also

ATTENDANCE AT SPECIAL SERVICES

Type of service	Whether attended	General sample No.	%	Church sample No.	%	Total sample No.	%
Wedding,	Yes	238	70	127	86	365	75
baptism, funeral	No	98	29	21	14	119	24
Christmas	Yes	133	39	118	80	251	51
	No	204	60	30	20	234	48
Easter	Yes	83	24	106	72	189	39
	No	254	75	41	28	295	60
Harvest	Yes	105	31	105	71	210	43
	No	232	68	43	29	275	56
Remembrance	Yes	67	20	79	53	146	30
	No	269	79	66	45	335	68
Total		341		148		489	

Note: The totals do not add up to 100 per cent because a small number of people, never more than 2 per cent, did not answer.

Source: Davies, Watkins and Winter, *Church and Religion in Rural England*, p. 216.

raises the question as to whether on special occasions (such as Easter) it should be parish policy to put on a service in every single church at 10.00 a.m. (or thereabouts). This was done in the Queen Thorne benefice in Dorset in 1990 and twice as many attended as in 1989, when there had been a more variable timetable to enable the rector to take most of the services.

It also underlines the importance of these services as an opportunity for evangelism. Indeed, it could be argued that in villages the top priority for direct 'word' evangelism must be to capitalize on the very high level of 'occasional attendance'. This can only happen if local lay people assist with the conduct and preparation of worship – and the more effectively they do so, the more likely people are to be 'touched by God'.

How such a calendar of worship can be made to come alive is itself the subject for a book. It is well covered in *Faith in the Countryside*, van de Weyer's *The Country Church* and Cutts's Grove booklet on *Worship in Small Congregations*, but a few principles may be helpful:

(1) In terms of mission, whether a service is sincere and obviously means something to the congregation is usually more important than the form of words used.

(2) A tiny congregation has few advantages, but one is that everyone who wants to can contribute to the service. This is more likely to happen if there is a worship group which helps to set up the service and gets people 'to do things' – as for family services.

(3) Another advantage of village worship is that it can be local. If local people can give out the notices and contribute to the intercessions, this will strike the right note; and the suggestion that those who take the services should normally be 'locally rooted' should ensure that the preaching is appropriate.

(4) Coffee after the service is the authentic village version of the 'kiss of peace'.

(5) All worship should be child-worthy, and this can be achieved even at the most adult service if the children present are asked to do something responsible.

(6) Many young people today play instruments. With a little preparation, these can help to lead the singing with or without the organ. Village congregations can learn to sing and enjoy choruses if the words are realistic and if there is a small group to teach them.

The great rural parish priests of the past were people of prayer, and congregations need to look to their own private prayer life if there is to be holiness in the village. A regular house group, a weekly Bible study, a course giving guidance in spiritual reading, a simple form of morning and evening prayer – these will all help those who see rural ministry as their vocation.

Local ministry groups will soon discover how much parishioners value intercessory prayer, and though the theology may be primitive, it is sincere. This is why the intercessions at Sunday worship are so important; and the obvious need for upholding individuals in prayer may lead to the formation of a Healing Intercession Group.

Teaching

Most people at some stage of their lives want to 'make sense of it all' and to learn to articulate their beliefs. Providing the opportunity for this is an essential item on any agenda for evangelism. The opportunity for this in villages is generally provided by sermons, baptism and marriage preparation, confirmation preparation and house groups.

On the face of it, this is the part of ministry which should be left to the stipendiary who is the trained theologian. The trouble is that statistics show that the present system does not seem to work well. Francis and Lankshear have shown that the churches' contact with young people has dropped dramatically since 1945; and the Rural Church Project reveals an extraordinary variety of belief and unbelief even among Anglican attenders. This may be partly a result of the academic world-view of most stipendiaries, and that as paid professionals their own witness is not heeded; partly it is that, as is increasingly being recognized, most people learn by 'teaching themselves'. So, at least in the iniital stages, people best learn the Christian faith and how to articulate it in groups, and in conversation with friends. *The People, the Land and the Church* (p. 202) bears witness to the exciting missionary results of the experiment of allowing people to think through life for themselves in the light of theology. Local ministry groups (on the Lincoln model) will learn their 'theology' in this way, and the last module of the three-year course seeks to help them to tell their own Christian story to others. It is to be hoped, therefore, that this will make them particularly well suited to helping with teaching and training in the parish. Certainly many urban parishes who use lay people to help with baptism and confirmation preparation find it 'effective'.

Direct evangelism

Concentration on pastoral and social mission should not rule out direct evangelism if it is done with sensitivity for the rural context. The Federation for Rural Evangelism has produced excellent material on how to do this in villages, and organizations such as Rural Sunrise are available to lead local missions. The witness of young people to their peers and to adults is particularly effective, as was found in a series of village missions in Cumbria. Some parishes have found a visit to Taizé, Iona or some other Christian centre (where again the witness of young people is often so challenging) has been particularly helpful. Within the diocese, and perhaps even the deanery, events can be organized which justify a major speaker and give people the chance to join in crowded, charismatic, exuberant worship which is not available in the village and which can move its participants greatly. Within the parish, a 'Songs of Praise' service is not only found to be popular, but also gives local people the chance to tell their story, often to great effect.

Indirect evangelism

Joint-benefice magazines which cover a group of villages are often easier to sustain than separate ones for single villages; and a joint-benefice magazine is the best tool available for creating a 'family of villages'. A 'community' magazine must, almost by definition, be one which goes free to every house in the area covered, and this is bound to mean that it is relatively cheap. It need not, however, be shoddy if one person can be found to raise sponsorship and encourage village organizations to make realistic contributions. Since the magazine is the chief means for creating 'community', for furthering co-operation with communities beyond the parish boundary, and for straightforward Christian evangelism, it is vital that it has a high place on the agenda of the local ministry group.

The church building, if properly presented, can be a potent agency for the evangelization of visitors. The dioceses of Canterbury, Bradford and Gloucester have pioneered 'Ministry to Visitors' and the publications *Helping the Stones to Speak* by Moya Feehally and *Churches and Visitors* by Chris Richards are cheap, easy to read and say virtually all that needs to be said on the subject. A few useful guidelines:

(1) A locked church is a theological nonsense and a denial of 'mission'.

(2) During the daytime the church tower is, as it were, the 'pillar of cloud', symbolizing God with his people. A floodlit tower, particularly if the church is near a busy main road, can be a 'pillar of fire by night'.

(3) Do not be cynical about churchyards, because the nearest many people come to 'experiencing God's love as real' is in personal

relationships. The headstones are a memorial to that profound experience.

(4) Burn the old guidebook and write something which leads the visitor to worship God and to wonder at creativity.

(5) The noticeboard is the last thing locals look at and the first thing visitors read.

(6) Why are churches on postcards always empty and usually flowerless? There should be something in the church which shows the visitor what happens there on a Sunday.

(7) Every visitor is a potential pilgrim: does your church encourage them to pray and worship?

Conclusion

Such an agenda for evangelism would appeal to most rural PCCs as being down-to-earth and realistic; and, if implemented – a bit here and a bit there, as and when the resources are available – it would help along the process of 'transfiguration'. Inevitably, in such a chapter as this there is a danger that the reader (and the potential member of a local group) ends up more exhausted than encouraged. The reason for making suggestions is because somewhere some parish has already proved that it can be done, and to show what could flow from accepting the principle that the parish rather than the individual stipendiary is committed to prayer, teamwork, mission and evangelism.

If just one person glimpses 'the vision' and begins to pray daily for the needs of the parish, that, church has started to grow and the angels of God rejoice.

Bibliography

The best public collection of books, articles and documents on rural ministry in the English churches is held by the Arthur Rank Centre at Stoneleigh. Readers and students are welcome to use the library there, which has recently been recatalogued and indexed. The Library at St. Deinol's, Hawarden, has recently created an impressive rural section to service the Rural M.A. course being offered there. For an extended bibliography on local ministry, see Bowden and West (2000).

The best source for reports on Total Ministry Unit in New Zealand is Canterbury Rural Ministry Unit, PO Box 8471, Christchurch. For the USA, contact the Diocesan Office of North Michigan, 131 East Ridge Street, Marquette, MI 49855.

Acora (1990) *Faith in the Countryside*. Arthur Rank Centre, Stoneleigh Park, Warwickshire: Acora Publishing.

Acupa (1986) *Faith in the City*. London: Church House Publishing.

—— (1991) *Local NSM – Policy Paper No. 1*. London: Advisory Board for Ministry.

—— (1992) *Development of Models of Ministry and Training in Recent Diocesan Proposals for LNSM Policy Paper No. 4*. London: Church House Publishing.

—— (1998) *Stranger in the Wings*. Policy Paper No. 8. London: Church House Publishing.

Advisory Board for Ministry (1998) *Shaping Ministry for a Missionary Church ABM Ministry Paper No. 18*. London: Church House Publishing.

Alexander, M. and Martineau, J. (2002) *So the Vicar's Leaving* (second edition). Arthur Rank Centre, Stoneleigh Park, Warwickshire: Acora Publishing.

Ambrose, P. (1974) *The Quiet Revolution*. London: Chatto & Windus.

Archbishop's Council and Trustees for Methodist Church Purposes (2001) *An Anglican-Methodist Covenant*. London: Church House Publishing.

Archbishop's Council (2001) *Public Worship with Communion by Extension*. London: Church House Publishing.

Archbishop's Council (2001). *Mind the Gap – Integrated Continuing Ministerial Education for the Church's Ministers*. London: Church House Publishing.

ARCIC (1982) *The Final Report*. London: CTS/SPCK.

Bailey, E. (1986) *A Workbook in Popular Religion*. Dorchester: Partners.

—— Various papers on implicit {popular) religion. Network for the Study of Implicit Religion, The Rectory, 58 High Street, Winterbourne, Bristol.

Baker, J. (1992) *Salisbury Diocese: Ministerial Resource and Deployment,* Green Paper. Salisbury: Diocesan Office.

Baker, N. (1990) 'Eastington: a living theodicy'. Dissertation for Advanced Diploma. Bristol: Trinity College.

Baptist Church (1983) *Half the Denomination*. Report of the Department of Ministry Working Group. London: Baptist Church House.

Beaminster Parish (1982) *Team Handbook*. Beaminster: Parish Office.

Beckwith, I. (1979) *The Lincoln Consultation on Rural Society*. Lincoln: Bishop Grosseteste College.

Bennett, B. (1997) *Listen to the Shepherd*. Palmerston North, New Zealand: Church Mouse Press.

—— (1997) *The Role of the Local Priest in Total Ministry.* Napier, New Zealand: Waiapu Diocesan Office.

—— (2001) *Seasons of the Land.* Palmerston North, New Zealand: Church Mouse Press.

Berger, J. (1967) *A Fortunate Man: The Story of a Country Doctor.* London: Allen Lane.

Borgeson, J. and Wilson, L. (eds) (1990) *Reshaping Ministry: Essays in Memory of Wesley Frensdorf.* Arvada, CO: Jethro. Available from the Dioceser of the North Michigan.

Blunden, J. and Curry, N. (1988) *A Future for Our Countryside.* Oxford: Basil Blackwell.

Blythe, R. (1969) *Akenfield.* London: Allen Lane, The Penguin Press.

Bowden, A. (1985) 'Why so difficult? Rural evangelism' , *Partners* no. 11 (Summer). Dorchester: Partners.

Bowden, A. and West, M. (2000) *Dynamic Local Ministry.* London: Continuum.

Bradbury, N. (1993) 'The minister as midwife', *Theology,* vol. XCVI, no. 774 (November), pp. 444–7.

Brierley, P. (1991) *Christian England.* London: MARC.

British Council of Churches (1945) *The Land, the People and the Churches.* London: SCM.

Buchanan, C. (1987) *Anglicans and Worship in Local Ecumenical Projects.* Nottingham: Grove Books.

Calvert, I. (ed.) (1977) *A Workbook in Rural Evangelism.* London: Archbishop's Council on Evangelism.

—— (ed.) (1984) *A Second Workbook in Rural Evangelism.* Durham: Partners.

Cantrell, R. and Krile, J. (1980–81) 'Church activity and the yoked parish: a structural adaptation to scarcity', *Sociology of Rural Life,* vol. 3, no. 4 (Winter).

Carroll, J. W., Hargrove, B. and Lummis, A. T. (1983) *Women of the Cloth.* San Francisco: Harper & Row.

Central Board of Finance (1991) *Church Statistics.* London: Central Board of Finance.

Chelmsford, Diocese of (1993) *Sharing Faith in the Countryside.* Chelmsford: Council for Mission and Unity.

Chesters, A. (ed.) (2000) *Celebrating the Rural Church*. Arthur Rank Centre, Stoneleigh Park, Warwickshire: Acora Publishing.

Church Commissioners (1983) *The Historical Resources of the Church of England*. London: Church Commissioners.

Church and Religion in Rural England: see Davies, Watkins and Winter.

Church in Wales (1992) *The Church in the Welsh Countryside*. Report of the Board of Mission (Wales) Rural Commission.

Clark, D. M. (1991) *Good Neighbours*. York: Joseph Rowntree Foundation.

Clarke, J. E. (1989) 'What does a "successful" rural church look like?' Unpublished paper submitted to Acorn.

Clarke, J. N. and Anderson, C. L. (1986) *Methodism in the Countryside – The Horncastle Circuit 1786–1986*. Horncastle: Clarke & Anderson.

Cloke, P. and Edwards, G. (1986) 'Rurality in England and Wales 1981: a replication of the 1971 index', *Regional Studies*, no. 20, pp. 289–306.

Collis, J. S. (1975) *The Worm Forgives the Plough*, London: Penguin.

Cope, S. (1987) 'The role of the laity in the rural Church'. BTh thesis, University of Southampton.

Council for the Care of Churches (2002) *Church Extensions and Adaptations* (second edition). London: Church House Publishing.

Coventry, Diocese of (1991) *Guidelines for the Ministry*. Coventry: Diocesan Office.

Crighton, R. (1964) *Commuters Village*. Newton Abbot: David & Charles.

Croft, P. (ed.) (1988) *A Workbook for Deaneries*. Dorchester: Partners.

Croft, S. (1999) *Ministry in Three Dimensions*. London: D.L.T.

(2002) *Transforming Communities*. London: D.L.T.

Cutts, D. (1989) *Worship in Small Congregations*. Nottingham: Grove Books.

Davies, D. J., Pack, C., Seymour, S., Short, C., Watkins, C. and Winter, M. (1990) *The Rural Church Project:* vol. 1: *The Rural Church: Staff and Buildings;* vol. 2: *The Clergy Life;* vol. 3: *Parish Life and Rural Religion;* vol. 4: *The View of Rural Parishioners*.

Royal Agricultural College, Cirencester, and Nottingham: Rural Church Project.

Davies, D. J., Watkins, C. and Winter, M. (1991) *Church and Religion in Rural England*. Edinburgh: T. & T. Clark.

Department of the Environment, Farming, Fisheries and Rural Affairs (2002) *Farming and Food – a sustainable future* (The Curry Report). London: Crown.

Department of the Environment, Transport and the Regions (2000) *Our Countryside: The Future*. London: Crown.

Diocese of ... see under name of diocese.

Dodds, A. (1993) *Desert Harvest*. Cirencester: Collectors Books.

Dogar, V. S. J. (2001) Rural Christian Community in North West India. Dehli: ISPCK.

Donaldson, C. (1992) *The New Springtime of the Church*. Norwich: Canterbury.

Dorey, T. (1979) *Rural Ministries*. Oxford: Oxford Institute of Church and Society.

Dudley, C. S. (1978) *Making the Small Church Effective*. Nashville, USA: Abingdon.

Ecclestone, G. (ed.) (1988) *The Parish Church?* London: Mowbray.

Edrnondson, C. (1989) *Strategies for Rural Evangelism*. Bramcote: Grove Books.

Ely, Diocese of (1988) *Ministry: A Report to the Bishop from the Ministry Advisory Group*. Ely: Diocesan Office.

Evangelical Council of the Church of England (1988) *A Gospel for the Countryside*. Submission to Acora. Salisbury: Canon Askew.

Evreux, Diocese of (1990) *La Pastorale Rurale d'accompagnement* (*Église en marche*, no.12). Evreux: Diocèse d'Evreux.

Fairbrother, N. (1970) *New Lives, New Landscapes*. London: Architectural Press.

Feehally, M. (1989) *Helping the Stones to Speak*. Durham: Tortoise-shell Publications.

Forster, P. G. (1989) *Church and People on LonghillEstates*. University of Hull, Dept of Sociology and Social Anthropology, Occasional Paper no. 5.

Francis, L. J. (1985) *Rural Anglicanism*. London: Collins.

—— (1991) 'The personality characteristics of Anglican ordinands: feminine men and masculine women?' *Personality and Individual Differences,* vol. XII, pp. 1133–40.

—— (1999) 'The Benefits of Growing up in Rural England: a study among 13–15 year old females.' *Educational Studies,* vol. 25, no. 3, pp. 335—41.

Francis, L. J. and Lankshear, D. W. (1988) *Continuing in the Way: Young People and the Church.* London: The National Society.

—— (1990) 'The impact of church schools on village church life', *Educational Studies,* vol. 16, no. 2, pp. 117–29.

—— (1990) 'The rural factor: a comparative survey of village churches and the liturgical work of rural clergy'. Unpublished paper on work carried out in the diocese of Chelmsford.

—— (1991) 'Do small churches hold a future for children and young people?', *Modern Churchman,* vol. XXXIII, no. 1.

—— (1991) Faith in the Isle of Wight: a profile of rural Anglicanism' , *Contact: The Interdisciplinary Journal of Pastoral Studies,* no. 105, 2, pp. 28–33.

—— (1992) 'The rural rectory: the impact of a resident priest on local church life', *Journal of Rural Studies,* vol. 8, no. 1, pp. 97–103.

—— (1992) 'The impact of children's work on church life in hamlets and small villages', *Journal of Christian Education,* vol. XXXV, part I, pp. 57–63.

—— (in press), Ageing clergy and the rural church', *Ageing and Society.*

Francis, L. J. and Martineau, J. (1996) *Rural Praise.* Arthur Rank Centre, Stoneleigh Park, Warwickshire: Acora Publishing.

—— (2001a) *Rural Visitors.* Arthur Rank Centre, Stoneleigh Park, Warwickshire: Acora Publishing.

—— (2001b) *Rural Youth.* Arthur Rank Centre, Stoneleigh Park, Warwickshire: Acora Publishing.

—— (2002) *Rural Mission.* Arthur Rank Centre, Stoneleigh Park, Warwickshire: Acora Publishing.

Francis, L. J. and Williams, K. (1990) *Churches in Fellowship: Local Councils of Churches in England Today.* London: BCC/CCBI.

Frankenberg, R. (1966) *Communities in Britain.* London: Penguin.

Gatward D. (2000) *See You Down the Bus Shelter.* Arthur Rank Centre, Stoneleigh Park, Warwickshire.

General Synod (1974) *Deployment of the Clergy* (The Sheffield Report). Report of the House of Bishops' Working Group. London: GS 205.

—— (1985) *All Are Called. Towards a Theology of the Laity,* London: CIO.

—— (1991) *Team and Group Ministries: Report of the Working Party.* London: GS 993.

—— (1992) *Team and Group Ministries Measure.* London: GS 994.

—— (1997) Eucharistic Presidency. London: Church House Publishing.

General Synod Board of Education (1988) *Children in the Way.* London: Church House Publishing.

General Synod Board for Mission and Unity (1987) *The Measure of Mission.* London: Church House.

General Synod Ministry Co-ordinating Group (1985) *Team and Group Ministries.* London: GS 660.

—— (1988) *The Ordained Ministry: Numbers, Cost and Deployment.* London: GS 858.

Gill, R. (1989) *Competing Convictions,* London: SCM.

—— (1992) *Beyond Decline,* London: SCM.

—— (1993) *The Myth of the Empty Church.* London: SPCK.

Gloucester, Diocese of (1993) *Local Ministry Scheme – Presentation to ABM.* Gloucester: Diocesan Office.

Greenwood, R. (1994) *Transforming Priesthood.* London: SPCK.

—— (1996) *Practicing Community.* London: SPCK.

—— (2000) *The Ministry Team Handbook.* London: SPCK.

Hall, P. (ed.) (1977) *Europe 2000.* London: Duckworth.

Harnilton-Brown, J. (1992) *Folk Religion and Evangelism.* Banbury: Parish and People.

Herbert, G. (1652) *A Priest to the Temple, or the Country Parson, his Character and Rule of Holy Life* (1986 edition). Oxford: OUP.

Hodge, F. V. (1986) *The Newly Ordained and Other Clergy.* London: Mowbray.

Jacobs, M. (1989) *Holding in Trustt: The Appraisal of Ministry.* London: SPCK.

Jefferies, R. (1909) *The Hills and The Vale* (1980 edition). Oxford: OUP.

Jenkins, T. (1984) 'The country church – the case of St Mary's, Comberton'. Unpublished paper presented to Acora.

Jung, S. *et al.* (1998) *Rural Ministry – the Shape of the Renewal to Come.* Nashville, USA: Abingdon Press.

Kent Agricultural Chaplaincy (1980) *Local Ordained Ministry.* Pluckley: Revd J. Sage.

Kirkham, J. (1991) *A Pattern of Rural Ministry for the Future.* Salisbury: Diocesan Office.

Kuhrt, G. W. and Nappin, P. (eds) (2002) *Bridging the Gap – Reader Ministry Today.* London: Church House Publishing.

Lankshear, D. W. and Francis, L. J. (1988) *Diocesan Profile: A Companion to Continuing in the Way.* London: The National Society.

Lathe, A. (1986) *The Group: The Story of Eight Country Churches.* Norwich: The Hempnell Group Council.

Lawson, J. (1955) *Green and Pleasant Land.* London: SCM.

Legg, R. (1989) *Lay Pastorate.* East Wittering: Angel Press.

Leominster Team Ministry (1992) *Annual Report.* Leominster: The Rectory.

Lewis, C. (1982) 'The practice of the absence of the priest', *New Fire* (Winter).

Lewis, R. and Talbot-Ponsonby, A. (1987) *The People, the Land and the Church.* Hereford: Hereford Diocesan Board of Finance.

Lima Text (1990) *Baptisim, Eucharist and Ministry: 1982 to 1990.* WCC

Lincoln, Diocese of (1990) *Exploring Local Ministry.* Lincoln: Diocesan Office.

—— (1990) *Five Course Books in Local Ministry.* Lincoln: Diocesan Office.

—— (1990) *Local Ministry Scheme. Submission to ABM.* Lincoln: Diocesan Office.

—— (1991) *New Times. New Ways – Report by Bishop to Synod.* Lincoln: Diocesan Office.

Lincoln, Diocese of, St Hugh Missioner (no date) *Using the Vacancy Constructively.* Lincoln: Diocesan Office.

Living Churchyard and Cemetery Project (1989) *A DIY Information Pack.* Arthur Rank Centre, Stoneleigh Park, Warwickshire: Acora Publishing.

Living Churchyard and Cemetery Project (1998) *Hunt the Daisy.* Arthur Rank Centre, Stoneleigh Park, Warwickshire: Acora Publishing.

Lloyd, R. (1946) *The Church of England in the Twentieth Century,* vol. 1. London: Longman.

—— (1950) *The Church of England in the Twentieth Century,* vol. 2. London: Longman.

Macquarrie, J. (1972) *The Faith of the People of God.* London: SCM.

Marsh, J. (1982) *Back to the Land: The Pastoral Impulse in Victorian England .from 1880 to 1914.* London: Quartet Books.

Martineau, J. (1992) *Report of Two Years as Archbishops' Rural Officer.* Stoneleigh; Martineau:

Mason, K. (1992) *Priesthood and Society.* Norwich. Canterbury.

Mathieson, M. (1979) *Delectable Mountains: The Story of the Washington County Mission Program.* Cincinnati; Forward Movement Publications.

Methodist Church (1968) *Border Experiment.* Report by Home Missions Department. London: Methodist Church.

—— (1970) *Country Pattern.* First Report of the Church in Rural Life Cornmittee. London: Methodist Church.

—— (1989) *Mission Alongside the Poor Programme: Seeing and Hearing.* London: Methodist Home Mission Division.

Methodist Conference (1988) *Let the People Worship.* Report of the Commission on Worship. Peterborough: Methodist Publishing House.

Morley Report (1967) *Partners in Ministry.* Report of the Commission on Deployment and Payment of the Clergy of the Church of England. London.

Bibliography

Napier, C. and Hamilton Brown, J. (1994) *A New Workbook on Rural Evangelism*. The Old Mill, Spettisbury, Blandford Forum: Partners.
Newby, H. (1977) *The Deferential Worker*. London: Allen Lane.
—— (1979) *Green and Pleasant Land? Social Change in Rural England*. London: Hutchinson.
Newton, C. (1981) *Life and Death in the Country Parish*. London: Board of Mission and Unity of Church of England.
Norwich, Bishop of: see Nott.
Nott, P. (1989) *Moving Forward*. Norwich: Diocesan House.
—— (1991) *Moving Forward II*. Norwich: Diocesan House.

Orwin, C. S. (ed.) (1944) *Country Planning: A Study of Rural Problems*. London: OUP.
Osbome, B. (1992) *The Key to Effective Rural Evangelism*. Hastings: Sunrise Ministries.

Pahl, R. E. (1965) *Urbs in Rure*. London: Weidenfeld & Nicolson.
Partners, The Old Mill, Spetisbury, Blandford Forum, Dorset. See Bailey; Calvert; Croft; Hamilton-Brown; Napier.
Paton, D. M. (ed.) (1968) *Reform of the Ministry: A Study of the Work of Roland Allen*. London: Lutterworth.
Paul, L. (1964) (Paul Report) *The Deployment and Payment of the Clergy*. London: CIO.
Paul, L. *et al.* (eds) (1977) *The Hereford Consultation*. Hereford: Hereford Diocesan Board of Finance.
Phillips, D. and Williams, A. (1984) *Rural Britain: A Social Geography*. Oxford: Basil Blackwell.
Poulter, P. and Towell, G. (1992) *Local Ecumenical Projects in Rural Areas*. Paper presented to Group for Local Unity of Churches Together in England. London: CTE.
Poulton, J. (1985) *Fresh Air: A Vision for the Future of the Rural Church*. Basingstoke: Marshall Pickering.
Pretty, J. (2002) *Agri-Culture Reconnecting People, Land and Nature*. London: Earthscan.

Pyke, A. (1985) 'Where are we going in rural ministry?' Unpublished dissertation on a survey of archdeacons in three rural dioceses.

Rahner, K. (1974) *The Shape of the Church to Come*. London: SPCK.

Richards, C. (1986) *Churches and Visitors*. Gloucester: Gloucester Diocese Church and Visitors Group.

Richardson, J. (ed.) (1988) *Ten Rural Churches*. London: MARC.

Ripon, Diocese of (1985) *Two Years On – Local Ministry in 1985*. Ripon: Diocesan House.

—— (1989) *Review of the Local Ministry Scheme*. Ripon: Diocesan House.

Robertson-Glasgow, N. (1976) 'Rural ministry in the 1980s'. Unpublished paper.

Robinson, P. W. (1991) *Gods People at Worship*. London: Methodist Church Division of Education and Youth.

Royle, S. (1992) *A Theological Basis for LNSM*. Salisbury: Canon S. Royle.

Rural Church Project: see Davies, D. J. *et al.*

Rural Churches in Community Service (1991) *Open All Hours*. Arthur Rank Centre, Stoneleigh Park, Warwickshire: Acora Publishing.

Rural Theology Association (1985) Journal *A Better Country* and various occasional papers. Bulwick Rectory: Rural Theology Association.

—— (1989) *The Rural Church: Towards* 2000. Bulwick Rectory: Rural Theology Association.

Russell, A. (ed.) (1975) *Groups and Teams in the Countryside*. London: SPCK.

—— (1975) *The Village in Myth and Reality*. London: Chester House Publications.

—— (1979) 'The countryside and its church', *Crucible* (October–December). London: Church House.

—— (1980) *The Clerical Profession*. London: SPCK.

—— (1985) *Christian Unity in the Village*. London: Bristol.

—— (1986) *The Country Parish*. London: SPCK.

—— (1993) *The Country Parson*. London: SPCK.

Rutter, C. (1989) *Local Ordained Ministry*. Salisbury: Diocesan Office.

Salisbury, Diocese of (1990) *Going with God –Together*. Salisbury: Diocesan Office.

—— (1992) *Ministerial Resources and Deployment. A Green Paper on Long Term Planning*. Salisbury: Diocesan Office.

Salsbury, J. (1985) *And Is There Honey Still?* London: URC.

Searle, H. (1988) 'Evaluating the rural church'. Unpublished paper presented to Acora.

Sheffield Report: see General Synod (1974).

Sherborne, Bishop of: see Kirkham.

Skilton, C. (1999) *Ministry Leadership Team*. London: Grove.

Simpson, D. (1990) *Team Missions*. North West Evangelistic Trust, Warehouse Centre, Preston Street, Camforth, Lancs.

Smethurst, D. (1986) *Extended Communion: An Experiment in Cumbria*. Nottingham: Grove Books.

Smith, A. C. (1960) *The South Ormsby Experiment: An Adventure in Friendship*. London: SPCK.

Stewart, J. (1988) *Parson to Parson*. Langton Matravers: The Rectory.

Thomas, R. S. (1968) *Selected Poems 1946–1968*. London: Granada.

Tiller, J. (1983) *A Strategy for the Church's Ministry* (Tiller Report). London: CIO.

Tiller, J. and Birchall, M. (1987) *The Gospel Community and Its Leadership*. Basingstoke: Marshall Pickering.

Toennies, F. (1955) *Community and Association,* trans. C. P. Loomis. London: Routledge.

Toffler, A. (1981) *The Third Wave*. London: Pan.

Tovey, P. (2001) *Public Worship with Communion by Extension*. Cambridge: Grove.

Towler, R. (1984) *The Need for Certainty*. London: Routledge & Kegan Paul.

Truro, Diocese of (1992) *Local Non Stipendiary Ministry in the Diocese of Truro: Report by Bishop of Truro' s Working Party*. Truro: Diocesan Office.

Turner, H. J. M. (1987) 'Ordination and vocation', *Sobornost*, vol. 9, no. 1. London: Fellowship of St Alban and St Sergius.

United Reformed Church (1986) *Stepping Forward: A Scheme for Youth Work in Rural Areas*. London: URC.

Van de Weyer, R. (1991) *The Country Church*. London: Darton, Longman & Todd.

West, F. (1960) *The Country Parish Today and Tomorrow*. London: SPCK.

West, M. (1994) 'Second class priests with second class training? A study of LNSM'. PhD thesis, University of East Anglia.

Williams, R. (1973) *The Country and the City*. London: Chatto & Windus.

—— (1992) *People of the Black Mountains: The Beginnings*. London: Paladin.

Williams, W. M. (1956) *The Sociology of an English Village: Gosforth*. London: Routledge.

Winchester, Diocese of (1984) *Lay Pastors Training Course*. Winchester: Diocesan Office.

—— (1990) *A Church for the World. Report of the Ordained Ministry Review Group*. Winchester: Diocesan Office.

Winter, M. (ed.) (1990) *Stress and the Parochial Clergy: Conference Proceedings of the Clergy at Work Conference*. London.

Winter, M. and Short, C. (1993) 'Believing and belonging: religion in rural England', *British Journal of Sociology* (September).

Zabriskie, S. C. (1995) *Total Ministry*. New York: The Alban Institute.